**Antebellum
Politics
in
Tennessee**

ANTEBELLUM POLITICS IN TENNESSEE

Paul H. Bergeron

THE UNIVERSITY PRESS OF KENTUCKY

Scholarly publisher for the Commonwealth,
serving Berea College, Centre College of Kentucky,
Eastern Kentucky University, The Filson Club,
Georgetown College, Kentucky Historical Society,
Kentucky State University, Morehead State University,
Murray State University, Northern Kentucky University,
Transylvania University, University of Kentucky,
University of Louisville, and Western Kentucky University.

Editorial and Sales Offices: Lexington, Kentucky 40506-0024

Library of Congress Cataloging in Publication Data

Bergeron, Paul H., 1938–
  Antebellum politics in Tennessee.

  Bibliography: p.
  Includes index.
  1. Tennessee—Politics and government—To 1865.
I. Title.
F436.B46 1982 976.8'04 82-40170
ISBN 0-8131-1469-1

To my wife,

Mary Lee

Contents

Preface

There seems to be little ground for disputing the point that the Volunteer State was in its political zenith in the antebellum period. This study of politics in Tennessee begins with the 1830s when Andrew Jackson was president and concludes on the eve of John Bell's abortive quest for that office in 1860. In the interval, Hugh Lawson White unsuccessfully sought the presidency in 1836 and James K. Polk won it eight years later. And Andrew Johnson, an eminent figure in state politics even before the Civil War, was to become president in 1865 upon the death of Abraham Lincoln. Judged simply in terms of political luminaries on the national scene, Tennessee enjoyed an enviable position in the prewar decades, and national observers regularly deemed the state a crucial one, in terms of leaders and votes.

Monographic literature appearing during the past fifteen years has also served as both a stimulus and a guide to my own examination of antebellum politics. Richard P. McCormick's pathbreaking study, *The Second American Party System: Party Formation in the Jacksonian Era,* has been particularly influential. I have therefore directed a good bit of attention toward party organization and the mechanics of conducting canvasses in Tennessee, with an emphasis on the presidential contests. I have presented the view that in the campaigns the parties were essentially electoral machines, not given to notable ideological differences.

As a natural by-product of my concern with party structure, I have investigated and discussed intraparty frictions. No sooner were the parties actually established in Tennessee than feuding broke out within them—sometimes serious, sometimes simply annoying. Students of the state's political history have had little or nothing to say about disharmony and rivalry within the political organizations, but this dimension of the story needs explication, for it indicates among other things how difficult it often was for the parties to put forth a united effort during a given campaign.

Another topic demanding attention is the constancy and fidelity of the voters. Repeatedly the electorate "behaved" in ways almost rigidly consistent with previous actions. In fact, once the two parties were securely organized the variations were so slight as to be noteworthy. The disruptions of the 1850s brought about some alterations of voting patterns, but nothing like what one might have expected. In

nearly all statewide contests, the percentage and aggregate vote differ-
entials between the winners and losers were incredibly narrow, so the
claim that the two parties were evenly balanced and fiercely competitive seems completely justified.

One of the visible threads that ties together the chronicle of politics
in the Volunteer State is intrastate sectionalism. Originally prescribed
by nature, Tennessee's tripartite division invariably had an impact
upon the socioeconomic and political ways of the people. On the eve
of the development of the two-party system in the state, it was clear
that sectional loyalties frequently prevailed over commitment to Tennessee's general welfare and needs. From the mid-1830s until the Civil
War intrastate sectionalism influenced and shaped two-party politics,
for almost from the beginning the eastern and western thirds of the
state joined hands in the political arena in an attempt to offset Middle
Tennessee's dominance and power. It is not surprising to find the two
ends of the state embracing, leading, and sustaining the "revolt"
against Jackson and his party. In the mid-1850s the sectional alignments underwent transformation, however, as West Tennessee abandoned its traditional loyalties and became Democratic.

I have restricted myself to an investigation and discussion of statewide contests, that is, gubernatorial and presidential races. But since
the election of United States senators by the legislature often took on
the coloration and significance of statewide competition, I have also
studied the battles for Senate seats. Gubernatorial, presidential, and
senatorial contests are examined within a basic chronological framework, although there are topical arrangements within each chapter.
Since I believe that each of the three decades under study exhibited
certain features around a general theme, I have devoted a separate
chapter to each of them, with the chapter titles announcing the thesis
or theme. The first major chapter, Chapter 2, examines all the statewide elections together in terms of electoral behavior across twenty-
five years. A longitudinal overview, mainly in empirical terms, is the
focus of this chapter. In the concluding chapter, the social composition of the parties is dealt with in order to say something about the
voters and leaders who have been discussed in the earlier chapters.
Finally, it should be noted that instead of focusing upon either the
Jacksonian or the anti-Jacksonian party, as has been done in several
studies of other southern states, I have chosen to scrutinize both
parties as they fought against each other for the prizes of political
office.

Except for passing references to congressional and legislative races,
I have left those contests unexplored, nor have I dealt with city and

county elections in the antebellum period. I would argue not that such races lacked importance but that the quantity and nature of them placed them beyond my scope. Another worthy area of investigation not touched upon in this study is the behavior of the two parties in the General Assembly toward various pieces of legislation.

Anyone familiar with McCormick's *Second American Party System,* with William J. Cooper, Jr.'s *The South and the Politics of Slavery, 1828-1856,* and with studies of other states knows that many of Tennessee's political experiences were not unique but instead conformed to developments in the South and elsewhere. Yet from time to time and in certain ways the state did seem to exhibit unusual political behavior. Moreover, the establishment of a clearly defined and vigorously active two-party system was unique in the annals of Tennessee politics and thereby brought a new day in partisan competition. This study is therefore directed toward showing this new style and manner of conducting politics, unraveling its complexities, and discovering and identifying themes in that story.

It is a distinct pleasure to acknowledge my indebtedness to institutions and persons. I have depended on a number of libraries and archives, but the two that have been the most important are the Tennessee State Library and Archives in Nashville and the Special Collections Department of the University of Tennessee Library. The latter, headed by John Dobson, has not only helped me with various materials but has also provided me with a convenient and hospitable place in which to work. University of Tennessee summer research grants have expedited progress on this project.

Individuals who have assisted me through constant encouragement and support include Professors Sarah R. Blanshei, LeRoy P. Graf, and Ralph W. Haskins, all of the History Department of the University of Tennessee at Knoxville. Years ago my mentor and friend, Herbert Weaver of Vanderbilt University, directed my attention to Tennessee's antebellum politics and subsequently helped me in numerous ways with my efforts to understand this complex topic. Professors Donald L. Winters and V. Jacque Voegeli, both of Vanderbilt University, have urged me along with my task and have provided direct assistance from time to time. I am immensely grateful for the critical reading and important suggestions made by Professor Paul J. Kleppner of Northern Illinois University and Professor Ralph A. Wooster of Lamar University. Naturally none of these professional colleagues should be held culpable for any of the deficiencies of this study.

My final bouquet goes to my family. My sons, Pierre, Andre, and Louis Paul, have not fully understood my research and writing on this book, but they have been good natured about my time away from them and their activities. Words fail when I try to acknowledge my debt to my wife, Mary Lee, except to say that the emergence of this book is testimony of her commitment to me and to my professional career. My family has been a continual source of inspiration, respect, and love.

Antebellum
Politics
in
Tennessee

I Introduction

Before the mid-1830s it had been the custom in Tennessee to conduct politics on the basis of factional and personal rivalries. In that regard Tennessee did not differ greatly from the other new western states. It entered the union in 1796 strongly disposed toward the Jeffersonian Republican party in presidential contests and for years never wavered in that loyalty. After the Federalist party disappeared, the nation's politics at all levels lapsed into a one-party or no-party status. But Tennessee had been in that mold from the very beginning. That factional and personal antagonisms were the rule of politics should not be surprising if one considers the two prominent figures at the time Tennessee gained statehood—John Sevier and William Blount. At most, they tolerated each other when it was politically expedient, but generally their well-known mutual hostility shaped and informed politics throughout the state.

In many respects Blount was an interloper. In 1790 President Washington had appointed him governor of the newly created Southwest Territory. From the moment of his arrival from North Carolina, Blount was a force to be reckoned with in the territory. His almost unrestrained domination of the territorial government constituted a principal theme of the 1790-96 period of Tennessee history. Yet try as he might, he could not rid himself of the disquieting reality that John Sevier was always waiting restlessly to reassert leadership. Long before Blount set foot on Tennessee soil, Sevier had been winning fame for himself as an Indian fighter and, during the period of the State of Franklin, as a fighter against North Carolina. No one could match his well-deserved role as a western frontier leader. From time to time in the 1790s when it was mutually advantageous to do so, Blount and Sevier patched up their differences; but most citizens understood that such reconciliations were mere window dressing. By the time the decade ended Sevier was clearly the most popular figure in the infant state, while Blount clung tenaciously to his position as most powerful man in the region. It was altogether fitting that upon its admission into the union, Tennessee should choose Sevier to be the first governor and Blount to be United States senator.[1]

Naturally these two leaders spawned followings that soon became identified as factions in state politics. Sevier's clique was based exclusively in the eastern section of the new state and for a time this served

Sevier and his allies very well. After all, the state's population and resources were concentrated in this area. This important fact, plus Sevier's popularity, assured him the governorship from 1796 until 1809 (with the exception of a two-year interlude, 1801-3). Judging by Sevier's monopoly of the governor's chair during the state's early years, one senses the political attractiveness of this man and his followers. Despite his long occupancy of the state's highest office, though, Sevier never revealed great astuteness as a politician. Instead, he relied repeatedly upon personal fame and popularity. It appears that he failed to organize his political cohorts into a cohesive, enduring faction, and after Sevier's death in 1815, one is hard pressed to find evidence of the continuing vitality of his faction in Tennessee politics.

The group which coalesced around William Blount, on the other hand, offered a contrasting picture. One important difference was that although Blount resided in the eastern part of the state his principal support was in the Cumberland Basin area of Middle Tennessee. With the passage of time as this region caught up with and then surpassed the eastern section in both population and resources, it became extremely important to have a stronghold in the middle portion of the state. Furthermore, Blount seems to have attracted the younger, more aggressive figures to his side—not the least of whom was Andrew Jackson. In short, the Blount faction developed a strong sense of identity and correspondingly a concern about organizing itself for the political battles.[2] Consequently, although Blount died in 1800 (after a brief and inglorious career in the United States Senate) his clique did not weaken and vanish but instead became a strong competitor in state and local politics. With the election of Willie Blount (William's half brother) as governor in 1809 the Blount faction began its long tenure at the head of state government.

In the absence of Andrew Jackson, who was busy with various successful military exploits (for example, the War of 1812 and the 1818 invasion of Spanish Florida), leadership of the Blount group rested upon the very capable shoulders of Hugh Lawson White of East Tennessee, and John Overton, William B. Lewis, and John H. Eaton, all of Middle Tennessee. They guided the faction to repeated gubernatorial victories with Willie Blount (1809-15) and then Joseph McMinn (1815-21). But both the Panic of 1819, which had a serious impact upon Tennessee's economy, and the Blount faction's longevity in office strengthened the hands of its opponents. Andrew Erwin of Bedford County emerged as the primary leader of a new rival group and was soon joined by William Carroll, Newton Cannon, John Williams, and others. Many of those who flocked to this anti-Blount contingent did so because of personal antagonisms toward Jackson himself. Subsequent political conflicts, however, would give them even more reason to oppose the old Blount clique.[3]

The governor's race in 1821 quickly became a test for the competing factions, for it represented the first serious threat in many years to the Blount group. The Erwinites offered William Carroll as their contender, while the Blount faction backed Edward Ward. In this contest Ward took a stance that was resistant to the democratizing, liberalizing winds blowing in the state and nation. Meanwhile Carroll shrewdly depicted himself as being in the vanguard of these new impulses, though actually he was anxious to stem the more radical measures advocated by Felix Grundy in response to the economic crisis. Carroll easily defeated Ward, thus dealing a body blow to the Blount-Jackson-Overton faction. Also, as Thomas P. Abernethy observed many years ago, Carroll brought to an end the short-lived democratizing phase begun by Grundy's work in the state legislature and thereby inaugurated a new era which emphasized retrenchment of government spending and economic involvement, on the one hand, but progressive social measures, on the other.[4]

The 1821 contest was the opening gun of intensified rivalry in state politics. Hardly had the noise of this campaign subsided than the Blount faction began plotting a return to power through the device of pushing Jackson for the presidency in 1824. But before this strategy could be implemented, Overton, Eaton, and Lewis agreed on the necessity of getting Jackson into public office. Their calculating eyes naturally fell upon the United States Senate seat then held by John Williams, whose term would expire in 1823. This attempt to wrest the seat away from Williams was a bold move indeed, reflecting perhaps both the determination and desperation of the Blount-Jackson partisans. When the General Assembly convened in Murfreesboro in the fall of 1823, a pitched battle between the two political cliques took place, with the result that Jackson walked off with the coveted prize by a scant ten votes and in the process stirred fierce antagonisms. Andrew Erwin, Governor Carroll, and especially John Williams renewed their vows to thwart the activities of the Blount-Jackson-Overton crowd.[5] But their voices were muted by Jackson's success in winning a national following that catapulted him into the 1824 presidential contest.

Although the alleged "corrupt bargain and intrigue" between John Quincy Adams and Henry Clay deprived Jackson of the presidency in 1824, he merely bided his time, certain of triumph in 1828 which in fact did come. His removal to the seat of government at Washington and his activities and appointments once there left an imprint upon Tennessee's political scene. For one thing, some of his devoted followers became increasingly irritated at the pervasive influence of Overton, Lewis, and Eaton. Salt was rubbed into the wounds when Jackson took Lewis and Eaton to Washington with him as a part of his administration. As a result, a new pro-Jackson faction evolved which depended upon Hugh Lawson White, James K. Polk, Felix Grundy, and Cave Johnson for guidance and leadership. Another motivation was the concern felt by these Jacksonians over the steadily developing pronational bank posture of the Overton faction.[6]

The various contests for office added to the interplay of factional politics in the state. In 1826, for example, Governor Carroll frightened the Overton group when he announced his candidacy for the Senate seat occupied by John H. Eaton, but the old Blount faction rallied enough strength in the legislature to defeat Carroll's challenge by nine votes. The 1829 governor's race presented other intriguing possibilities, for when the new year dawned, there was every reason to believe that Sam Houston would seek reelection. Closely identified with the Blount-Jackson-Overton group, Houston was vulnerable only if the other pro-Jackson faction and the Erwin clique decided to unite in opposition to him, and that is precisely what began to shape up after Carroll revealed his desire for the gubernatorial post again. Then suddenly and dramatically the whole political complexion changed when Houston resigned as governor in mid-April and promptly left the state. This incredible turn of events enabled Carroll to win the governor's office unopposed and also blocked a potentially dangerous union between the Erwin faction and the Grundy-Polk group.[7]

In the early 1830s, on the eve of the two-party development in Tennessee, other changes in factional politics occurred. After the establishment in Nashville of a branch of the Bank of the United States, the Erwin and Blount groups inched closer and closer to each other, both being favorably disposed toward the national bank. Certainly the Blount group realized the danger it courted, given the president's avowed hostility toward the bank. Needless to say, Jackson's veto of the bank rechartering bill in 1832 stunned its Tennessee proponents, especially those in the Nashville mercantile community. The Erwinites and the old Blount crowd also found themselves in harmony on the topic of Calhoun and nullification as they staunchly opposed South Carolina's nullifying sentiments, largely because of personal dislike for Calhoun. Of course, on the matter of Jackson's attack upon the nullifiers, all factions in Tennessee concurred, though the Grundy-Polk group had earlier been friendly toward Calhoun.[8]

Perhaps exerting the greatest impact upon factional alignments was the movement to promote Van Buren for the vice presidential spot in 1832. Alfred Balch, a little-known but apparently persuasive Nashville lawyer, is usually credited with launching the Van Buren cause in Tennessee. Not the least important of Balch's converts was Governor William Carroll, who gravitated to the Jackson ranks primarily because of his desire to see Van Buren secure the vice presidency and eventually the presidency itself. Testimony of Carroll's considerable political skills is found in the fact that he continued to enjoy the backing of the Erwin group despite his jump to the Blount-Overton faction. In large measure the Van Buren movement succeeded in reuniting the two Jackson cliques in the state, the Grundy-Polk group having joined after Van Buren's nomination as minister to Great Britain was rejected by virtue of Calhoun's tie-breaking vote in the Senate in January 1832. Oddly enough, at the eleventh hour on the eve of the Democratic national convention Eaton and Overton, apparently fearful of Van Buren's forthright position against the bank, attempted to have him dropped from contention for the vice presidential nomination. But with Jackson's blessing, Van Buren easily won the second post on the Democratic ticket.[9]

Paradoxically, the victory of the Jackson-Van Buren slate in 1832 planted the seeds of discontent and eventual revolt against the Jackson movement in Tennessee. The president's obvious intention to groom Van Buren as his successor did not set well with many of the state's citizens who had no great affinity for the New Yorker. Moreover, Van Buren's concurrence in Jackson's internal improvements veto in 1830 and his bank recharter veto in 1832 further disturbed those already irritated with Jackson's actions in the economic sphere. Although the two Jackson factions in the state endorsed Van Buren in the 1832 election and carried the state without difficulty, there were latent fears that all was not well. The precipitous drop in voter turnout in 1832, as compared to 1828, indicated, among other things, some degree of voter dissatisfaction in the state.[10] Two short years after the election, the incipient rebellion against Jackson and Van Buren began.

For almost forty years Tennesseans waged political battle without benefit of a two-party or even one-party system. In fact, the state seemed little affected by national political organizations (with the obvious exception of the Jackson campaigns). The two or three factions in Tennessee were surrogate parties, to be sure, but they were not parties in the generally accepted meaning of that term. One has only to look at the experience of the late 1830s and the following two decades to see the contrast. As subsequent chapters show, two-party politics with its conventions, committees, candidates, and the like was the warp and woof of state political contests during the twenty-five years leading up to the Civil War.

Slightly more than three decades ago, an eminent scholar of the South, Charles S. Sydnor, declared that "party conflict south of the Potomac, from nullification to the late 1840's, had the hollow sound of a stage duel with tin swords."[11] The following survey of Tennessee politics during the second party system should stand as refutation of Sydnor's bold generalization. By no stretch of imagination or historical evidence could it be argued that the Whigs and Democrats were engaged in a game of charades during the approximately twenty years they were locked in combat in Tennessee. Moreover, as the review of politics in the 1850s shows, even the absence of the Whig party did not greatly diminish the two-party struggle in the state, the Know Nothing and the Opposition parties having risen to the challenge. The great numbers of voters who swarmed to the polls apparently did so with some intensity of feelings about their parties, candidates, or issues—thereby testifying that there was something more involved than the hollow sounds of tin swords.

The succeeding chapters discuss and analyze six presidential and thirteen gubernatorial elections. Attention is also given to the battles over the United States Senate seats in the 1840s and 1850s, because they constitute an inseparable part of two-party politics in those years. From about 1834 to the end of that decade Tennessee politics was shaped by two primary developments: the "revolt" against Jackson, evident in the 1835 governor's race and reinforced by the Hugh Lawson White candidacy in the 1836 presidential contest; and then the somewhat uncertain, jerky starts toward a genuine two-party system. The decade ended with the startling and all-important reversal of the Whig tide by James K. Polk, who in 1839 triumphed over incumbent governor Newton Cannon.

The two-party system blossomed in the 1840s. In a short span of time the rival parties structured themselves with the requisite paraphernalia of party organization. From that moment on to the Civil War, Tennessee politics would be conducted by clearly defined (in terms of leadership personnel if not in other ways), effectively organized, and highly visible parties which were tied to the national political scene. Counterbalancing this theme of the regularization of two-party competition was the unsettling reality of intraparty friction and division. Both the Whig and Democratic parties were afflicted, and one cannot fully comprehend the story of the gubernatorial and presidential elections apart from the internal bickerings that often eroded the strength of the parties. A review of state politics in the 1840s leads to another conclusion; namely, that the Whig party held the upper hand—a total of six Whig victories (three presidential and three gubernatorial) versus two Democratic wins (both gubernatorial).

The succeeding period of the 1850s offers a different picture in several respects. The emphasis on party organization and the besetting problem of internal friction continued, to be sure, but in somewhat diminished fashion. One of the major developments of the period, of course, was the demise of the Whig party nationally and locally, thereby destroying the previous symmetry of two-party rivalry. Naturally these circumstances played into the hands of the Tennessee Democrats who reaped repeated victories in the period. As it turned out, the decade brought Democratic domination (five victories out of the seven presidential and gubernatorial contests) in the Volunteer State—the best showing for the Democrats since the beginning of the two-party system. But this should not obscure the point that the Democrats did not go unchallenged after the collapse of the Whig party; instead, the American (Know Nothing) and eventually the Opposition parties fought against the Democrats. Two-party competition was thus kept alive, though on a modified basis. Declining levels of voter participation in Tennessee elections during this period bespoke voter confusion, to some extent, and also perhaps the lack of excitement resulting from the breakup of the old Whig-Democratic rivalry.

As one looks across twenty-five years (1835-60) of Tennessee's political landscape, another prevalent theme can be seen: the competition among the three sections of the state. Considering the rivalry manifested since the earliest days of statehood, it is not surprising that intrastate tensions carried over into politics. By the mid-1830s Middle Tennessee towered over the other two sections in terms of population and economic well-being. According to the federal census of 1830, Middle Tennessee had 50.5 percent of the state's total population, while East had 28.8 percent and West 20.6 percent. Small wonder that the eastern and western parts of the state looked upon Middle Tennessee with envy and resentment. Although all three sections steadily gained population during the three decades after 1830, both East and Middle lost ground in a relative sense. The 1860 census, for example, reveals that by that time Middle Tennessee had 46.1 percent and East

Tennessee 26.9 percent of the state population. West Tennessee, which more than doubled its population in the 1830-60 period, possessed 26.9 percent of the state's population by 1860.[12]

What is surely one of the ironies in the saga of sectional rivalry in state politics is that although East and West yoked themselves together to challenge the Jackson party in the antebellum period they continually depended upon the middle section of the state to furnish leadership. Only in the 1850s did the eastern and western regions sufficiently exert their influence in both parties to put forth candidates for governor and United States senator. And one should not forget that although East and West Tennessee were anti-Democratic until very late in the two-party period they nevertheless evinced much support for the Jacksonian party. Conversely although Middle Tennessee was the principal stronghold of the Democrats, it gave healthy percentages to the Whig, American, and Opposition parties. Thus no party could count on carrying any given section of the state without working diligently for it. In the mid-1850s West Tennessee abandoned its traditional political party allegiance and went into the Democratic camp, thereby enhancing the possibilities of victory for that party. But throughout the entire quarter century, the eastern and middle thirds of the state (with the exception of two or three elections) remained true to their traditional party alignments.

The various matters of two-party formation, such as party machinery, internal dissensions, the elections themselves, sectional antagonisms, and personal ambitions all comprise intriguing parts of the story of two-party politics in Tennessee. But one is also drawn to this history of political combat because the state's electoral behavior did not conform to the anticipated pattern. Tennessee's contribution of two Democratic presidents during the period might easily lead to the expectation that the state would be a pillar of the Jacksonian edifice. As the state's most prominent Democratic newspaper, the *Nashville Union,* declared in near exasperation shortly before the fifth consecutive Whig presidential victory in Tennessee: "This State was never intended to be anything but democratic. . . . It is impossible that a State, whose history is identified with that of Jackson could ever really affiliate with the whig party."[13] Statements such as these constituted a deliberate glossing over of political realities. In fact it was only after the mid-1850s that one could talk in terms of Democratic party hegemony. Since relatively little attention has been directed to the puzzle of Tennessee's political loyalties during the two-party period, the chapters which follow seek to redress the neglect.

II Electoral Behavior
An Overview

One way to remedy the surprising disregard Tennessee's antebellum political history has experienced is to begin with a longitudinal view that utilizes an empirical analysis of the elections from 1835 to 1860. To that end voting data and related information are offered which make possible specific and general observations. This chapter is arranged according to the size of the units being discussed and analyzed: first the three sections of the state, then the congressional districts, and finally the counties. These three components lend themselves to comparisons and contrasts, and the reader should be able to see how the electoral behavior of one relates to the others.

My premise is that once a quantitative overview is established, then one can turn more profitably to an examination of the specific decades with their various electoral contests. Therefore this chapter provides a general background of the entire period against which subsequent detailed chapters on discrete decades can be placed and measured. Certain points and observations made here are further substantiated in the subsequent, more qualitative, chapters.

Stability and consistency were hallmarks of the antebellum two-party system in Tennessee. After the early days of "revolt" against Jackson and his party in the mid-1830s, the political process moved quickly, but not automatically or smoothly, to the establishment of a clearly recognizable two-party rivalry by the end of the decade. During the approximately five-year transitional phase, there was a great deal of fluctuation and change in voter responses. But from the 1840 election to 1860 the state's electoral scene was one of fierce, evenly balanced two-party competition that saw the voters adhere to their chosen parties with incredible fidelity. Even the disruption of parties in the mid-1850s did not greatly disturb the stability-consistency pattern, although it did contribute to Democratic hegemony.

One approach to voter constancy is to examine the nineteen statewide elections (thirteen gubernatorial and six presidential), with an eye on the percentages of support enjoyed by the parties. It is instructive to analyze proportional strengths in the three divisions of the state. It is almost a truism that antebellum East and West Tennessee were Whig or anti-Democratic, while Middle Tennessee was a pillar of Jacksonianism, yet careful scrutiny of electoral statistics tells us much more about how these sections reacted and how they compared to each other. One must bear in mind that within each of the three divisions there were strong contingents of *both* parties and there were counties which regularly deviated from the norm.

The peculiarities of Tennessee's political behavior come more sharply into focus when we consider the gubernatorial and presidential elections consecutively (see Table 2.1).[1] It might be helpful to look at East Tennessee first and then make some comparisons among the sections. As was true elsewhere, the eastern third of the state experienced some notable changes in the latter half of the 1830s not to be duplicated again after the 1840 election. What is most startling about the trend in East Tennessee during the period 1835-39 is that it was decidedly favorable to the fortunes of the *Democratic,* not the Whig, party. The Democratic percentage increased steadily from 22.6 in 1835, to 34.8 in 1836, to 42.6 in 1837, and to 49.4 in 1839. It looked as if the region, originally in the vanguard of the anti-Jacksonian rebellion, were about to leap into the arms of the enemy, but luckily for the Whigs the 1840 presidential election came along in time to reverse the pattern.

Surely one of the surprises is the voter reaction in the 1836 election, for when East Tennessean Hugh Lawson White sought the presidency in opposition to the Jacksonian candidate, Martin Van Buren, the Democratic percentage *increased* by 12.2 in White's home region. White easily carried East Tennessee (65.2 percent of the vote), but he did not sweep it as impressively as the anti-Democratic candidates had in the 1835 gubernatorial contest. Even so, in East Tennessee, as well as in the statewide vote, White polled the highest percentage of all presidential contenders from 1836 through 1860. His 58 percent of Tennessee's vote was not matched again by any presidential candidate, regardless of party, until after the Civil War.

Part of the explanation for East Tennessee's leanings in the direction of the Democratic party rests in the region's disenchantment with the Whig governor, Newton Cannon. The proportional figures make obvious Cannon's declining appeal in the eastern third of the state. In the 1837 gubernatorial race against a very weak opponent, Robert Armstrong of Nashville, Cannon polled 57.4 percent of the vote. Although Cannon was clearly a winner, his showing was much poorer than in 1835. To put it into perspective, East Tennessee returned a higher Democratic percentage in 1837 than did Middle or West. And East Tennessee was the only section to register a percentage increase for the Democratic party in 1837 compared to the 1836 election.

Table 2.1. Percentage of Democratic Vote by Section, 1835–59

Year	East	Middle	West	STATE
1835	22.6	51.7	39.7	40.3
1836	34.8	48.3	34.3	42.0
1837	42.6	39.3	33.8	39.3
1839	49.4	54.5	45.1	51.1
1840	40.5	49.0	39.2	44.3
1841	45.1	53.1	43.8	48.8
1843	45.3	51.5	45.2	48.3
1844	46.7	53.4	46.3	49.9
1845	47.2	54.2	47.8	50.7
1847	46.3	53.0	47.0	49.7
1848	42.8	51.5	45.0	47.5
1849	46.2	55.0	47.3	50.6
1851	44.8	53.2	48.3	49.6
1852	44.8	52.6	47.6	49.3
1853	49.3	53.1	48.8	50.9
1855	47.1	53.2	49.6	50.5
1856	48.6	56.0	51.5	52.7
1857	50.8	57.4	53.0	54.3
1859	48.2	56.1	52.6	52.8

When faced with a stiff challenge from James K. Polk in 1839, Cannon came dreadfully close to losing East Tennessee (50.6 percent). The combination of Polk's highly effective campaigning and the continuing discontent with Cannon almost sent the region into the Democratic column. But with the regularizing and tightening of the two-party system, East Tennessee quickly settled down to permanent quarters in the Whig household.

The mention of Polk brings to mind his four (three gubernatorial, one presidential) statewide campaigns. In 1839 Polk registered substantial percentage gains in the Democratic vote in all three sections. In fact, his proportion of the vote in East Tennessee was not to be matched or surpassed by a Democrat until Isham Harris carried that section with 50.8 percent of the vote in 1857. In Middle Tennessee, where Democratic strength had been seriously eroded by the 1836 presidential election and by the inept candidacy of Armstrong in

1837, Polk's gain (15.2 percent) was the highest in the state. Polk swept Middle Tennessee with 54.5 percent of the vote—a figure not to be equalled until William Trousdale got 55.0 percent ten years later. In West Tennessee, where Democrats had fared badly ever since the revolt against Jackson, Polk posted an 11.3 percent increment over the 1837 Democratic vote. Statewide Polk pushed the Democrats into the victory column in 1839 with 51.1 percent of the vote, an increase of 11.8 percent over the party's poor 1837 showing. His percentage was not matched or surpassed by a fellow Democrat until 1856, when presidential candidate James Buchanan captured 52.7 percent of Tennessee's vote.

While these statistics suggest the importance of Polk's victory in 1839 they also hint at his inability to duplicate his achievements in subsequent elections. As a matter of fact, Polk attained his highest percentage in East and Middle Tennessee and in the statewide vote in 1839. Only in West Tennessee did Polk improve on his record, for in both 1843 and 1844 (but not 1841) he achieved higher percentages than he had in 1839. There is little doubt that Polk's 1841 governor's race was hurt by the intervening 1840 presidential contest, in which the Democrats lost ground, relatively speaking, in all three sections. Yet Van Buren ran better in 1840 than he had in 1836, perhaps benefiting from Polk's stirring victory in 1839. Although Polk made gains in 1841 in all sections, compared to Van Buren's 1840 record, in none of them was he able to match the percentages he had captured in 1839. Polk enjoyed slight increases in 1843 in East and West Tennessee but suffered a slippage of 1.6 percent in Middle Tennessee. Finally, Polk as a presidential contender in 1844 improved on his 1843 record everywhere, but only in West Tennessee did he surpass his 1839 showing. Although the matter is not clear, it appears that Polk shouldered the burdens of the 1840 presidential contest—when the Democrats failed to carry any section of the state—for several years.

Actually Polk's difficulties with seeking reelection were not unique. In fact, a survey of the twenty-five years from 1835 to 1859 impresses one with the liabilities of incumbency. In the most heated moments of two-party rivalry, James C. Jones was the only one to succeed himself. Cannon won twice but lost the third time; Polk won once but lost thereafter. Aaron V. Brown, Neill S. Brown, and William Trousdale all managed to win their first statewide bids for office but failed on their second efforts. Andrew Johnson (in 1855) and Isham Harris (in 1859) broke the curse of incumbency—aided by the emerging Democratic domination in the 1850s. Not only did candidates have problems winning reelection, but also they seldom improved on their proportional strength. At the statewide level, Cannon gained a greater share of the vote in 1837 than he had in 1835 but then slipped 11.8 percentage points in 1839. James C. Jones increased his proportion of the state vote in 1843 by a scant .5 percent over his 1841 race. Otherwise no gubernatorial candidates received higher percentages in their second or third attempts for the office. All these facts bespeak the highly competitive nature of the political process in the two-party system.

One other sure sign of the balanced rivalry between parties is the frequency with which extremely small alterations in party vote occurred. Table 2.2 conveniently lists, by sections and statewide, the instances in which there was a 2.0 percent or less variation in the Democratic vote.

The symmetry is quite noticeable; more often than not the minuscule fluctuations were experienced in all sections of the state simultaneously. Even more striking is the number of elections characterized by very minor alterations in party vote. If one considers, for example, the fourteen elections in the 1841-59 period, there was a fluctuation of 2.0 percent or less in the statewide vote ten times. In 1841 Polk enjoyed a 4.5 percent gain over the 1840 Democratic vote, but afterward the Democratic vote varied more than 2.0 percent on only three occasions: 1848 (-2.2 percent); 1849 (3.1 percent); and 1856 (2.2 percent). No wonder political leaders took nothing for granted and considered virtually every election a toss-up.

In the discussion above of Polk's campaigns, reference was made to the 1840 presidential election sandwiched between gubernatorial contests. Other clusters of elections should be examined briefly. Table 2.1 shows, for instance, that the percentage of Democratic vote in the sections, as well as the state, improved both before and after the 1844 presidential race (Middle Tennessee in 1843 being the exception). The chief beneficiary of this trend was unfortunately not Polk himself but his close political ally, Aaron V. Brown, who reaped victory in 1845 from the seeds sown by Polk. For the 1847-1848-1849 cluster, in all three sections in 1847 and again in 1848 the Democratic proportion of the vote diminished; in both contests the pulling power of Whig Zachary Taylor exerted its influence. (Taylor's likely candidacy in 1848 was a strong selling point for Tennessee Whigs in the 1847 governor's campaign.) But surprisingly, in 1849 Democrat William Trousdale reversed the pattern, posting percentage gains in all sections of the state; Taylor's coattails apparently were not available for the Whigs once he was in the White House.

Table 2.2. Fluctuations of 2.0 Percent or Less in Democratic Vote, 1836–59

	1836[e]	1837[e]	1843	1844	1845	1847	1848	1851	1852	1853	1855	1856	1857	1859
East[a]			1843	1844	1845	1847		1851	1852			1856		1859
Middle[b]			1843	1844	1845	1847	1848	1851	1852	1853	1855		1857	1859
West[c]		1837[e]	1843	1844	1845	1847	1848	1851	1852	1853	1855	1856	1857	1859
STATE[d]	1836[e]		1843	1844	1845	1847		1851	1852	1853	1855	1856	1857	1859

[a] All these elections in East Tennessee were Democratic defeats.

[b] All these elections in Middle Tennessee were Democratic victories.

[c] All these elections in West Tennessee were Democratic defeats until 1856; the 1856, 1857, and 1859 elections were Democratic victories.

[d] Statewide the 1836, 1843, and 1844 elections were Democratic defeats; the 1845 election was a Democratic victory; the 1847, 1851, and 1852 elections were Democratic defeats; the 1853, 1855, and 1859 elections were all Democratic victories.

[e] The 1836 and 1837 elections occurred before the two-party system was actually established, though it was in the process of evolving.

The 1851-1852-1853 grouping offers a similar picture. In 1851, thanks partly to the strong candidacy of Whig William B. Campbell, the Democrats lost ground in East and Middle but not in West Tennessee. More surprising is that in the 1852 presidential contest, the Democratic percentage vote *decreased* everywhere except in East Tennessee, where it remained the same as in 1851. Considering the controversial candidacy of Whig Winfield Scott in 1852 one would have expected gains, not decreases, for the Democrats. Andrew Johnson in 1853 broke the downward movement and made percentage gains in all sections, especially East Tennessee, his home region.

After the collapse of the Whig party in 1854, the complexion of state politics changed in various ways. Hence the 1855-1856-1857 cluster does not reveal much, except that Democrats were establishing themselves in the driver's seat in Tennessee. The only exception was the percentage decrease experienced by Johnson in East Tennessee in 1855. Otherwise the party's candidates enjoyed gains, with the result that West Tennessee went Democratic in 1856 for the first time and East Tennessee went Democratic in 1857 for the first and only time. Johnson's campaigns in 1853 and 1855 were instrumental in effecting the shift of West Tennessee. West Tennessee stayed in the Democratic camp, but East Tennessee in 1859 abandoned its momentary flirtation with the Jacksonians. Isham Harris benefited throughout the state from the impetus of the 1856 contest and also from the weakness of his gubernatorial rival, Robert Hatton, in 1857. But Harris, like many other candidates, suffered slight percentage decreases in every section of the state in his 1859 reelection canvass.

One final and significant observation about the state's political behavior over the 1835-59 span is shown by the data in Table 2.1. Submitting those statistics on Democratic percentages in the various elections to a linear regression test of voting strength on time, one derives the equation: $Yc=39.8 + .45x$, with $r^2=.64$ This particular finding strongly suggests that the growth of Democratic support in the state was a long-term, gradual, and steady process. The .45x figure indicates that the underlying trend of Democratic support was one of increase at an average of .45 percent per year. Moreover since a perfect fit on the line would be represented by the figure $r^2=1.00$, the finding of $r^2=.64$ means that there was relative little deviation from the perfect trend. Therefore, the underlying trend across the 1835-59 period is strong and shows, as mentioned above, a slow and steady growth of Democratic support.[2] All of these findings support the view that there were no dramatic shifts in Democratic support in the Tennessee elections and therefore there were no really pivotal or critical elections that account for the emergence of Democratic strength.

To illustrate the important point that there were variations in political behavior within the three sections of the state, Table 2.3 shows the percentage of Democratic vote for the thirteen districts from 1835 to 1841.[3] Generally an analysis of the congressional districts corroborates much of what has previously been said about the electoral reactions of the state's three divisions, but there are some differences worth commenting upon.

For East Tennessee, Table 2.3 offers few surprises—with one significant exception. Though all four congressional districts started out as strongly anti-Democratic, the Second District quickly moved in an opposite direction. In the 1837 governor's race that district went into the Democratic column for the first time and stayed there through the 1841 election. Armstrong carried only two Tennessee congressional districts in 1837, the Second being one of them. The ineffectual Democratic candidate clearly profited from the anti-Cannon sentiment which erupted in parts of East Tennessee. The substantial Democratic majorities in Sullivan and Hawkins counties shoved the Second District into the Jacksonian camp and kept it there. Oddly enough, Armstrong ran better in the First District in 1837 than did Polk in 1839—the only district in the entire state to show this pattern; but of course neither Armstrong nor Polk carried that district. Finally, the strongest Whig congressional district in the entire state during the 1835-41 period was the Third District, located in East Tennessee. Prominent in that district were such counties as Knox and Blount.

Table 2.3 shows that there were four Democratic and three Whig districts in Middle Tennessee. Districts 6, 7, and 8 were consistently Whig during the six elections analyzed. The Seventh District (Davidson and Wilson counties) was John Bell's home district; and while it sent Bell, leader of the anti-Jackson movement, back to Congress in 1835 without opposition, it voted ever so slightly for the Democratic gubernatorial candidate, William Carroll. But the 1836 presidential election ruined the Seventh District for the Democrats, and from then through 1841 the district never gave as much as 40 percent of its vote to the Democratic presidential or gubernatorial candidates.

Of the four Democratic districts, there was none stronger in Middle Tennessee or the entire state than the Fifth District, a five-county district located in the eastern Highland Rim region. It always went into the Democratic column during the 1835-41 period and by extremely high percentages. The Ninth District (Bedford and Maury

Table 2.3. Democratic Percentages of Votes by Congressional District, 1835–41

District	1835	1836	1837	1839	1840	1841
First	24.0	37.1	47.3	41.7	35.0	39.1
Second	28.1	43.6	52.3	63.7	53.6	57.6
Third	17.7	19.2	30.9	37.7	27.2	31.6
Fourth	21.3	28.6	38.3	48.8	41.6	45.7
Fifth	63.9	56.8	55.8	68.7	64.3	66.4
Sixth	46.2	38.9	43.9	45.1	38.8	41.3
Seventh	50.5	34.3	33.1	39.9	32.2	35.5
Eighth	37.0	34.4	25.9	43.7	36.6	41.0
Ninth	42.7	57.1	48.4	59.4	55.3	58.5
Tenth	59.4	54.1	39.7	59.9	56.3	59.5
Eleventh	55.3	54.5	39.4	58.2	52.7	57.2
Twelfth	33.5	29.7	33.1	45.7	38.2	43.3
Thirteenth	46.9	38.7	33.4	44.3	39.4	43.5
STATE	40.3	42.0	39.3	51.1	44.3	48.8

counties), Polk's home district, must have been a source of keen embarrassment to him in the 1835 and 1837 gubernatorial contests, but he won reelection to Congress on both these occasions. His hard work in behalf of Van Buren in 1836 paid off in his district with a 57.1 Democratic percentage that year, and, happily, Polk's district avidly supported him when he himself sought the governor's office. Two of the Democratic districts in Middle Tennessee, the Tenth and the Eleventh, experienced serious difficulties with the Armstrong candidacy in the 1837 race, as Table 2.3 suggests, but in 1839 Polk was able to turn both districts back to their customary allegiances and they did not stray again. Polk's poorest showings in the 1839 contest were in the Third District (the state's strongest Whig district) and the Seventh District (home district of arch-rival John Bell). The "revolt" against Jackson did not affect all portions of Middle Tennessee, so far as electoral behavior indicates, certainly as applies to the Fifth, Tenth, and Eleventh districts.[4]

In West Tennessee the two congressional districts were consistently and strongly Whig. Table 2.3 adds little to what has been claimed earlier about West Tennessee's political loyalties, but it does show that

Tennessee's Congressional Districts, 1832-1841

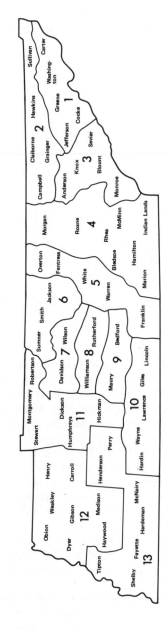

Map adapted from Stanley B. Parsons, William W. Beach, and Dan Hermann, *United States Congressional Districts, 1788-1841* (Westport, Conn., 1978), p. 363.

initially the Thirteenth District was less enthusiastically Whig than it subsequently became. The voting pattern of both districts was remarkably similar, except for the 1835 and 1836 elections.

Other points of analysis are provided by Table 2.4, which indicates the population of the various congressional districts, as well as the actual number and percentage of slaves in each of them. Although there was some variation in the sizes of the districts, it was not substantial. Perhaps more informative are the data on the districts when adjusted to subtract 40 percent of the slave population (since the national constitution prescribed that only three-fifths or 60 percent of the slave population could be counted for purposes of representation in Congress.) Given the total statewide population (with 40 percent of the slave population subtracted) the average size congressional district shoud have been 48,093. Of the thirteen districts, however, only six more or less conform to this; they are the First, Third, Fourth, Fifth, Twelfth, and Thirteenth districts. Four of the districts (the Second, Sixth, Seventh, and Eighth) were essentially overrepresented—that is, their adjusted population figures fell noticeably below the so-called average size of approximately 48,100. Of these four districts, three were Whig in loyalty and one was Democratic. There were three Tennessee districts that were underrepresented, their populations exceeding the norm. They were the Ninth, Tenth, and Eleventh districts, all of which were Democratic in political commitment in this period. In sum, there seems to be little discernible pattern to the whole matter of the size of the given districts, except that there were variations across the state with most of it occurring in the Middle Tennessee districts.

Considering the data on the percentage of slave population in each district (see Table 2.4) and the percentage of Democratic support (see Table 2.3), one can derive correlation coefficients for the 1835–41 period. The election years of 1835 and 1837 return correlation coefficients that suggest the possiblility of some causal relationship between the two sets of data. The coefficients are +.412 for 1835 and -.407 for 1837; but the small number of cases (thirteen districts) may rule against attaching much significance to these findings. On the basis of what is discussed in Chapter 3 about those two elections, there is no readily available explanation of why there *might have been* some relationship between slave population concentration and Democratic support in 1835 and a change in the relationship in 1837. The coefficients of correlation for the other four elections in this particular time span are too low to support the contention that there was any connection between slave percentages and Democratic percentages.[5]

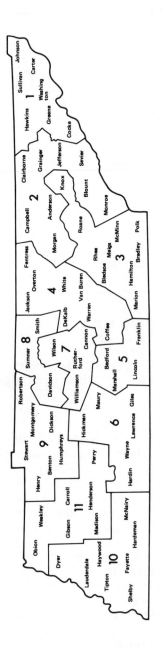

Tennessee's Congressional Districts, 1843-1851

Table 2.4. Data on Total and Slave Populations by Congressional District, 1835–41

District	Total population	Adjusted population	Slave population	Percentage slave	Political loyalty
First	49,636	47,876	4,400	8.9	Whig
Second	47,402	45,556	4,615	9.7	Democratic
Third	50,261	48,276	4,963	9.9	Whig
Fourth	49,001	47,438	3,909	8.0	Whig
Fifth	51,787	48,993	6,986	13.5	Democratic
Sixth	50,173	45,109	12,660	25.2	Whig
Seventh	53,594	46,552	17,606	32.8	Whig
Eighth	52,772	45,111	19,154	36.3	Whig
Ninth	58,061	52,026	15,087	26.0	Democratic
Tenth	57,070	52,552	11,296	19.7	Democratic
Eleventh	56,160	50,401	14,398	25.6	Democratic
Twelfth	53,175	47,697	13,695	25.7	Whig
Thirteenth	52,811	47,736	12,939	24.5	Whig
STATE	681,903	625,220	141,708	20.8	

Source: District population data in this table are drawn from Parsons et al., *Congressional Districts*, pp. 362–65. The slave population figures include free blacks. The figures on adjusted populations represent my own calculations. Political loyalty has been derived by examining the data provided above in Table 2.3.

Based on the new federal census of 1840 and the requirements of Congress, Tennessee's representation dropped from thirteen to eleven. This necessitated, of course, a redrawing of congressional districts, an action carried out in 1842 by the legislature (Democratic control of Senate, Whig control of the House). The first election affected by the new redistricting was the gubernatorial contest in 1843. Table 2.5 conveniently shows the percentages won by the Democratic gubernatorial and presidential candidates during those years. A remarkable picture of stability and consistency emerges from these data. Of the state's eleven districts, only one—the Tenth—fluctuated in its party loyalty, voting Whig four times and Democratic three times. Setting aside that particular district, there were five Democratic (1,4,5,6, and 9) and five Whig districts (2,3,7,8, and 11). Since Table 2.5 does not show the results of elections for congressmen, it should be pointed out that five of the eleven districts were noncompetitive in this period; and

Table 2.5. Democratic Percentages of Votes by Congressional District, 1843–51

District	1843	1844	1845	1847	1848	1849	1851
First	51.7	53.9	54.1	51.9	50.2	54.2	51.0
Second	37.6	38.9	40.9	39.3	34.6	38.9	37.9
Third	46.8	47.1	46.6	47.8	43.5	46.0	45.7
Fourth	58.6	60.9	61.6	59.5	57.0	61.7	58.7
Fifth	65.1	67.8	67.9	66.5	66.6	68.2	65.6
Sixth	53.3	57.6	58.0	55.7	54.8	56.5	55.4
Seventh	38.8	38.5	41.0	40.9	38.0	40.9	42.7
Eighth	44.4	45.0	44.7	44.4	43.9	48.6	44.8
Ninth	51.9	53.9	54.7	54.0	52.0	55.3	55.1
Tenth	48.5	49.7	51.7	49.8	48.6	51.2	51.2
Eleventh	38.0	39.9	40.1	40.7	37.3	39.9	42.3
STATE	48.3	49.9	50.7	49.7	47.5	50.6	49.6

of the remaining six, only three districts ever changed hands from one party to the other. In 1843 and again in 1851, the Third District, for example, elected a Democratic congressman—albeit by painfully small margins. The Eighth District deviated once from its normal pattern by electing a Democrat in the 1849 election. The Tenth District began choosing Democrats for Congress in 1845 and continued through the 1851 contest.[6] Seen in this light, the Tenth District certainly appears to be more Democratic than Whig.

It is obvious from Table 2.5 that the strongest Democratic district in the state was the Fifth District—composed of four counties from the lower part of Middle Tennessee: Franklin, Lincoln, Bedford, and Marshall. In all seven of the elections reviewed here, the best showing for the Democratic gubernatorial or presidential candidates was in this district. Conversely, the strongest Whig district was the Second District—an East Tennessee district of nine counties located mainly in the central portion of that region. The poorest showing for the Democratic candidates occurred in this district five of the seven times; but in 1844 and in 1845 this distinction went respectively to the Seventh and the Eleventh districts. Further analysis shows that Aaron V. Brown and William Trousdale did better than the other Democratic candidates in securing high percentages for their party. For example, the strongest Democratic percentages during this period were achieved by Brown in 1845 in the Second, Sixth, and Tenth districts and in 1847 in the Third District. The highest Democratic percentages in the First, Fourth, Fifth, Eighth, and Ninth districts occurred in Trousdale's 1849 race and in the Seventh and Eleventh districts in his 1851 bid for reelection. The lowest percentages, on the other hand, are seen in the 1848 presidential race when Lewis Cass achieved this dubious honor in seven of the eleven districts (1,2,- 3,4,7,8, and 11). The lowest Democratic percentages in the Fifth, Sixth, Ninth, and Tenth districts were in the 1843 gubernatorial election, when Polk again went down in defeat at the hands of James C. Jones.

In his study of the 1843-51 period, Brian G. Walton lends further weight to the theme of voter constancy, finding that the "three levels of party strength, presidential, gubernatorial, and congressional, tended to coincide to a remarkable degree." Of the forty instances during this period when a direct comparison between the guber-natorial and congressional races was possible, Walton found that the difference between the two performances was 1.0 percent or less in twenty-three cases, and in only nine instances was the difference 3.0 percent or more. Moreover, "in only six out of forty-four cases did the presidential election differ more than 3.0 percent from the guber-natorial elections preceding and succeeding it at the congressional district level in the 1840's." Walton also found that generally the Democratic gubernatorial candidates ran ahead of their congressional tickets in the Middle Tennessee districts but trailed in the East and West Tennessee districts. On the matter of voter participation in the districts, Walton found "strikingly similar" levels in gubernatorial, presidential, and congressional races—though generally participation in the latter contests was not quite as high. Obviously, the noncompet-itive districts, so far as congressional races were concerned, accounted for most of the noticeable differences in voter participation among the three different kinds of elections. It should also be noted that there was a tendency for voter participation in gubernatorial (but not in presidential) contests in the West Tennessee districts to trail that seen elsewhere; this was likewise true of the Eighth District in Middle Tennessee. Walton suggests that "geographical location . . . was often more significant than the presence or absence of competitiveness in determining the degree of participation within a particular district."[7] All in all, his analysis of the congressional districts demonstrates that a given party could, more often than not, depend upon the voters of a certain district to react with consistency, regardless of the type of election being held.

Table 2.6 shows clearly that there was considerable disparity in the population of the districts in the 1840s, unlike the preceding decade. For whatever reason the legislators doing the redistricting in 1842 apparently paid little or no attention to the population data in the 1840 census; they seemed to have had no concern about the equal apportionment of districts. This appears to be the case, whether one examines the total population of each district or the adjusted population figures. Considering the latter, the so-called average district in this period should have had an adjusted population of 79,796. Yet, Table 2.6 shows that only the Second and Seventh districts out of the eleven conformed to this norm. Thus nine of the districts were either underrepresented or overrepresented, when measured against the average adjusted population of approximately 80,000.

Five of the districts were overrepresented; that is, their population figures fell considerably below the theoretical average. These were the First, Fourth, Fifth, Eighth, and Ninth districts. With the exception of the Eighth, all of the overrepresented districts were Democratic in political loyalty. One of the so-called overrepresented districts, the First, had been redrawn in 1842 through the influence of Andrew Johnson in the state senate so as to create a congressional fiefdom for himself. It became a Democratic district, rather than Whig as it had been in the preceding decade, simply by the addition of the strongly Democratic counties of Sullivan and Hawkins. There were four underrepresented districts: the Third, Sixth, Tenth, and Eleventh. Their adjusted population figures stood considerably higher than the norm. Two of these four districts were Whig districts, one was Democratic, and one had a mixed voting record. From the point of view of the three sections one can enter a tentative claim that Middle Tennessee had the presumed benefit of overrepresentation, whereas West Tennessee was underrepresented. It is nearly impossible to establish, however, whether such considerations played much part in the deliberations of the legislature when it devised the districts in 1842. Given the overall lack of conformity to the theoretical norm for population size, it seems that the legislators did not concern themselves with the matter of fair apportionment of the districts.

If one takes the data in Table 2.6 on the percentage of slave population and the figures in Table 2.5 on the percentage of Democratic support in the congressional districts, it is possible to derive correlation coefficients for each election during the 1843-51 period. As indicated below, the coefficients for all of the elections are so low that there is no possibility for maintaining, quantitatively, any relationship

Table 2.6. Total and Slave Populations by Congressional District, 1843-51

District	Total population	Adjusted population	Slave population	Percentage slave	Political loyalty
First	75,098	72,365	6,834	9.1	Democratic
Second	82,597	79,505	7,730	9.4	Whig
Third	95,137	91,066	10,178	10.7	Whig
Fourth	72,002	68,708	8,236	11.4	Democratic
Fifth	74,387	66,928	18,648	25.1	Democratic
Sixth	92,644	81,667	27,442	29.6	Democratic
Seventh	92,748	79,331	33,544	36.2	Whig
Eighth	80,011	68,826	27,962	34.9	Whig
Ninth	86,283	76,301	24,956	28.9	Democratic
Tenth	125,872	104,089	54,457	43.3	Mixed
Eleventh	98,211	88,978	23,083	23.5	Whig
STATE*	974,990	877,762	243,070	24.9	

*These totals exclude the six counties established after the 1842 redistricting but before the 1850 census. They had an aggregate population of 27,727 and a slave population of 2,811.

between Democratic support in the districts and the concentration of black population.[9]

In early 1852 the Tennessee legislature redrew congressional district lines, mainly out of necessity since the number had been reduced from eleven to ten, but partly out of political spite. The Whig-controlled legislature was especially intent on restructuring Andrew Johnson's home district—the First—so as to make it very difficult for him to be reelected to Congress (delayed revenge for Johnson's efforts ten years earlier to carve out a political preserve for himself in the First District). To that end, the heavily Whig counties of Jefferson and Sevier were tacked on to that district; otherwise, the district was essentially what it had been in the 1840s. As noted below in Chapter 5, Johnson was indeed forced to reassess his political career; poetic justice (or revenge) was his when he successfully ran for governor in 1853 and 1855. Ironically, the First District exhibited mixed political behavior in the statewide elections in the 1850s.

As Table 2.7 clearly shows, the decade of the 1850s was unlike that

Table 2.7. Democratic Percentages of Votes by Congressional District, 1852–59

District	1852	1853	1855	1856	1857	1859
First	46.3	50.9	48.7	50.1	52.1	49.0
Second	42.7	47.2	45.3	48.5	51.5	48.3
Third	49.6	53.5	53.0	52.3	53.7	52.0
Fourth	46.0	48.8	52.8	54.6	56.0	53.4
Fifth	44.5	46.1	44.2	47.6	49.4	49.1
Sixth	64.7	64.8	61.9	66.7	67.2	66.4
Seventh	54.0	53.6	56.8	59.3	61.7	58.7
Eighth	46.7	46.7	42.2	45.8	48.0	46.9
Ninth	47.0	48.2	50.6	51.3	51.9	51.5
Tenth	47.6	49.7	46.5	50.3	52.4	52.2
STATE	49.3	50.9	50.5	52.7	54.3	52.8

of the 1840s, principally because the incredible stability of congressional voting behavior disintegrated. One simple illustration makes the point: in 1852 there were two Democratic and eight anti-Democratic districts; but in 1859, there were seven Democratic and only three anti-Democratic districts. Admittedly, this was not a fixed pattern throughout the period, but it is indicative of the transformation that took place across the state. Another way of pointing out the fluidity of electoral behavior is to note that there were three districts that were anti-Democratic: the Second (but it went Democratic in 1857); the Fifth and the Eighth (they never voted Democratic). By the same token, there were five Democratic districts: the Third (anti-Democratic in 1852); the Fourth (anti-Democratic in 1852 and 1853); the Sixth (always strongly Democratic); the Seventh (always Democratic); and the Ninth (anti-Democratic in 1852 and 1853). Finally, there were two districts which exhibited quite mixed behavior: the First (voted Democratic three times and anti-Democratic three times); and the Tenth (likewise voted Democratic three times and anti-Democratic three times).[10]

Much of the transformation of politics in this decade was the direct result of the demise of the Whig party and the consequent turmoil and confusion among the voters. The disappearance of the Whig party meant that Tennesseans of that persuasion had to seek shelter in new quarters or else change their spots and move into the Democratic camp. With these kinds of decisions staring many Tennessee voters in the face, it is small wonder that political allegiances experienced twists and turns and also that the Democratic party reaped favorable results from these events. Looking again at Table 2.7, one can see that District 3 went into the Democratic column in 1853 and remained there for the duration of the decade, District 4 shifted in 1855, as did District 9, while District 10 waited until the 1856 election to make the shift. The districts not only exhibited changing loyalties, they also showed a pronounced trend toward the Democratic party.

But some things remained constant in the electoral behavior of the districts in this period. As noted above, the Fifth and Eighth districts stayed with the anti-Democratic party (whatever its label) through thick and thin. The Fifth was a crescent-shaped district, composed of five Middle Tennessee counties. Except for the addition of Sumner County, this district had the same composition as the Seventh District had had during 1843-51, when the Seventh had been one of the strongest Whig districts. Sumner was a heavily Democratic county, but it could not offset the usually strong anti-Democratic votes of the other counties. Contiguous to the Fifth District was the Eighth, a Middle Tennessee district of five counties led by Davidson, renowned for its notable anti-Democratic majorities; Davidson's pattern was closely imitated by Robertson and Montgomery counties in that district. The Democrats on their side could always count on the Sixth and Seventh districts, which never wavered in their loyalty. The Sixth, unquestionably the strongest Democratic district in the state, was composed of the same four Middle Tennessee counties that had constituted the Fifth District in the 1840s—the most devoted Democratic district in that period. The only difference was that the Sixth had an additional county, Maury, a traditional Democratic stronghold. The Seventh was a sprawling district of eleven counties (seven Middle and four West Tennessee) that took in most of the southern and western part of Middle Tennessee and then crossed the Tennessee River to include four counties on that side. Since it bore no relationship to any single district in the 1840s, there is no basis for comparison. In sum, Districts 5,6,7, and 8 managed to remain true to their political colors, despite the changing political milieu. The total population and the adjusted population figures in Table 2.8 show readily the disparity in sizes of the districts. Theoretically each district should have had a population of 97,036 (counting whites plus 60 percent of the slave population) but in the 1850s not a single district came close to matching that norm. The admitted gerrymandering of the First District doubtless contributed to that district's emerging as the second largest,

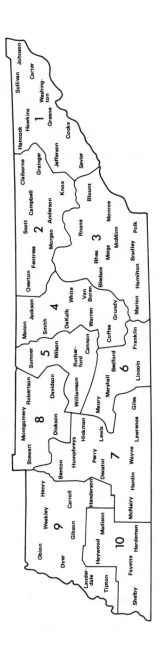

Tennessee's Congressional Districts, 1852-1861

Table 2.8. Total and Slave Populations by Congressional District, 1852-59[11]

District	Total population	Adjusted population	Slave population	Percentage slave	Political loyalty
First	118,282	113,924	10,895	9.2	Mixed
Second	81,761	78,730	7,577	9.3	Anti-Democratic
Third	107,007	101,711	13,241	12.4	Democratic
Fourth	81,836	76,458	13,445	16.4	Democratic
Fifth	109,356	92,295	42,653	39.0	Anti-Democratic
Sixth	105,350	90,701	36,622	34.8	Democratic
Seventh	111,977	103,050	22,317	19.9	Democratic
Eighth	103,093	88,994	35,248	34.2	Anti-Democratic
Ninth	132,671	118,007	36,660	27.6	Democratic
Tenth	130,955	106,493	61,156	46.7	Mixed
STATE*	1,082,288	970,363	279,814	25.8	

*These totals exclude the five countries created after the 1852 reapportionment and prior to the 1860 census, which had an aggregate total population of 27,513 and a total slave population of 3,205 (including free blacks).

in terms of adjusted population, in Tennessee. Across the state, there were five districts that were underrepresented—that is, their adjusted populations exceeded the norm of approximately 97,000: the First, Third, Seventh, Ninth, and Tenth. The other five districts were overrepresented, with the Second and Fourth being the most blatant examples. From the geographical point of view, West Tennessee again was underrepresented when compared to the theoretical norm. With regard to political loyalties, not much can be made of the fact that of the five underrepresented districts three were Democratic and two were mixed in their political behavior, while the five overrepresented districts were divided into three anti-Democratic and two Democratic.

In the final decade before the Civil War, as in the 1840s, the ideal of somewhat equally apportioned congressional districts received scant attention from the Tennessee legislature. It appears that, of the three decades under review, only the 1830s came close to having fairly evenly divided districts, in terms of population. The districts in that decade, it should be noted, were drawn prior to the revolt against Jackson and the development of the two-party system. A chronologically broader and more comprehensive study of Tennessee's congressional districts would be necessary to determine whether the experience of the malapportioned districts in the 1840s and 1850s was unique or, on the contrary, fairly traditional.

Despite all the changes taking place in the decade of the 1850s, an examination of the data on slave percentages (see Table 2.8) and Democratic percentages (see Table 2.7) again leads to the conclusion that there really was no relationship between the two sets of information. The correlation coefficients for all six of the elections in the 1852-59 period are very low.[12] Therefore, as in the preceding decades, the concentration of black population in the districts appears not to have had an impact upon political behavior.

One final observation about the congressional districts should be made. Utilizing the data found in Tables 2.3, 2.5, and 2.7 on Democratic percentages in the various districts from 1835 through 1859, one can calculate the Democratic mean and the standard deviation for each election with the object of establishing some notions about electoral behavior. As shown below in Table 2.9, there are some noteworthy points to be made here. With a few exceptions, the Democratic mean continued to increase over time from 1835 (40.5 percent) to 1859 (52.8 percent). The standard deviation figures (which measure the degree of variation around the mean) steadily decreased from 14.9 in 1835 to only 5.8 in 1859. This indicates that over time there was increasing uniformity in voting among the districts, a narrowing of the spread between relatively high percentage districts and relatively low percentage Democratic districts. Democratic strength increased across the years, and it was more uniformly distributed among the congressional districts. These particular findings relative to the districts seem to conform well to the earlier mentioned linear regression test for the statewide voting data.

The next unit to be examined after the three sections and the congressional districts is the county, the smallest entity for which voting returns are available for Tennessee in the antebellum period.[13] Any analysis of electoral reactions of individual counties during most or all of the twenty-five years from 1835 to 1859 is rendered nearly impossible by the legislature's creation of about twenty new counties during this period. With only one exception, Bradley County (1836), all of the counties established after 1835 were carved out of already existing counties; in fact, in most instances the new counties were formed by lopping off portions of two or more counties. Hence the pitfalls are many in attempting to analyze a given county's voting behavior over an extended period. For the 1835-59 span, one might separate out those counties unaffected by the legislature's penchant for establishing new counties, but such a procedure would yield a

Electoral Behavior   31

Table 2.9. Democratic Means and Standard Deviations, 1835–59

Year	S.D.	Mean	Year	S.D.	Mean
1835	14.9	40.5	1848	9.6	47.9
1836	12.0	40.5	1849	9.3	51.0
1837	8.9	40.1	1851	8.3	50.0
1839	10.1	50.5	1852	6.3	48.9
1840	11.2	43.9	1853	5.5	51.0
1841	10.8	47.7	1855	6.1	50.2
1843	8.7	48.6	1856	6.2	52.7
1844	9.6	50.3	1857	5.9	54.4
1845	9.2	51.0	1859	5.8	52.8
1847	8.6	50.0			

disappointingly small list of approximately thirty counties scattered around the state. Another alternative would be to divide the twenty-five years into smaller chronological segments so as to minimize the problem of new county creation, but this defeats the purpose of a long-range examination. One could, of course, utilize county aggregate voting data as a means of circumventing the problems of individual county analysis. In any event despite the obvious difficulties, a number of rewarding lines of inquiry may be pursued to show how counties responded to the competitiveness of the two-party system.

In view of what has already been said about the three sections and the congressional districts, it is not surprising to learn that the counties showed remarkable voting consistency and stability during the antebellum period. Using presidential election returns from 1840 to 1860, for example, to determine the percentage of Democratic support on a county by county basis, Frank M. Lowrey III found that in only twenty-four instances (or about 7 percent of all the cases) did the Democratic proportion shift in two successive elections as much as 10 percent. In about 65 percent of the cases, the percentage changes were less than 5 percent.[14] Lowrey offers another approach by comparing two successive presidential elections on the basis of the percentages captured by the Democratic party in the counties. The extremely high coefficients of correlation from 1840-60 (.99 the highest, and .94 the lowest) show the stability of the Democratic vote in the presidential contests. A comparison of Democratic percentages in the 1836 and 1840 elections, however, yields a correlation coefficient of .76, indicating that prior to 1840 there was relative instability and flux in county voting behavior. An analysis of the percentages of the anti-Democratic party support in presidential elections from 1848 to 1860 reveals extraordinarily high coefficients of correlation, again demonstrating party stability and voter consistency.[15]

Examining Democratic percentages in the counties during gubernatorial elections affords another point of analysis. To accommodate the problems of new county creation, Lowrey divided the two-party period into three blocs: 1837-43, 1845-51, and 1853-59. Not surprisingly, the only relatively low correlation coefficients were found for the comparisons of the 1837 Democratic percentages with those of 1839, 1841, and 1843; this suggests a time of fluidity as compared to the constancy of the post-1839 period. From 1839 through 1859, the correlation coefficients were very high, never dropping below .94. Consequently, it is indisputable that the performance of the Democratic ticket in the counties in one governor's race was very closely matched by that in a succeeding contest.[16] In his study of the 1840s, Brian Walton likewise found barely measurable differences in the counties' support of a given party.[17] Even a comparison of presidential and gubernatorial elections, on the basis of Democratic percentages in the counties from 1843 to 1860, merely confirms the remarkable consistency of the voting behavior of the counties across the state (.95 was the lowest coefficient of correlation).[18] There is no room to doubt the near rigidity quickly established by the parties, so far as the electoral behavior of the counties in gubernatorial and presidential contests goes.

Other avenues of investigation include an assessment of the relationship between economic status and party allegiance. The hoary contention that prosperous counties voted Whig and poorer counties voted Democratic can be tested in a quantitative framework. To make his analysis more manageable, Frank Lowrey initially focused on the 1844 presidential election, since by that year the two-party system was firmly entrenched in Tennessee.

Lowrey arranged seventy counties into three categories based upon average real estate values: low, medium, and high. Statewide he found that 43 percent of the counties voting Democratic and 37 percent of those voting Whig fell into the low-land value group, while 38 percent of the Democratic counties and 43 percent of the Whig counties were in the medium bloc. The third category—high value—included 20 percent of both the Democratic and the Whig counties. Thus, on a statewide basis, it is impossible to make much of the relationship between land values and party preferences. This is further borne out by a mean square contingency coefficient test, utilized by Lowrey. Statewide the coefficient was .03, and only Middle Tennessee showed a relatively stronger association, with a .20 coefficient.[19] But in truth that section's coefficient is too low to claim a relationship between economics and politics.

To follow still further the quest for economic-political relationships in the counties in the 1844 election, Lowrey tested the percentages of Democratic vote against twelve different economic characteristics in order to arrive at coefficients of correlation. For the state as a whole and for each of the sections the correlation coefficients for the bivariate associations were all extremely low. When seven economic characteristics (total population, percentage of slaves, value of farms, cattle per capita, swine per capita, bushels of corn per capita, and population density) were combined to yield multiple coefficients, something of note emerged—but only for Middle Tennessee. That section's correlation coefficient was .68, suggesting that Democratic strength was at least somewhat related to these economic indicators. To put it another way, about half of the variation (.68 coefficient equals 46 percent) in aggregate political behavior among Middle Tennessee counties can be attributed to these seven combined economic factors. Statewide, however, the coefficient was a scant .27, showing a very weak association between economic patterns and politics in 1844.[20]

While this multifaceted analysis of the 1844 presidential election is instructive and perhaps typical of what one would find for nearly all of the elections of this period, additional understanding may be furnished by broadening the coverage to include presidential elections from 1844 to 1856. Lowrey has done this on the basis of counties that experienced rapid, moderate, and slight increases in land values from 1850 to 1860. The analysis is confined to the fifty-four counties unaffected by new county creation during this time span. Statewide Lowrey found that the Democratic percentage net gain for the counties experiencing rapid increases in land value was 3.3, for counties with moderate increases 5.6, and for counties with slight increases 2.8. This general pattern was adhered to in each of the three sections; nowhere in the state did the percentage net gain for the Democrats in rapidly increasing value counties vary from that in slightly increasing value counties by as much as one percentage point. A mean square contingency coefficient test yielded a statewide figure of .06—which shows the almost nonexistent relationship between changing land values and Democratic preferences in the counties in the 1844-56 elections. The -.29 coefficient for West Tennessee is a faint hint that increasing land values were associated with Whig votes there. Ralph

A. Wooster reports that in 1850 a majority of the counties in Tennessee with farms valued above the state average were represented by Whig legislators.[21] All in all, however, the picture remains pretty much the same: there is little empirical basis for seeing county electoral behavior solely in economic terms.

These aspects of electoral behavior that have been examined at the statewide, congressional district, and county levels reveal an impressive picture of balanced competitiveness. Very gradually and by small increments, however, the Democratic party regained strength so that by the mid-1850s it was able to dominate the political scene. In that sense, after some twenty years of intense rivalry and many defeats, the Jacksonians in Tennessee ended the period by taking control—a position they had enjoyed before the two-party system developed. Having established in this chapter something of the empirical background of the state's antebellum political experiences, it is appropriate now to turn to a more qualitative narrative of elections that ushered in the two-party system and sustained it until the Civil War.

III   Political Revolution 1834-39

In the early 1830s Tennessee seemed a most un-
likely place for a political insurrection among its citizenry. After all,
Andrew Jackson, the state's most famous individual, was serving as
president, and most Tennesseans took great pride in his accomplishments. But midway through his second term, Jackson suffered the
profound embarrassment and displeasure of witnessing a widespread
"revolt" in his home state. His vice president, Martin Van Buren of
New York, served unwittingly as a focal point of much of the unhappiness among Tennessee voters. By the time of the 1835 gubernatorial
campaign, Jackson partisans could not shut their eyes to the reality
of the rebellion. Once launched, this sudden anti-Jackson movement
swept everything along the way—gubernatorial and presidential contests. So menacing did it become that only James K. Polk's return to
Tennessee in 1839 and his successful governor's race prevented the
state from establishing itself as a bastion of Whiggery.

The anti-Jackson plotters quickly latched on to the highly popular
Senator Hugh Lawson White. The distasteful irony of this hastily
formed alliance was that White had long been identified, both personally and politically, with the career and policies of Andrew Jackson.
A reluctant leader of "revolution," White nonetheless threw himself
into the thick of battle and carried the state in the 1836 presidential
canvass. The repercussions of White's accomplishment were to be felt
for the next two decades in Tennessee.

But the spotlight did not shine only upon Jackson and White, for
John Bell and James. K. Polk nearly stole the show with their intense
personal rivalry, which soon blossomed into the beginnings of two-
party development in Tennessee. Personal allegiances, not ideological
commitments, were often the sinews that gave strength to the emergence of a rivalry in Tennessee. That Polk and Bell were patently
ambitious seems indisputable, and that they were to be thrown into
conflict with each other seems to have been almost inevitable. As their
antagonism grew, Polk and Bell went separate ways on supporting
Jackson and his policies, for there did not seem to be room enough
for both of them in the Jacksonian household. In fact, as early as 1833

the two congressmen were moving in different directions. Polk was becoming more and more the man upon whom the White House depended for leadership in the House of Representatives, especially on the all important bank question. John Bell, on the other hand, took the path of silence, which was interpreted subsequently and correctly as opposition to the Jacksonian position on the national bank. Because Bell did not subscribe to this essential dogma of the Jacksonian faith, he would soon find himself excommunicated from the Democratic church. Thus whatever misgivings he might have had about making the break from Jackson vanished when the president's group expelled him, although there is the lingering suspicion that somehow in the early 1830s Bell sensed that Jackson liked Polk more than Bell and therefore his political future would have to be attached to some group other than the Jacksonian.[1] It is difficult to determine, of course, whether the Bell-Jackson alienation and divorce were first related to personality or to principles, but eventually the two men differed on both counts.

The contests for the speakership in 1834 and 1835 brought to the surface the smoldering hostility between Polk and Bell. The persistent rumor in the 1833-34 session of Congress that Andrew Stevenson would resign as speaker in order to accept a diplomatic appointment excited the ambitions of both Polk and Bell. In fact, as early as the summer of 1833 Polk had corresponded with various Tennessee and out-of-state friends about the possibility of his seeking the speaker's chair.[2] But not until the summer of 1834 did the time seem propitious for Stevenson to submit his resignation, whereupon Polk and Bell launched their campaigns for the speakership. Jackson and his followers lost this round of the battle as Bell, depending largely upon anti-Jackson support, emerged victorious.[3] But in many respects it was a hollow triumph for him: it pushed him to the brink from which very shortly he would have to leap into the anti-Jacksonian camp, and it meant that in Tennessee political controversy would dog his steps from this point forward.

Immediately upon their return to Middle Tennessee, Polk and Bell unleashed their attacks. Polk was particularly eager to broadcast the message about Bell's alleged apostasy, but he discovered in the fall of 1834, as he would frequently, that he was hamstrung by the lack of an effective, friendly newspaper, for both the *Nashville Banner* and the *Nashville Republican* showed their pro-Bell colors at this time. After Bell's somewhat rash speech in Murfreesboro in October, Polk was greatly agitated to have a full and correct copy of it printed in one of the Nashville papers, but he finally had to settle for the less prestigious *Murfreesboro Monitor.*[4]

Bell quickly assumed leadership of the successful, but potentially dangerous, promotion of White for the presidency. When the congressmen returned to Tennessee in the spring of 1835, they discovered how widespread was the pro-White crusade they had fostered. But Polk, who had refused to support his colleagues' endorsement of White, soon enlisted others in the strategy of trying to defeat Bell's bid for reelection to Congress in 1835, surmising that if they were successful, the White cause would be seriously weakened if not fatally wounded. At first they tried to persuade William Carroll, the popular governor, to run, but he backed away from the daring opportunity and determined instead to seek the gubernatorial office again. Robert M. Burton, a Wilson County lawyer and friend of Jackson, finally consented to the unenviable assignment, but he withdrew from the race in June because of personal difficulties. Time did not then permit another candidate to come forth, so ironically both Bell and Polk ran unopposed in their respective congressional districts.[5]

Had either man been defeated in the August 1835 elections, there would have been no showdown in December over the speakership. Two or three weeks after the elections, *Nashville Union* editor, Samuel H. Laughlin began reminding Polk of the crucial importance of his winning the speaker's chair. Meanwhile, Andrew J. Donelson tried to impress upon Van Buren the beneficial effect in Tennessee that Polk's selection as speaker would have. The state's Democrats fervently desired a Polk triumph in December in Washington to prove that the White movement was dissipating in Tennessee. By the time members of the House were ready to make their decision, an obvious choice lay before them: Polk was the administration's candidate, whereas Bell represented the opposition. When the votes were counted, Polk was the winner by a decisive margin.[6] This victory meant that the White cause would have diminished appeal in 1836 at the national level, though the same could not be said about Tennessee.

Not surprisingly, the state's Jacksonians drew joy and encouragement from Polk's success. Their extravagant celebrating indicated both their elation and their hunger for something to be jubilant about. Many were quick to claim that Van Buren's cause had been materially enhanced in Tennessee by the election of Polk as speaker. As Polk's fellow townsman Andrew C. Hays declared: *"Van Buren will get the State!!!"* And Polk's brother-in-law insisted that the speakership outcome was "conclusive evidence of the utter hopelessness of Judge

White's prospects of Success in the Presidential canvass." In its report of victory celebrations the *Nashville Union* interpreted Polk's triumph as the demise of the influence of John Bell in Tennessee: "The bells were rung, indicating, in no very mournful notes, the approaching dissolution of *Bell*-ism in this State."[7] The exuberant Democrats were whistling in the dark, however, for there was still plenty of evidence that the steam had not gone out of the White machine. In the September 1837 speakership contest Polk defeated Bell again, but this victory did not stir as much reaction as the earlier battles had. Perhaps there was an awareness on both sides that capturing the leadership post in Congress could not readily be translated into votes in Tennessee. Certainly there is no denying that the Polk-Bell public and private clashes were a pivotal point in the evolution of two-party politics in their home state.

But the changes which took place in Tennessee politics in this period were not the result solely of the activities and policies of aggressive leaders who excited and wooed the electorate. There were other vital components of the story, such as the new constitution drafted in 1834 and ratified in 1835. The state had functioned under only one constitution since its admission into the union in 1796, but that original document had become more antiquated with each passing year. As early as the economic crisis of 1819 voices were raised on behalf of a constitutional convention, but even in that critical year the voters soundly defeated a proposal for a convention. A decade later the General Assembly passed a resolution providing for a vote by the people two years later on a constitutional convention, yet in 1831 the voters rejected it. Shortly thereafter the legislature agreed to resubmit the question to the voters in 1833, who did in fact favor a call for a convention. The legislature then set the first week of March 1834 as the time for the election of delegates.[8]

In mid-May of 1834 sixty delegates assembled in Nashville to devise a new instrument of government.[9] Apparently not feeling the urgency of their 1796 predecessors, who had taken only four weeks to write a constitution, the 1834 convention consumed some fourteen weeks. But judging by their corporate decisions, one would have to concede that the framers were hard working and serious minded.

The writing of new more egalitarian constitutions has often been viewed by historians as one of the hallmarks of the Jacksonian era, and Tennessee's new document fits fairly well into this interpretation. Property qualifications for state representative, state senator, and governor, for example, were eliminated, as were property qualifications for voting rights. Apportionment of representation in the General

Assembly was now to be based on "qualified voters," rather than "taxable inhabitants" as the 1796 constitution had required. At the county level, most of the officials were now to be elected by the voters of the county. The legislature retained the right to appoint state judges and state attorneys, but this provision was subsequently altered by amendment in 1853 to permit the direct election of judges and attorneys. Clearly the major reason for a convention in the mid-1830s was the increasing uproar over the taxation of property. The 1796 document had provided that all property be taxed on a uniform and equal basis, and by the 1830s a very vocal group was urgently demanding a change and crusading for taxation to be based on the value of property. This movement may well be viewed as a manifestation of the democratic impulses of the decade and certainly as a recognition of economic reality.[10] The advocates of change won this major battle and interpreted their victory as a blessing for the common folk. The democratizing changes implemented by the 1834 constitution writers indicated that they dined at the Jacksonian banquet table.

But for some of Tennessee's residents, crumbs and only crumbs fell from that table in 1834. For example, one of the decisions agreed upon, albeit by a close vote, was that free blacks should now be deprived of the suffrage—a right they had held since 1796. By simply inserting the word "white" into the suffrage clause (Article IV, Section 1) the convention delegates testified that in Tennessee so-called Jacksonian democracy would be "for whites only." The convention also decreed that free blacks should be denied the right to vote for or against the constitution in 1835.[11]

Upon receiving thirty memorials from sixteen different counties urging some kind of emancipation of slaves, the convention was forced to treat this extremely sensitive subject. The president, William B. Carter, appointed a three-man committee to consider these petitions. This special committee confessed that slavery was an evil but protested that the question of how to eliminate this blight was one that the "wisest heads and the most benevolent hearts have not been able to answer in a satisfactory manner." A group of five delegates, dissatisfied with the report, responded eloquently and poignantly: "Viewing the report (as we do) a kind of apology for slavery, we have thus raised against it our feeble testimony, in discharge of a duty we owe, not only to the memorialists, but to that degraded people whose voice cannot be heard here."[12] Such words fell on deaf ears as the convention adopted Article II, Section 31: "The General Assembly shall have no power to pass laws for the emancipation of slaves, without the consent of their owner or owners." Thus for slaves, as well as for free blacks in Tennessee, the 1834 constitution held no promise of better things.

With its virtues and its vices, the constitution was judged by the voters during the first week of March 1835, of whom 71.4 percent favored the new constitution. Fifty-eight of the sixty-two counties approved the new document; the four opposing counties—Davidson, Robertson, Smith, and Williamson—were all in Middle Tennessee. The contest was close in several other counties in the middle portion of the state, but East and West Tennessee generally voted heavily in favor of the new instrument of government.[13]

One section written into the constitution in 1834 seemed at the time to have been hortatory, but subsequent developments proved it to be the springboard for increased governmental activity in Tennessee. Article XI, Section 9 read: "A well-regulated system of internal improvement is calculated to develop the resources of the State and promote the happiness and prosperity of her citizens; therefore it ought to be encouraged by the General Assembly." This statement reflected the swelling tide of interest in improving transportation facilities—a concern that was becoming more apparent in the early 1830s. Tangible, visible signs of railroad fever first appeared in East Tennessee, a region that felt increasingly isolated economically, and politically. Meanwhile West Tennesseans were stirred by a vision of Memphis becoming the western terminus of an extensive stretch of rails extending from Charleston, South Carolina. In Middle Tennessee interest in railroad construction was exhibited in the Maury County area, but the influential and powerful Nashville interests, already enjoying the benefits of traffic on the Cumberland River, looked with disdain upon these railroad proponents. In a desire to link other Middle Tennessee counties more closely to Nashville, business leaders there proposed the construction of a series of turnpikes radiating out from the city.[14]

Such was the prelude to the constitutional convention's decision to incorporate the internal improvements section into the new constitution. After its ratification in the spring of 1835 and the gubernatorial-legislative elections in August, it was fairly clear that additional steps would be taken by the General Assembly to promote the development of railroads and turnpikes. Newly inaugurated governor Newton Cannon reminded the legislators in October 1835 that the constitution placed an obligation upon them to devise a program of internal improvements. This admonition fell upon already receptive ears and shortly the legislative chambers echoed with debates over an internal improvements bill. Much of the expressed opposition was based upon a fear of saddling the state with a debt that would require new taxation. The bill, as originally devised, was solely for the benefit of railroad companies, but the Middle Tennessee "turnpike lobby" exerted its muscle, and the bill was expanded to include turnpike companies.[15]

The internal improvements bill finally passed both houses in mid-February of 1836. Simply stated, it committed the state to subscribe one-third of the stock of chartered railroad or turnpike companies; this payment might be withheld, however, if the improvements board decided that the other two-thirds of the company's stock was not "well secured." A brief analysis of the alignment of ballots on the final vote is instructive. Since it is not possible to determine accurately the political predilections of the legislators in 1835-36, given the beginnings of the political rebellion, one can say only tentatively that the *recognizable* Jacksonians voted against the measure, whereas the anti-Jacksonians supported it. More important, however, is the sectional vote: East and West Tennessee legislators heavily favored the measure, while those from Middle Tennessee voted strongly against it. The internal improvements question was not an identifiable partisan issue; instead sectional allegiances were more significant.[16] It is not difficult to comprehend the strong desires of both East and West Tennessee to reap economic advantages resulting from better access to other regions, especially adjoining states. Quite understandably, Middle Tennessee was not disposed to invite the rest of the state to feast at the economic barbecue. Thus began the initial phase of the battle over internal improvements.

But partly because of Governor Cannon's puzzling lack of enthusiasm for carrying out the provisions of the 1836 law, railroad and turnpike companies were not noticeably helped by it. In certain quarters, especially East Tennessee, internal improvements were an important issue in the 1837 legislative and gubernatorial races; and in response to worsening economic situations, an insistent demand was made that the state should take an even more active role in promoting internal improvements. These considerations merged in the 1837-38 legislative session to support new proposals, and eventually both houses of the legislature reached agreement in January 1838 on a bill that went considerably beyond the 1836 law. The new one provided for state government expenditures up to $4,000,000 as the state agreed to subscribe one-half of the stock of qualified railroad and turnpike companies. In addition, the 1838 law created a state bank with a maximum capitalization of $5,000,000—to be acquired by several means, including the selling of bonds at 6 percent interest.[17]

As with the 1836 legislation, the 1838 bill enjoyed support that corresponded to sectional rather than party allegiances. The total Whig vote in both houses, for example, favored the measure by a close 35-31 vote, while the Democratic ballots approved by an equally narrow 18-15 vote. But from a sectional analysis, East Tennessee and West Tennessee were solidly in favor of the new legislation, while Middle Tennessee voted against the bill.[18] Ironically, this 1838 law represented the apogee of the internal improvements movement for several years to come.

The successful coalition between East and West Tennessee which enabled the passage of the 1836 and 1838 improvements laws oc- curred simultaneously with the political alliance between these two regions. In truth, it seems that both economic and political consider- ations were involved as the eastern and western thirds of the state sought to bring Middle Tennessee under some restraints. (The strat- egy, if such it be, shortly backfired as Middle Tennessee began furnish- ing most of the leadership of the anti-Jackson element, much as it did for the Jackson group.) It is virtually impossible to say which came first, economics or politics, to convince East and West Tennessee to spearhead a rebellion against the entrenched Jacksonians. It is clear, however, that both sections were inclined toward a feeling of aliena- tion—a feeling fostered by both economic and political disadvantages. Doubtless East Tennessee looked back longingly to earlier days when it had enjoyed the role of preeminent leader of the state, while West Tennessee looked forward to the time when it might realize its great potential for economic and political leadership. It should be pointed out, however, that the election results from the first two or three contests held after the anti-Jackson rebellion began did not show that East and West were to be yoked together against Middle Tennessee, but that is the way the alliances soon formed.

Seemingly indispensable to the political revolution and the forma- tion of new political groups were the partisan newspapers. Given the already established prominence of Nashville, the state's capital city, it was natural that most of the attention of the press centered there. On the eve of the rebellion there were two newspapers in Nashville: the *National Banner,* edited by Samuel H. Laughlin, was considered to be the most dependable Jacksonian paper, whereas the *Nashville Republican,* edited by Allen A. Hall, had gravitated to the pro-Bell and probank position. In the fall of 1834 both papers suddenly under- went leadership changes. *Banner* publisher W. Hassell Hunt dis- missed Laughlin as editor, because Hunt was himself steadily moving toward the anti-Jackson cause, and placed George C. Childress in the editor's chair. About two months later Hall of the *Republican,* apparently very much in debt, put his paper up for sale, causing a scramble among Nashvillians of opposing political sides to purchase it. Not unexpectedly, Hall finally sold out to John Bell and a group of his supporters, who installed Washington Barrow as the new editor of the *Republican.* When these swift developments ended, Bell and his backers were in the enviable position of controlling directly or indirectly both of the Nashville papers.[19]

Greatly perturbed by this turn of events, Polk and other Jacksonian leaders quickly agreed to establish a new paper in Nashville, one that would do their bidding. Thus in the spring of 1835 the *Nashville Union* was born, with Polk and Donelson as two of the most important attending midwives. Despite clearly expressed misgivings by certain Nashville leaders, a decision to name Laughlin as editor of the *Union* was reached. From the outset, the paper was hard pressed financially, for subscriptions and commercial advertising never seemed adequate sources of revenue. Compounding the *Union*'s plight were the inebriated condition and irresponsible personal habits of editor Laughlin.[20] With these manifold difficulties besetting the fledgling Democratic newspaper, it was able to contribute relatively little to the 1835 and 1836 statewide campaigns.

The next couple of years unfortunately witnessed even more problems at the *Union* office. The situation was so bad in 1837 that for a time Laughlin did not even publish the paper. Those who continued to add to the *Union*'s coffers finally forced Laughlin out in July. He was followed by two men who did not give much evidence of the leadership and talents the *Union* so desperately needed. Accordingly, Polk and other Jacksonian leaders gave top priority to finding a new editor for the floundering paper. Jeremiah George Harris, a Massachusetts Democrat, finally yielded to the pleas of Tennessee Democrats that he take over the *Union* and moved to Nashville in February 1839.[21] Luckily for Polk and the Jacksonian cause, they had at long last a man who could get the job done.

Interestingly enough, not all of the exasperations over the press were solely in the Democratic camp, for the crosstown rivals had their problems as well. Right after the 1837 elections, Bell decided to merge the two anti-Jackson papers, thus establishing the new *Republican Banner;* he designated Hall as editor of this paper. That not all of the anti-Jackson forces in Nashville were pleased by Bell's monopoly of the press was indicated by the movement among Ephraim Foster and his friends to found a paper of their own. Their negotiations culminated in the establishment of the *Nashville Whig,* edited by Caleb C.

Norvell, which began publication in January 1838.[22] These twists and turns in the journalistic world reflected the growing tensions between the two prominent Whig leaders in Nashville, Bell and Foster, whose rivalry would continue to generate internal frictions within the party for at least a decade. Democrats, absorbed by the dimensions of their own problems with the press, doubtless took some delight in the antagonisms stirred in the Whig ranks by the two Whig newspapers in Nashville.

But journalistic wars, economic concerns, a new constitution, and clashes between leading political figures did not necessarily insure an insurrection against Jackson and his lieutenants. They were all integral parts of the drama, to be sure, but the reality of rebellion had to be tested in actual contests for political office. The three gubernatorial races provided such an opportunity. They show that initially there was no clearly defined and established two-party system. The 1837 election and the confusion surrounding the candidates indicate that at that date the system was still in the process of becoming. While it is true that by 1837 most of the anti-Jackson element was employing the label "Whigs," they still had not yet developed party apparatus. In fact, in none of the three governor's races was a nominating convention utilized by either Democrats or Whigs; this would not happen until the 1840s.[23] Instead, the aspirants simply entered the races upon the urgings of friends or upon some personal whim. In 1837 neither candidate actively electioneered—a situation related in part to the personal dispositions of the contenders but also to the puzzling alignment of support for both men. That Newton Cannon competed in all three contests is somewhat striking, given the rapid changes occurring in state politics at this time. In 1835 he was helped considerably by the transitional phase and its accompanying push of Hugh Lawson White for the presidency, and in 1837 he had the good fortune of having an opponent who had little to offer. When Cannon ran into stiff opposition from Polk in 1839, he simply could not measure up to the challenge. One final generalization is that all of the contenders in these three races, with the exception of a minor candidate in 1835, were from Middle Tennessee, a pattern that continued to hold until the 1850s.

Some clues about the voters' response to the political revolution in the 1830s are provided in Tables 3.1, 3.2, and 3.3.[24] One cannot say for certain what was responsible for bringing out 38,000 additional voters in the 1835 gubernatorial canvass, as compared to 1833. Doubtless the highly competitive nature of the 1835 race, in contrast to Carroll's running without opposition in 1833, stirred eligible citi-

Table 3.1. Total Votes, 1833–39

Party	1833	1835	1836	1837	1839
Whig	——	53,255*	36,058	55,462	51,790
Democratic	51,184	35,901	26,120	35,909	54,177
Total	51,184	89,156	62,178	91,371	105,967

*In 1835 there were two anti-Jackson or Whig candidates: Newton Cannon received 44,123 votes, West Humphreys received 9,132. Cannon, the winner, was slightly short of having a majority of the statewide vote.

Table 3.2. Percentage of Democratic Vote by Section, 1835–39

Section	1835	1836	1837	1839
East	22.6	34.8	42.6	49.4
Middle	51.7	48.3	39.3	54.5
West	39.7	34.3	33.8	45.1
STATE	40.3	42.0	39.3	51.1

zens to participate at the ballot boxes, and the excitement of the "revolt" against Jackson perhaps shook some of the voters from their earlier indifference.[25] The substantial decrease in voter participation in the 1836 presidential contest (see Tables 3.1 and 3.3), though somewhat disturbing in view of White's candidacy and widespread interest in the contest, actually followed a well-established pattern in Tennessee whereby presidential elections pulled fewer voters than the governors' races. In 1837 the pendulum swung widely back the other way to approximate the percentage of turnout in the 1835 contest. There is no question that the Polk-Cannon battle in 1839 generated a vast outpouring of voters (see Tables 3.1 and 3.3). As Tables 3.1 and 3.2 clearly indicate, Polk was the beneficiary—both absolutely and relatively—of this new army of voters. Never again in the antebellum period did the total statewide vote drop below the 100,000 level in either gubernatorial or presidential elections. No wonder Democrats heaped praise upon Polk in 1839, for he not only won but also attracted unprecedented numbers to the polls and a percentage of eligible voters unrivaled in the state's electoral history.

Table 3.3. Percentage of Statewide Voter Turnout, 1835–39

1835	1836	1837	1839
78–80	55.2	80–82	89

Tennessee's political revolution had its tangible beginnings in the 1835 election. That contest experienced the added complication of serious questions surrounding the eligibility of William Carroll. Both the 1796 and 1835 constitutions restricted governors to three consecutive terms, but in 1835 Carroll was seeking his fourth. Though professing neutrality in the governor's race, the *Nashville Republican* ran several articles that concluded that Carroll could not constitutionally run for another term in 1835. The paper did, however, reprint a lengthy essay from the *Nashville Union* which expounded the expected argument in favor of the legality of Carroll's reelection bid.[26] Carroll's justification was based on the somewhat feeble contention that since the 1835 election was being conducted under the new constitution he was actually running for a first term under its provisions. Carroll's strained logic was difficult to articulate to the voting public and did little to push away the legal cloud that hovered over his candidacy.

Meanwhile, the incipient Whig element sought a strong competitor to field against the very popular Carroll. Richard G. Dunlap of Knoxville was the first to take the plunge, but after apparently finding the water not very inviting, he withdrew in midsummer, pleading ill health.[27] In late April Newton Cannon of Williamson County agreed to challenge Carroll. Cannon was well known as antagonistic toward Jackson—the two had quarreled a number of years earlier—and Van Buren. Moreover, he was an emerging leader of the pro-White forces at this time. In his "Circular to the Citizens of Tennessee" Cannon depicted himself as a zealous advocate of a system of public education and of state-sponsored internal improvements. More important, he questioned the legality of Carroll's candidacy and, with regard to the presidential race, proclaimed himself to be "decidedly and unequivocally in favor of our distinguished fellow citizen, Hugh L. White."[28] A third candidate who persevered in 1835 was the little-known West H. Humphreys of Fayette County, whose purpose in seeking the state's highest office remains a mystery. The real contest, of course, was between Carroll and Cannon.

It was inevitable that this gubernatorial campaign would focus almost exclusively upon the forthcoming 1836 battle between White and Van Buren. Significantly, nine days before the *Nashville Republican* carried an announcement of Carroll's gubernatorial candidacy, it declared its endorsement of White for the presidency.[29] A survey of newspapers in the spring and summer of 1835 leads to the inescapable conclusion that the governor's race was relegated to a noticeable backseat vis-à-vis the pending national campaign. The importance of the Carroll-Cannon battle was viewed in terms of how it was related to the White–Van Buren contest. Cannon and his backers generally eschewed criticism of Jackson and stuck to the more positive strategy of promoting state loyalty to White's claims for the presidency. Carroll meanwhile got mixed results when he waved the Van Buren flag from time to time. At Athens in East Tennessee, for example, Carroll's advocacy of Van Buren was greeted with shouts of "Huzza for White" and an accompanying departure of some of the crowd.[30]

The voters rendered their decision in early August and gave Carroll the first defeat of his long career. As Table 3.1 shows, although Cannon fell short of a majority of the statewide vote, the White forces were clearly triumphant, for both Cannon and Humphreys were White backers. Five days before the election an apparently nervous *Republican* editor, Washington Barrow, contended that even if Carroll did win his victory would not constitute evidence of Van Buren's strength because there were White men who, from personal considerations, intended to vote for Carroll. But after Carroll's defeat was an accepted fact, the paper still maintained that the outcome did not show the relative appeal of the presidential contenders, although it averred that "his Van Burenism operated against Carroll in many parts of the State." Democrats naturally were quick to claim that Carroll had been defeated by the eligibility question; while there was some truth in this explanation, it glossed over the importance of the presidential preference issue. As the *Nashville Republican* editorialized with some exaggeration, the legality argument did have some impact against Carroll but it would not have if Carroll had expressed a preference for Hugh Lawson White. Had Carroll done so, he would have been reelected, perhaps without opposition.[31] In any event, the contest foreshadowed what was to come a year hence. Furthermore, it marked the end of Carroll's public career—a regrettable development in view of his twelve years of excellent service as governor.

Several factors operated in 1837 to make that election quite different from the preceding gubernatorial contest. For one thing, it came after the presidential election, so the momentum of the successful White movement was almost irrepressible. And by the summer Tennessee was definitely experiencing the squeeze of the nationwide economic panic, for most of the banks had suspended specie payments. The White juggernaut and the economic panic combined to make the gubernatorial nomination very unattractive to ambitious Democrats. Despite Polk's best efforts to line up candidates for all statewide posts, including governor, he was hampered by the unwillingness of friends to stake their fortunes on the 1837 elections. There had been some hope that the old warhorse, William Carroll, would answer the call once more, but after having seen President Van Buren award to another man the diplomatic appointment he had long sought, Carroll went into a sort of political exile and refused to campaign. Less than a week after Carroll's public announcement that he would not be a candidate, Governor Cannon indicated that he would seek reelection.[32]

All was quiet thereafter on the campaign front until mid-April, when stirrings in behalf of Gen. Robert Armstrong were reported in the *Knoxville Register*. But no further activity seems to have taken place until a month later when the *Nashville Union* published letters to Armstrong urging him to be a candidate and from Armstrong responding affirmatively. Polk and other Democratic leaders were pleased with Armstrong's decision and routinely predicted success for him at the polls. Armstrong, Nashville postmaster and longtime friend of Andrew Jackson, was naturally assumed to be the Jacksonian candidate against the incumbent Cannon. Yet the already murky picture of state politics took on additional cloudiness when several prominent Whig leaders, such as John Bell, Ephraim Foster, and Allen Hall, pledged their support to Armstrong. Earlier, John Catron, Nashville jurist who had recently been appointed to the national supreme court by Jackson, indicated his reservations about Armstrong on the grounds of his close ties with John Bell and friends.[33] In any event, Armstrong's popularity among many Tennesseans and a certain unspecified dissatisfaction with Cannon among the Nashville leadership of the Whig element pushed a number of anti-Jacksonian people into the Armstrong camp.

Although neither Cannon nor Armstrong campaigned actively or directly for the governor's chair, the press devoted a great deal of attention to the race. In fact, the 1837 canvass received more journalistic coverage, oddly enough, than did the more exciting 1835 campaign, because the 1837 race was not directly tied to a forthcoming presidential election. Beginning in late May and continuing until early

August, the papers around the state attempted to stir voter support for one candidate or the other. Among the usual topics treated, the press took due notice of Armstrong's personal popularity and his military fame. Armstrong had served as brigadier general of the Tennessee Volunteers in the Florida campaign against the Seminole Indians during the preceding year. The *Paris West Tennessean* declared that had it not been for Armstrong's Florida activities no one would have considered running him for governor. The *Knoxville Register* went a bit further when it asserted that in military qualifications Carroll was superior to Armstrong and that even Cannon did not suffer by comparison to Armstrong. During the gubernatorial race there was a flap over the lack of pay for some of the Tennessee Volunteers who, though not seeing active service in the Seminole campaign, were away from their homes for some time. Money was eventually appropriated for these Volunteers, and Cannon and his supporters were quick to take credit for this happy turn of events. According to some observers, there was considerable opposition to Armstrong among the Volunteers in various parts of the state.[34] Thus, apparently, Armstrong's hopes of winning widespread backing because of his military fame were not realized.

The chief campaign tactic of the Armstrong people, however, was to promote him as a no-party candidate. Allen Hall, *Banner* editor and erstwhile devoted Whig, indicated his support of Armstrong on this basis. Seemingly the belief that Armstrong would not be a mere party governor, plus his own personal popularity, was persuasive to a number of anti-Jacksonian leaders. The *Nashville Republican* and other pro-Cannon papers spent a great deal of space attacking this particular point of view. To them, Armstrong was the obvious Van Buren party contender and to back him would be to abandon or upset the political revolution that had already taken place in Tennessee. Cannon was praised for his identification with the principles of Tennesseans and for having discharged the duties of his office "with fidelity and impartial justice."[35]

In early August the journalistic winds died down and the voters went to the polls. Hardly a better illustration of the importance of gubernatorial vis-à-vis presidential elections can be found than to note that this very quiet and lackluster 1837 governor's race attracted a voter turnout of approximately 80 percent, in sharp contrast to the 55 percent brought out by the more exciting 1836 presidential campaign (see Tables 3.1 and 3.3). The voters gave Cannon a winning margin of nearly 20,000 votes or 60.7 percent of the statewide total. In the process of achieving this stunning victory margin—never to be duplicated by any candidate, gubernatorial or presidential, in any succeeding election in antebellum Tennessee—Cannon carried all three sections of the state (see Table 3.2). In view of his compelling victory, Cannon is due more respect as a politician than he is usually given.

There are several possible explanations for Cannon's success or Armstrong's failure. Cannon was helped by the caliber of his opponent, for while Armstrong had admirable personal qualities he seemed ill-suited for the political canvass and perhaps for gubernatorial politics. In a scathing assessment of Armstrong's abilities, Catron commented that his friend Armstrong "cannot speak, and is radically defective in intelligence." Doubtless the impact of the economic crisis in 1837 caused some voters to steer away from a candidate identified with Van Buren, whose administration reaped the blame for the financial woes. Polk was convinced that Armstrong made a fatal mistake by agreeing with Cannon not to travel around the state, and that the Bell and Foster support of Armstrong hurt him among some of the Van Buren people. The antagonism of some Volunteers toward Armstrong was singled out by some observers as detrimental to the Jacksonian cause. Finally, Cannon was assisted substantially by the pronounced Whig trend evident in the legislative and congressional elections occurring simultaneously with the governor's race. The *Nashville Republican* eagerly summarized its analysis with the claim that "despite of the trickery and malevolence of 'the party,' [Cannon] has been nobly sustained by THE SOVEREIGN PEOPLE."[36] His victory was the third consecutive triumph for the state's Whigs—a disturbing fact for the Democrats to contemplate.

Hence, the importance of the 1839 governor's race can hardly be exaggerated. In that year Polk was willing to risk his entire political future by making his first statewide race, and the missionary zeal he displayed signified the importance he attached to this redemption crusade. A year before election day, Polk finessed Carroll out of the race and announced in Murfreesboro his intention to seek and win the governor's chair.[37] Discouraged Democrats immediately had new life and energy breathed into them, and they responded enthusiastically to Polk's declaration of war upon the Whigs.

Once more there was discontent among some of the Whig leaders over the prospects of Cannon's candidacy. Bell in particular seemed to retain his earlier unhappiness with Cannon, complaining to Henry Clay that "Our Gov. Cannon is too sluggish and self-sufficient, or we might do better." After Polk's bold announcement, there was some scurrying among Whigs to find a stronger candidate to pit against

Young Hickory; the *Knoxville Register* expressed its preference for Bell. But all this came to naught, because when faced with the battle against Polk no courageous Whig, other than Cannon, was willing to enter the lists. Besides, the Whigs discovered that Cannon was "too much of a mule to give way."[38] It remains something of a mystery why Cannon's fellow Whig leaders demonstrated little enthusiasm for him each time he put on the armor; luckily for him the voters did not seem to share this feeling.

For four solid months the candidates took their message directly to the people. Sometimes jointly, often separately, they went into virtually every part of the state. Cannon easily tired of such exertions, especially since Polk seemed to be gaining ground and thriving, and even though he left the campaign trail from time to time, Cannon could not afford to leave Polk unattended for any length of time. People all over the state learned what Polk's congressional constituents had long known; namely, that he was a masterful campaigner on the stump. They also learned that Cannon was no match for Polk in this rough and tumble kind of electioneering. The spectacle of Polk's cracking open a barrel of whiskey for his supporters in Rogersville late in the campaign is almost more than one can believe about the usually circumspect and reserved Polk.[39] But in 1839 he was fighting desperately for his political life, as well as for the governorship.

Amidst the hurly-burly of the campaign two issues dominated. At the local level there was much debate about the internal improvements and banking act passed by the legislature in January 1838. But after sifting through the rhetoric, one discovers that the two candidates voiced only procedural, not substantive, differences over this law. Polk conceded at a Coffee County rally that "there was but little difference between his notions and the present incumbent, as regarded State policy."[40] Realizing that he was making little headway on this issue, Polk shifted to a more promising matter—presidential preference. He and fellow Democrats asserted that the 1839 contest was really a battle between Van Buren (represented by Polk) and Henry Clay (represented by Cannon). It was risky business for Polk to embrace Van Buren, who was not widely admired in Tennessee (remember the 1836 election). But the gamble could possibly pay off, because antagonism toward Clay had been quite evident in the state since at least the 1824 presidential election. Of the three Nashville newspapers, only the *Union* emphasized the presidential question; the *Whig* and the *Republican Banner* were virtually silent on this matter. Cannon tried without much success to minimize the question of presidential preference and steadfastly refused to say he favored Clay for the 1840 nomination. About the only confession Polk finally extracted from his resistant and cagey opponent was that Cannon did not intend to support Van Buren in 1840. It is amusing to witness Polk's pro–Van Buren stance in the 1839 campaign if one recalls that he had worked frantically behind the scenes to keep Van Buren from visiting the state in the early part of that same year.[41] Although Polk knew that Van Buren was a heavy load to carry on his shoulders in 1839, he nevertheless was willing and even eager to do so because he had one eye riveted upon the vice presidential plum.

A vast army of nearly 106,000 voters, representing approximately 89 percent of the eligible electorate, swarmed to the polls when the campaign ended. As Table 3.2 shows, the 60.7 percent victory margin enjoyed by Cannon in 1837 was drastically reduced in 1839, when he garnered only 48.9 percent of the statewide vote. Polk made significant percentage gains in all three sections, although he carried only Middle Tennessee. Polk gained nearly 18,300 votes over what the Democratic candidate in 1837 had received (see Table 3.1). Polk had indeed triumphed.

Polk's surprising and remarkable victory may be attributed to several factors. First, he apparently made the presidential question work in his favor. Allen Hall, admittedly a biased observer, reported afterward that much feeling had been whipped up against Clay in the campaign. Furthermore, the Whigs were caught by surprise; they simply were not ready for the whirlwind, exhausting electioneering carried on by Polk and the Democrats. Instead, they were more content to rest on their laurels, hoping for a fourth consecutive victory. Also to Polk's benefit was East Tennessee's dissatisfaction over the lack of promised internal improvements; this unhappiness eroded Cannon's strength there (from 57.4 percent in 1837 to 50.6 percent in 1839). Moreover, one must not ignore the herculean exertions of Polk himself as a factor in his triumph. He proved to be a highly effective stump speaker and an ingenious mastermind of the entire Democratic campaign. So exhaustingly did he labor that his wife constantly worried about his health.[42] Polk was successful in part because his exciting canvass generated enough enthusiasm to stir the voters to get out on election day. So if democracy be understood as voter participation, then it was Polk, not Jackson, who made democracy manifest in Tennessee.

The legislative and congressional elections held simultaneously with the gubernatorial contest were interrelated with it in various ways. The 1835-36 General Assembly saw both houses controlled by the pro-White contingent, but because partisan alignments were still very fluid, it is not possible to give an exact accounting of the Jackson and anti-Jackson representation. By the time of the tremendous Whig sweep in 1837, however, party lines were more clearly drawn. Thus one can say with confidence that in the 1837-38 session the Whigs controlled both the lower and upper houses. But in 1839 the Democrats gained ascendancy in the General Assembly by a majority of nine in the lower house and three in the state senate.[43] Certainly for Polk and other state Democratic leaders this was one of the most gratifying results of the campaign. If the coattail argument has any validity, it might apply to the 1839 contest. Unlike Cannon, Polk appreciated the importance of winning on both fronts, and though burdened with his own demanding race he did not neglect the legislative contests.

For years the congressional races had enjoyed considerable prestige and importance, and the 1830s were no exception to the rule. In all three elections—1835, 1837, and 1839—Tennessee Whigs captured a majority of the congressional seats. Particularly impressive was their 1837 achievement in sweeping ten of the thirteen posts. The only victorious Democrats were Abraham McClellan, Hopkins Turney, and Polk; the redoubtable Cave Johnson was the most important Democratic casualty in that year. In 1839 the Whig stranglehold on the congressional seats was weakened by a Democratic trend, although the Whigs retained seven of the thirteen posts.[44]

During the early years of political revolution in Tennessee, Polk devoutly hoped to retire Bell from Congress. To that end, in 1839 Jacksonian leaders first flirted with William Carroll, but the former governor's rheumatism provided a convenient excuse for him to avoid a distasteful political endeavor. Finally Robert M. Burton enlisted, however reluctantly, to do battle with Bell. Although Polk did not get his greatest wish—to have Bell defeated—he at least succeeded in keeping Bell occupied during most of the 1839 campaign. Polk also intervened in other congressional districts as well. As Alfred Balch wrote: "Your election is dove-tailed into that of every candidate for Congress in our state." Polk pinned his hopes for the "redemption" of the state on the shrewd strategy of sweeping as many offices as possible; and given the results, one cannot quarrel with his plan of attack.[45]

At the top or very near the top of the political ladder was the much-coveted post of United States senator. And in the latter half of the 1830s the selection of senators by the legislature exhibited the impact of the pro-White movement. As a matter of fact, hardly had

the 1835-36 legislature convened in Nashville before it entertained a
motion to reelect White to the seat he had held since 1825. There
emerged no opponent to challenge the venerable White, and he was
returned to office with 98 of the General Assembly's 100 votes.[46]
Obviously, in this instance White ran far ahead of the actual strength
of the anti-Jackson cause. About ten days later this same legislature
recommended White for the presidency in 1836.

After their breathtaking triumph in the gubernatorial and legislative races (as well as congressional) in 1837, the Whigs were understandably anxious to fill the other Senate seat with a deserving Whig,
thus replacing the Democrat, Felix Grundy. But it was tricky and
potentially dangerous business that this General Assembly seemed
eager to engage in, for Grundy's term did not actually expire until
March 1839. Thus when various Whig leaders proposed that Grundy's seat be filled, they were really talking about making a decision
almost two years early, thereby ignoring the Tennessee tradition of
electing senators "late," that is, in the fall of the year after the term
had expired in the spring. Pushing the legislators into these questiona-
ble actions in 1837 were the ambitions of John Bell and Ephraim
Foster, both of whom had developed a sudden thirst for this high
office. That Bell and Foster were quite audacious must be conceded
in light of their having supported Armstrong (the Jacksonian), not
Cannon, in the 1837 gubernatorial election. Despite feeble efforts by
Democrats to halt or alter the General Assembly's plans, the legislature was soon ready to vote. But first the Bell-Foster rivalry had to
be resolved and finally was—in favor of Foster—whereupon the legislators chose Foster.[47] By this decision, Grundy became something of
a premature "lame duck," about one and a half years before his term
officially ended. In their haste to congratulate themselves upon their
successful tactics, the Whigs overlooked the antagonism they stirred
among many Tennesseans who felt that they had engaged in "over-
kill" and that they should have waited, as custom dictated, until 1839
to replace Grundy. The Democrats used this issue to some advantage
in the campaigning of 1839. Through an odd quirk of circumstances
the Democratically controlled legislature of 1839-40 was able to fill
both of the United States Senate seats, but that story belongs more
properly to the succeeding chapter. Suffice it to say, the Whigs' practice in 1837 of electing "early" was not followed again by either party
for twenty years.

That the gubernatorial, legislative, and congressional elections were
important components of Tennessee's political story in the 1830s

seems evident, but the 1836 presidential contest was the most critical and crucial one. After all, it was the willingness of Hugh Lawson White to be a contender for the presidency that emboldened the dissatisfied elements in the state to organize and promote a "revolt" against Jackson and his hand-picked successor, Martin Van Buren. White's electoral success gave an undeniable and enduring boost to the anti-Jackson cause in Tennessee, and from this flowed in time the development of the two-party system in the state.

Several features of the 1836 race cause it to stand out in comparison with previous and subsequent presidential contests. As incredible as it may seem, the White–Van Buren battle was the first truly competitive presidential election in Tennessee's history. Prior to that time the Jeffersonian Republican candidates faced no serious challenge, nor did Andrew Jackson in 1824, 1828, or 1832. Furthermore, White's candidacy in 1836 marked the fourth consecutive presidential race in which a Tennessean sought the nation's highest political office; perhaps the state's citizens were growing accustomed to having one of their own in these quadrennial battles. State pride played a part in influencing and attracting support to the side of White in 1836, much as it had done for Jackson. Likewise there was some regional loyalty evinced by White's backers who talked disparagingly of the New Yorker, Van Buren. The election results show that White trounced the opposition by capturing 58 percent of the statewide vote. While that figure does not compare favorably to the percentages won by Jackson in his three contests, still it does stand as the highest percentage for any presidential candidate in Tennessee from 1836 until after the Civil War.

As Tables 3.1 and 3.3 make clear, the 1836 race did not draw impressively large numbers of voters to the polls. In fairness to the White–Van Buren contest, though, it should be noted that 55.2 percent of the eligible voters participated in that year, whereas only 28.8 percent had done so in 1832. Admittedly, there was a "stay-at-home" vote in 1832, but even in 1828 Jackson had managed to get out only about 50 percent of the voters on election day.[48] Some have unfairly tried to compare the 1836 and 1840 voter turnouts to show that the voters stayed home in the former election or to demonstrate how remarkable the 1840 voter participation level was. One may simply compare the 1835, 1836, and 1837 results (see Table 3.3) to make the point that there was a decided drop in voter turnout in the presidential race. But again, there was really nothing unusual about this situation, for it was not until the two-party system was firmly established that presidential canvasses outpolled the gubernatorial.[49] Moreover, the extremely high voter participation in 1840 must be put in the perspective of the equally high turnout in the 1839 governor's election.

Regardless of how one analyzes the election statistics, the brilliance and cleverness on the part of John Bell and others who enticed White to enter the 1836 combat must be granted. Practically everyone was in agreement that White was second only to Jackson in statewide popularity. From 1801 to 1815 White had served as a judge on the state's highest court; from 1812 to 1827 he had functioned most impressively as president of the Bank of the State of Tennessee (a private corporation). Along the way he had held two terms in the state legislature and since 1825 had served with distinction in the United States Senate. Those who liked their politicians a little more rough-hewn could point out that White had had some experience as an Indian fighter. Considering all these accomplishments, it is little wonder that in the mid-1830s some politicians believed that White's time had come. And doubtless the ambitious White reckoned that it was now or never.

But why did White reach that conclusion and agree to tangle with Jackson and Van Buren? No simple or definitive answer is available. Though an ardent friend and follower of Jackson, White showed no signs of having surrendered his independence, and once Jackson was in the presidency White seemed more determined than ever to be his own man. On more than one occasion Jackson put pressure on White to accept a Cabinet post or to support an administration measure, and reportedly he even dangled a Supreme Court appointment or the vice presidency before White.[50] But each time White responded with something resembling defiance. This mood and temperament became even more pronounced after Jackson chose Van Buren to be his vice presidential candidate in 1832 and made apparent his intention to promote Van Buren for the presidency. Jackson's alleged remark that after Van Buren had served eight years as president then White would have his chance simply widened the breach between White and Jackson.

Although he at first resisted the overtures of those who wanted to push him into contention for the presidency, in December 1834 White yielded. In that month the Tennessee congressional delegation, with the exception of Grundy, Polk, and Cave Johnson, drew up a document entreating White to become a candidate in 1836. Whereas Johnson attended the delegation's meeting, he apparently had second thoughts shortly thereafter.[51] In any event, once White displayed his political colors in early 1835, a chain of events began which meant that for White there was no turning back.

Testimony of the somewhat painful period of confusion in the state after White's announcement is found in the failure of Tennessee to send delegates to the national Democratic convention at Baltimore in May 1835, which occurred despite Jackson's efforts to have the state represented at the convention. In the months immediately preceding the Baltimore conclave Jackson had tried to persuade Tennessee's political leaders to commit themselves to the support of the Baltimore presidential nominee. But they were busily testing the political waters and in the process learned that the White-for-president cause was strong and serious—a fact Jackson never seemed to appreciate, perhaps because of his geographical separation. Even so devout a Jacksonian as Polk told his hometown supporters that he actually preferred White but would, characteristically, wait until after the convention before making a final commitment. Cave Johnson conceded that public opinion favored White but argued also that the people did not want to see the party divided. The *Nashville Union* praised White while urging support of the Baltimore convention and its nominees. The *Nashville Republican,* on the other hand, declared its opposition to the national convention and its preference for White, "whose claims will be submitted—not to a packed jury, dignified with the name of a *National Convention*—but to the impartial decision of a free and enlightened PEOPLE." Given the decidedly mixed feelings across Tennessee, cautious politicians adopted a laissez-faire attitude toward the Baltimore meeting, and the state was therefore unrepresented. Upon learning of this development, an understandably incensed Jackson declared that if he could take action, Tennessee in six weeks "would be . . . erect upon her republican legs again."[52]

In the same month as the Baltimore convention, John Bell figuratively put his cards on the table in his notable Vauxhall Gardens speech. While proclaiming his loyalty to Jackson, Bell also contended that White, not Van Buren, should be Jackson's successor.[53] This argument became indispensable to the White cause from this point forward. These developments dovetailed neatly with Newton Cannon's desire for revenge against the Jackson crowd by running for governor on a pro-White platform. Cannon's success in the summer elections signaled that White was indisputably a leader of full-fledged rebellion against Jackson and his lieutenants.

As hinted at above, the 1835-36 legislative session was a noisy prelude to the forthcoming presidential race. The Jacksonian contingent reasoned that if it could exert political muscle at this critical time it could arrest the White movement. But in October the legislature reelected White to the United States Senate and then recommended him as a presidential candidate—actions which revealed the atrophied condition of the Jacksonian sinews. Significantly, the resolution endorsing White depicted him as the man most qualified to maintain Jackson's principles and carry out his policies.[54] Only Polk's victory in December for the speakership seemed to dampen the spirits of the Whigs.

The rapidly approaching presidential campaign did not permit the Jackson partisans the luxury of cursing their misfortunes nor allow the anti-Jackson men to bask in the glory of their accomplishments. Tennessee's congressmen were particularly anxious to break loose from Washington so they could get home to assist the claims of their presidential candidates. Even though Polk was speaker, he was able to do little toward hastening the adjournment of Congress. Since the congressional delegation contained the principal leaders of both sides of the emerging political struggle, most of the actual campaigning had to wait until these men returned to the state in early summer. Meanwhile the Jacksonians and anti-Jacksonians staged meetings in the thirteen congressional districts for the purpose of choosing presidential electors.[55] That neither side held a state party convention to set up the machinery and structure for the campaign is further evidence that at this date the two-party system had not yet arrived. By late spring both groups had their respective slates of electors. Nominally these were the men who were expected to shoulder the burdens of the campaign in their own locales, but whatever efforts they made paled in comparison to the labors of the congressmen.

In midsummer when the canvass began in earnest, the sheer power and prestige of the Jackson luminaries seemed to augur well for the Van Buren cause. Former governor Carroll, Felix Grundy, Cave Johnson, and Polk all took very active roles in the Democratic effort, and they were soon joined by none other than President Jackson himself, who worked the campaign trail from upper East Tennessee to his home outside Nashville. The strenuous efforts by Democratic leaders in Middle Tennessee stood in marked contrast to the floundering campaign in the other two sections of the state. In fact, Jackson's brief foray across East Tennessee was about the only serious work in behalf of Van Buren in that part of the state. Pro-White leaders, fearful that Jackson's activity for Van Buren and his vehement attacks upon White might swing voters away from their ticket, quickly and shrewdly took the offensive with the exaggerated argument that Jackson's visit was merely another example of his dictatorial ways. The President thundered and roared against such charges, but there was little doubt that the anti-Jacksonians had hit upon a good tactic to use among voters already sensitive about their freedom of choice in 1836. Meanwhile, Polk, Grundy, and other leaders attempted to switch emphasis from Van Buren (by now a decided liability) to Old Hickory, whose accomplishments they praised highly. The *Nashville Whig* noted this switch when reporting on the Jacksonian rally in Giles County; Van Buren's name was hardly mentioned, while Jackson's superior fitness for office was emphasized. In fact, at some of the political dinners and rallies it was difficult to tell that Jackson was not actually seeking a third term.[56]

Since custom dictated that presidential candidates should do little or no campaigning, White was not in a position to aid his own cause in Tennessee. He did, however, break with tradition on several occasions to make speeches in late summer and early fall. But it was John Bell and Balie Peyton, both Middle Tennessee congressmen, who emerged as the main campaigners for the anti-Jackson side. Their special mission was the erosion of Jacksonian strength in Middle Tennessee, and there they waged a hard-fought and sometimes vituperative campaign. Bell and Peyton left few Jacksonians untouched by their harsh criticisms. Peyton claimed, for example, that he would as likely find female virtue in a house of prostitution as to find political virtue in Felix Grundy. If one may judge correctly from comments in private correspondence and in the columns of Jacksonian newspapers, the activities of Bell and Peyton greatly annoyed the Democrats. Later these two White protagonists ventured into West Tennessee, where they continued to spread their theme of "revolt." Of incalculable value to all the White campaigners was their virtual monopoly of the newspapers in the state.[57] No wonder the anti-Jackson leaders soon thought that they smelled victory in the air.

But the 1836 canvass was not exclusively a clash of prominent campaigners, for debate over certain issues added another dimension. On basic economic matters such as protective tariffs, internal improvements, and a national bank there was hardly a discernible difference between White and Van Buren, since they both stuck to conventional Jacksonian thought on these points.[58] Actually there was a dimly perceived difference, as John Bell and other White leaders promoted the view that White favored an extended state banking system and might be malleable on the matter of a national bank, if elected president. Fearing Van Buren's doctrinaire hostility toward government-sponsored banks, men representing the financial interests in the state soon convinced themselves that they should endorse White. Because White was from East Tennessee, a region favorably disposed toward government-assisted internal improvements, it was generally assumed that he would approve of such legislation—at least at the state level, if not the national. Thus the White strategists effectively worked both sides of the street—persuading voters wedded to Jacksonian dogma on economic issues that White would continue to uphold those tenets much as he had done in the past, but convincing voters who wanted a friendlier attitude toward business and economic expansion that White was their man. White's strength in East and West Tennessee, as well as Nashville, was amply demonstrated at the polls in November.[59]

Of paramount importance to many Tennessee voters in 1836 was this question: Is Hugh Lawson White still a true Jacksonian? Thomas P. Abernethy once asserted that the answer determined the outcome in November.[60] His interpretation, of course, is rooted in the assumption that the voters were motivated by issues—a somewhat shaky premise, though a noble one. At any rate, so far as issues were involved in the 1836 contest, the question of White's fidelity to Jacksonian principles was the most significant one.

The President's personal declaration of war upon White gave this issue a very clear focus in Tennessee. Warming to this topic at Carthage, Jackson declared that no one could support him and not vote for Van Buren in November. One observer at that rally unimpressed by Jackson's assertion commented sarcastically, "*I believe Jackson is deranged* and therefore excuse his *folly & madness.*"[61] The contention that White had deserted the Jackson fold was not without considerable merit; after all, White had become a part of the national anti-Jackson strategy to defeat Van Buren, the duly nominated Democratic candidate. But Jackson partisans had trouble convincing the electorate that White could not and should not be considered a member in good standing in the Jackson camp. Here was an excellent example of the tenacity of voters' beliefs and perceptions: they knew that White had long been devoted and loyal to Jackson and hence refused to be shaken from this view, cogent arguments to the contrary notwithstanding. About all the exasperated Democratic leaders could do was applaud Van Buren as the man most likely to continue Jackson's work and program. But this encomium had to be used with caution, given the indifference and even antipathy toward Van Buren evident in the state.

The pro-White leaders tried to capitalize on this enduring debate. One approach, for example, was to portray White as a better Jacksonian than Van Buren, therefore reducing the Jackson-White conflict to a simple disagreement over who should succeed Jackson as president. At other times the anti-Jackson partisans frankly proclaimed that there were no genuine differences between the President and White. As the *Knoxville Register* editorialized: "In the main we believe the political doctrines of the President and Judge White are the same." Another argument, bolder and potentially more dangerous, declared that it was Jackson himself who had strayed from the original tenets, not White. If anything, so ran this line of reasoning, the Democratic party had deserted White, not vice versa. Doubtless either or all of these approaches helped shore up the wavering who might have been wondering if they could serve two masters in 1836. When the swirling currents of controversy subsided, it appeared that at the very least the pro-White people had neutralized this key issue, and at the very most they had succeeded in winning votes to their cause. Or as one of Polk's friends observed, the White forces gained strength "by palming themselves on the people as friends of Genl. Jackson and his administration."[62]

As a corollary to the debate over White's real or imagined tergiversation, the issue of presidential interference in Tennessee politics developed. As noted above, White's backers accused the President of attempting to dictate to the voters how they should vote. As one paper charged: "To bring those prejudices to bear upon the freedom of elections, and by the influence of Executive patronage, to control public opinion, he [Jackson] at once abandons the dignity of his station, and forfeits all claims to the confidence of a free people." William B. Campbell, a member of the legislature, protested "I shall be found opposing the attempt at dictation of the president—and I can find sufficient reason in sustaining White (if I had none other) in the fact that there is a direct & palpable attempt on the part of Jackson, to force this state to vote for Van."[63] That Jackson's efforts in behalf of Van Buren could be so strongly criticized was indicative both of the touchiness over the selection of Van Buren and of the growing prowess of the White cause. Had Jackson been playing from a position of strength in his home state, few voices would have been raised in 1836 to claim that he was interfering or dictating, but as long as the White leaders could keep alive the belief that their candidate was a committed Jacksonian, they could indulge in the rare luxury of directly criticizing Old Hickory himself.

The Democrats, on the other hand, got some mileage out of their accusation that White could not win the presidency and that in fact he was not even a serious candidate. The *Nashville Union* warned very early in the race "that his cause is desperate—that inevitable and unavoidable defeat awaits him." More telling blows were struck when Jackson leaders pointed out that on the national scene White was merely being exploited by the Whigs as the best way to divide the Democratic vote in the South. They vociferously declared that White was a part of the strategy to throw the presidential election into the House of Representatives, where the Whigs might hope to salvage a victory.[64] Despite the basic soundness of these Democratic arguments, it was apparently difficult to convince the voters that White was a meek pawn in the conspiratorial hands of the Whigs or that he was not really in the race to win. These notions seemed to fly in the face of facts as understood by Tennesseans in 1836.

Questions of slavery and abolition received some ventilation during the campaign, but they seem not to have been of major consequence. Being a New Yorker, Van Buren was naturally subject to some criticisms about his views on slavery. The *Columbia Observer* charged that Van Buren did not know whether Congress could interfere with slavery in the District of Columbia. The *Nashville Union* eagerly defended its candidate, rejecting any allegations that Van Buren had ever opposed slavery in Missouri or anywhere else. Van Buren sent his friend Gideon J. Pillow some information from an antiabolitionist meeting in Albany which contained a denial by Van Buren that government had the authority to disturb the institution of slavery. Hugh Lawson White meanwhile took a strong stance against the power of Congress to eliminate slavery in the District or to interfere with it in southern states. One White elector, Asa Faulkner, drew up a circular in which he stated, "I am for Judge White because he is identified with the south, in feeling, interest and patriotism, on the subject of abolition." This theme was echoed by the *Columbia Observer,* which urged its readers to cast their ballots "for a man whose interests are your interests."[65] Yet despite the noise that surrounded this controversy from time to time, it seems to have been little more than rhetorical flourishes designed by both parties to attract attention and perhaps support. In fact, one senses a quiet desperation as some campaigners latched onto this question for fear that nothing else was working right in the campaign.

The time for discussion and debate ended with the arrival of election day. Tennessee voters preferred White to Van Buren by a decisive margin. White's strength was statewide, though it was more pervasive in East and West Tennessee (see Table 3.2). It is fair to say that the electorate responded to White (or against Van Buren) for various reasons—state pride, economic questions, White's long-standing loyalty to Jackson, rejection of Jackson's alleged meddling in state politics, and doubtless others.[66] But whatever the motivation, very few voters were aware that they were helping to erect a new political party that would persist for two decades in challenging Jackson's party. Near the end of the decade of the 1830s, this development was clearer and more obvious, as leaders of the White movement linked hands with the national Whig managers. And thus the new two-party system evolved in Tennessee.

The gradual, but dramatic, shift from politics conducted on a no-party basis to genuine two-party conflict was a distinguishing characteristic of the latter half of the 1830s. To be sure, the two parties did not yet have all of the apparatus of party structure, but there was no question that henceforth Tennesseans would choose between parties rather than factions or personalities. By the conclusion of this decade, the labels "Whig" and "Democrat" were consistently being used to refer to the opposing groups, the chief leaders of each party were clearly identified, and seemingly both parties had attracted enough statewide support to insure a durable competitiveness.

The decade also shows another change in Tennessee politics; namely, the increasing importance of the presidential contests. This can be seen, for example, in the 1835 and 1839 gubernatorial races, in both of which the question of presidential preference was important to the gubernatorial aspirants and to the voters. Hence these battles over the governor's chair took on new national importance—especially as a barometer of the political climate. By the time of the 1840 presidential campaign this growing interest in national politics paid off; from that point on to the Civil War, presidential elections attracted higher voter participation in Tennessee than did the governors' contests. Quite clearly, the fact that the 1836 campaign was the first competitive presidential election in the state helped generate new concern and commitment to these national contests, and in turn the new two-party development gave added significance to the presidential battles.

IV   Political Maturity 1840-49

      Two-party politics in Tennessee came of age in the decade of the 1840s when, judging from various statewide elections, the revolt against Jackson was firmly secured. The incipient Whig movement of the late 1830s became the bona fide, loyal and noisy opposition party, compelling the Democrats to fight diligently to maintain a high level of competitiveness. In the process the two parties waged eight vigorous statewide contests (five gubernatorial and three presidential) in ten years' time. If the pace of politics in the 1830s was hectic, one must search for new phrases to describe the 1840s.

      As both parties refined their structural machinery (nominating conventions, statewide and district committees, and partisan newspapers), they regularized the political process in Tennessee. In addition to this evidence of two-party maturation, feuding within each party was an equally significant theme that expressed itself again and again throughout the decade. Thus both parties simultaneously developed survival techniques (more sophisticated ways of waging political battle) and self-destructive tendencies (factional infighting).

      The two parties were naturally dependent upon their leaders to guide them in the new phases of development. Death laid its hands on several top political figures, but new leadership quickly emerged to fill the void. On the Whig side of the aisle the most important new face was that of James C. Jones. But some of the Whig leaders of the 1830s, John Bell, Ephraim Foster, and Neill S. Brown, were still around to direct the party in the 1840s. Unquestionably the two most prominent new Democratic leaders were Andrew Johnson and Alfred O.P. Nicholson. As with the Whigs, some of this new leadership in the Democratic party generated the factional rivalry that characterized politics in the 1840s.

      That state politics had to take cognizance of national events is almost a truism. The tremendous territorial expansion and the accompanying Mexican War certainly affected Tennessee. The state, for example, clearly wanted Texas in the union (despite the votes against such a move by Tennessee's two U.S. senators, Ephraim Foster and Spencer Jarnagin, both Whigs). And in mid-1846 when fighting erupted, Tennesseans, anxious to answer the call for volunteers, did so by the thousands. Regardless of a commitment to arms and regardless of the fact that Tennessean James K. Polk was president, Tennessee did not unanimously condone this war or even the acquisition of vast new territories which resulted. Evidence of nagging reservations is found in the 1847 gubernatorial campaign and elsewhere.[1]

The national political scene yielded the only two victories enjoyed by the Whigs in presidential contests. In fact the party ushered in the decade with the startling and boisterous triumph of the "Tippecanoe and Tyler too" team. In 1848 the Whigs once more successfully championed a military folk hero. Considering the use of such appeals and the extraordinary campaigning, one is tempted to say (as has been said about the Progressives' relationship to the Populists) that the Whigs found the Democrats in swimming and stole their clothing.

The Democrats tasted victory only in the 1844 contest, but they savored its flavor, for they defeated the Whigs' great leader, Henry Clay. Perhaps it was fitting that "Young Hickory" should have been the one to accomplish this impressive feat. That Clay's opponent in 1844 was Polk, rather than Van Buren, was a somewhat surprising development. Almost until the eleventh hour Van Buren was a serious contender. While there was a strong undercurrent against his nomination, it did not succeed until Van Buren publicly announced his opposition to the annexation of Texas. This declaration set in motion the events which thrust upon Polk the burden of trying to turn the tide against the Whigs in November. Polk was indeed successful, though his failure to carry his home state made him the proverbial prophet without honor in his own country.

The national economic picture left its mark on Tennessee. The internal improvements ardor so evident in the state in the 1830s cooled in the early 1840s, partly as a result of economic hard times that began with the Panic of 1837 and continued for the next four or five years. When Polk became governor in October 1839, the General Assembly began a move toward revoking the 1838 improvements law, culminating in the successful repeal in January 1840. The repeal evinced sectional, more than partisan, attitudes. John Marshall, Whig senator from Williamson County in Middle Tennessee, introduced the repeal measure into the General Assembly. West Tennesseans in the legislature voted in favor of revocation, while East Tennesseans split 14 to 14 on the matter. As expected, the Middle Tennessee legislators voted strongly in support of the Marshall bill. The General Assembly's 70 votes for repeal and only 23 against signaled broad-based opposition to the previous improvement law.[2]

Eventually, however, enthusiasm for railroad construction was fostered by the great railroad convention held in Memphis in November 1845, which attracted representatives from six states, and by Georgia's resumption of work on the Western and Atlantic Railroad. Not surprisingly, then, in the latter half of the 1840s the Tennessee legislature began chartering railroad companies to build lines within the state's boundaries. Great encouragement came in 1848 when the legislators endorsed $500,000 of bonds for the Nashville and Chattanooga Railroad and $350,000 for the East Tennessee and Georgia Railroad. State support for such endeavors crossed party lines as well as sectional, so strong was the fervor for this new transportation network. But even at that, by 1850 Tennessee still did not have a single mile of an operational railroad line.[3]

Despite a noticeable lack of steam in the internal improvements program, plenty of heat was generated in other areas of concern—especially state politics. Throughout the decade, for example, the Tennessee legislature fought vehemently over the selection of United States senators. Wrapped up in these intriguing battles were personality clashes, sectional animosities, partisan infighting, and, of course, individual ambitions. The decade's intense rivalry over choosing senators began in the fall of 1839 and did not cease until some eight years later. And strangely enough, at one point during the fight Tennessee found itself without any representation in the United States Senate.

For many years it had been assumed that one Senate seat belonged to East Tennessee and the other to Middle Tennessee. This tacit understanding served well the interests of both regions, though newly emerging West Tennessee naturally took a dim view of such an arrangement. Throughout the 1820s and 1830s East Tennessee, deprived of a chance at the governor's chair, was placated to a degree by possession of one of the Senate positions, but in the hectic conflict of the 1840s the traditional geographical division of the two seats eventually broke down, with the result that by 1847 Middle Tennessee claimed both posts.

The decade's battle over Senate seats had its genesis in the shifting situation of the late 1830s. Felix Grundy, a Democrat, occupied the so-called Middle Tennessee seat, and Hugh Lawson White, a Whig, held the East Tennessee one. But Grundy resigned in September 1838 in order to become attorney general in the Van Buren Cabinet, precipitating much of the confusion that was to come in the next few years, for in 1838 Governor Cannon appointed Ephraim Foster to serve the remaining months of Grundy's term. One should also recall that in October 1837 the emboldened Whigs had chosen Foster to take over the Grundy seat in 1839 for a full six-year term, but now because of the unexpected appointment, Foster became a senator several months ahead of schedule.

After the election of Polk and a Democratically controlled legislature in August 1839, Jacksonians could hardly be faulted for looking at the two Whig senators, White and Foster, with jaundiced eyes. But the realities of politics seemed to be against the eager Democrats: White would serve until March 1841 and Tennessee customarily did not elect "early" (the blatant exception of 1837 was still fresh in the legislators' minds); furthermore, Foster's term would not end until March 1845. Exhilarated by their triumphs, however, Jacksonian legislators were determined to do something about the Senate seats. But any notion of electing someone "early" to take over White's chair was quickly jettisoned when Governor Polk, still critical of the Whig tactics in 1837, committed himself against any such strategy.[4]

Ironically, developments in Washington, rather than Tennessee, were instrumental in the unseating of Foster and White and the subsequent realignment that enabled the Democrats to secure both seats. It was widely known that both senators opposed the Independent Treasury proposal which President Van Buren had been trying to get Congress to adopt. This gave Polk and the Democrats in the legislature the break they needed, for they instructed the two senators to support the Independent Treasury measure. Almost immediately Foster submitted his resignation from the Senate; White, however, held out until January 1840, when the U.S. Senate passed the Van Buren bill.

In anticipation of this happy turn of events, several Democrats made known their desires to move to the U.S. Senate. So worried was Governor Polk about keeping harmony in the family that he went to great lengths to persuade Grundy and Van Buren to permit Grundy's name to be placed before the legislature. When chosen by the legislature to replace Foster, Grundy reluctantly surrendered his Cabinet post. Polk engineered the replacement of White with almost equal skill. He found an East Tennessean (a necessary prerequisite) willing to take the White post for the remainder of the term, that is until March 1841. The obedient and anxious tool of Polk's maneuverings was Alexander Anderson of Knoxville, whose credentials were stained by his earlier identification with the Whig party. Anderson was a weak choice, to be sure, but he could be sold to the Democrats in the legislature as a man who would not make trouble and who would leave in 1841 without a fuss. Accordingly, he was elected shortly after White stepped down. The Democrats justifiably took pride in their success at having wrested both Senate seats away from the Whigs.[5]

But such joy was short-lived, for the death of Senator Grundy in mid-December 1840 not only shocked and saddened Tennessee Democrats but also opened the senatorial controversy once again. Governor Polk, whose responsibility it was to appoint someone to the now vacant seat, moved quickly to designate A.O.P. Nicholson. Nicholson was not to serve the remainder of the Grundy term (that is, until March 1845) but only until the next session of the legislature met. Polk's selection of Nicholson is somewhat puzzling. Nicholson was a Middle Tennessean, one of the requirements to be considered; yet there were other individuals from that section who might have received the appointment. Moreover, for some time he had been an irritant to the party chieftains, especially when he backed Hugh Lawson White in 1836. But Nicholson had worked hard for the Van Buren ticket in the 1840 presidential contest and Polk wanted to reward him. Perhaps Polk feared that Nicholson might eventually disrupt the smooth workings of the party and become a serious rival to him. Polk did not commit himself to supporting Nicholson for election when the next session of the General Assembly convened.[6] When the new year, 1841, dawned Nicholson assumed the Middle Tennessee seat, while Alexander Anderson, occupying the East Tennessee post, had only three months remaining in his abbreviated term.

The decision by newly inaugurated President William Henry Harrison to call a special session of Congress to meet in May presented new complications. Since Anderson was to leave office in March, Tennessee would have only one Senator, unless the legislature met in special session. Consequently, much pressure was exerted upon Governor Polk to summon the General Assembly to Nashville. Should the legislature meet, it would also be responsible for filling the seat held by Nicholson. Despite the insistence of Polk's Democratic friends, including Andrew Jackson, that he convene the legislature and also that he be considered for one of the Senate posts, Governor Polk refused to accede to these demands. Apparently Polk's strong aversion to specially called legislative sessions, be they state or congressional, and his fear of arousing antagonisms should he be selected as senator were the factors in his steadfast negative decision.[7] At any rate, the state was represented by only one senator—Nicholson—during the special 1841 session of Congress; but that was somewhat better than having no senators at all, which is precisely what happened next.

For longer than anyone could remember it had been the practice of the General Assembly to elect U.S. senators on a joint vote of both the lower and upper houses. But the 1841-42 session represented a departure from this hoary tradition. The Whigs won the gubernatorial contest in August, secured a majority of three in the legislature's lower house, but achieved only a minority (by one vote) in the state senate. A joint ballot would give the Whigs the desired majority on any vote for senator. But the Democrats, smarting from the defeat of Polk by James C. Jones, pledged to make life unpleasant for the new governor and the legislature as well. Since both U.S. Senate seats were to be filled, Democratic leaders were particularly sensitive to the high stakes of politics.[8]

When the legislature assembled in Nashville much plotting and maneuvering had already taken place in the interim between August and October. Not surprisingly, both Alexander Anderson and A.O.P. Nicholson had indicated that they would be available for at least one of the Senate posts, should the Democrats be able to implement a compromise strategy to get one seat. Meanwhile, quite understandably, there was a wave of enthusiasm within the Democratic ranks in support of Polk for a U.S. Senate seat. In addition to these three possible contenders, Hopkins L. Turney, congressman from the Fifth District, emerged as a candidate whose aspirations were aided considerably when his brother, Samuel Turney, became speaker of the state senate. By October the field had become a bit crowded on the Democratic side of the aisle.

The Whigs, needless to say, were keenly anticipating the Senate battle. Ephraim H. Foster, "instructed" out of the Senate two years earlier, was a prime candidate for one of the posts in 1841. For the East Tennessee seat, Spencer Jarnagin was presented by his friends as the most suitable contender. Eventually two additional Whigs were brought into the circle of candidates: John Bell, who had just resigned his post as secretary of war in the Tyler Cabinet, and Thomas Brown, a little-known Whig politician from East Tennessee's Roane County. When Bell returned to Tennessee in late November, his supporters began feuding with the Foster advocates; meanwhile Democrats smugly looked on, content that they could reap advantages from Whig dissension. Former Governor Polk, lurking and working behind the scenes, and other like-minded Democrats vowed that they would never agree to a compromise arrangement whereby Bell would obtain a seat.[9]

A group of thirteen Democratic members of the state senate became the frustrating obstacle to the selection process. They stubbornly refused to meet with the lower house for purposes of carrying out the elections, thereby making it impossible for agreement. Samuel Turney, as a Democrat elected to the state senate with Whig support, was a man much tormented throughout the session. His position as senate speaker made him all the more vulnerable to entreaties from both political parties. Naturally his desire to see his brother, Hopkins Turney, chosen as senator merely compounded his discomfort. Occasionally Turney wavered and sided with Whig demands for a joint ballot, only to be snatched back just in time by nervous Democratic friends.[10] For the moment the "Immortal Thirteen," as the Democratic state senators were labeled, had their day, but the failure to select senators would soon become a heavy burden for the Democrats to carry.

Because of the necessity of redrawing congressional district lines, Governor Jones convened the legislature in October 1842. Knowing that the Senate seat controversy would again arise, Polk and other Democrats had urged all members of the legislature to resign en masse, thereby making it necessary to hold new elections before the special session met. Presumably this strategy was calculated to give the voters an opportunity to render a verdict on the activities of the 1841-42 session. The Democrats' bold, if not radical, plan got nowhere. The 1842 special session wrestled once more with the Senate seat conflict but was unable to reach any agreement.[11] Perhaps by this time the Whigs were guilty of foot-dragging; after all, they would likely profit in the 1843 elections from the debacle seen in the two sessions of the Twenty-fourth General Assembly.

And how right they were. The Whig party not only swept Jones back into office for a second term but also secured majorities in both houses of the General Assembly. Those who had liked the dramatic flair of the Senate battles felt some disappointment when the Twenty-fifth legislature quickly and quietly in October selected Ephraim Foster and Spencer Jarnagin. Foster took the Middle Tennessee seat for the rest of the term which ended in March 1845, while Jarnagin was to occupy the East Tennessee seat for the years remaining in the 1841-47 term. There had been some noise about elevating Bell to the Senate, but he magnanimously withdrew in deference to Foster's claim on that post.[12] The Whigs were definitely back in the driver's seat in Tennessee politics, but they were not to enjoy that advantage for long.

In fact, the elections of 1845 completely reversed the results seen two years earlier. A Democratic governor, Aaron V. Brown, was elected and a Democratic majority was achieved in both legislative houses. Obviously there was no hope that the Whigs would be able to retain Foster in the Senate seat that he had held until March 1845. (Of course, Foster's defeat in the August 1845 gubernatorial election ended his chances for future political rewards.) When the General Assembly met in October it faced the opportunity of electing a person to a full six-year term in the U.S. Senate—for the first time since the selection of Grundy in 1839. The legislature's eventual decision to place Hopkins L. Turney, in the vacant Senate post was actually an empty triumph for the Democrats, for oddly enough, he was elected with forty-seven Whig votes plus half a dozen Democratic votes. A.O.P. Nicholson, not Turney, had been designated by the legislature's Democratic caucus as the party's candidate for the Senate seat. But as in earlier days, Nicholson's name could be counted on to stir bickering among Democrats; dissident Democrats immediately fished about for a substitute nominee and agreed upon Turney. Whigs in the legislature, believing Nicholson, editor of the *Nashville Union,* to be the choice of President Polk, determined to thwart his elevation, and they backed Turney. Actually President Polk had taken a strict hands-off approach. He was still unhappy about Nicholson's activities in 1841-42 and now in 1845 he was equally peeved at Turney for his flirtation with the Whigs. Polk stayed above the battle, though the Democratic feuding pained him.[13]

As the balloting continued, Nicholson, realizing that he could not win without Whig votes, shrewdly withdrew from contention lest he add another blemish to his name. On the final vote, a coalition of Whig and six Democratic votes elected Turney. The selection of Turney under such circumstances engendered much hard feeling among important Democrats—not the least of whom was Nicholson. In fact in a document designed to oust Turney from the party, a group of thirty-one members of the legislature accused Turney of "political immorality." But with the intervention of Governor Brown and others, who urged restraint and harmony, Turney remained in the party and even managed to placate President Polk with subsequent pledges of support for the Democratic administration. Yet despite this hasty papering over by the party stalwarts, the fissures were still there. Whigs naturally tried to make the most of the 1845 situation by claiming that they had put Turney in office and had thereby defeated Polk's man.[14] Pleased with this turn of events, Whigs were content to wait for the opportunity to fill the other Senate seat.

The election results in 1847 favored the Whig party, presenting it with the chance to name a successor to the post vacated by Spencer Jarnagin. When the General Assembly completed its work, the cus-

tom of Middle and East Tennessee each having one of the Senate seats
was broken for the first time in recent generations. Jarnagin, an East
Tennessean, had managed to irritate a number of Whigs in the state
during his years in the Senate, especially with his support of the Polk
administration's Walker tariff in 1846. With Jarnagin out of contention, the new six-year term (1847-53) was available—a situation that
unleashed intrastate rivalries as well as some factional infighting.
William G. Brownlow, editor of the *Jonesboro Whig,* jumped into the
fray early by renouncing East Tennessee's special claim on the seat
and urging the selection of John Bell. That Brownlow did not reflect
unanimous Whig opinion in East Tennessee was shown when John
Netherland and William B. Reese, both of East Tennessee, entered the
competition for the Senate post. Meanwhile, Whigs at the opposite
end of the state agitated for long-overdue recognition and pushed two
candidates: Robertson Topp of Memphis and Christopher H. Williams of Lexington. Amidst such competing sectional claims, Middle
Tennessee Whigs sensed that through a strategy of watchful waiting
they might be able to secure the Senate trophy themselves. John Bell's
friends were anxious to capitalize on this situation, though they were
aware of the potential danger of supporting a Middle Tennessean to
take the traditional East Tennessee seat.[15]

When the joint balloting began on October 28, it was anybody's
guess about the eventual outcome. As Bell gained strength during the
days of voting, Ephraim Foster and James C. Jones conducted behind-
the-scenes maneuvers to block his election. Yet their activities seemed
to have accomplished nothing more than ruffling some feathers and
prolonging the agony of decision. Near the end, the race narrowed to
Bell and Netherland, but Netherland's backers unexpectedly shifted to
a fellow East Tennessean, James A. Whitesides, a somewhat independent Whig who was thus more palatable to Democrats. Suddenly
Whitesides's support evaporated and moved in the direction of William B. Reese. Finally on November 22 (after almost a full month of
abortive balloting) the legislature agreed on Bell, after his promoters
apparently had worn down the opposition during the lengthy ordeal.
In all likelihood East Tennessee Whigs had come around to Brownlow's point of view when they recognized, belatedly, that they did not
have a candidate who could win. Besides, it was infinitely better to
have Bell, a Middle Tennessee Whig, in the Senate seat than no Whig
at all.[16] So in 1847 the principal architect of the "revolt" against
Jackson achieved his highest political reward.

The evenly balanced two-party rivalry repeatedly seen in the contests over the U.S. Senate was likewise exhibited in the gubernatorial

elections. In fact, of the five contests in the 1840s, the Whigs captured three and the Democrats two; clearly neither party had a monopoly on the governor's office.[17] After James C. Jones's two consecutive terms no other governor served more than one term—a new "tradition" in state politics not broken until the reelection of Andrew Johnson in 1855. The narrow margins of victory in the gubernatorial canvasses were further indication of the tight competition. In the 1845, 1847, and 1849 races the victorious candidates secured less than 51 percent of the statewide vote. The 1843 election saw the largest victory margin (3,800 votes) and percentage (51.7), but hardly anyone would describe that outcome as a landslide; yet in relative terms perhaps it was.

Other points of comparison among the gubernatorial contests show, for example, that Middle Tennessee continued its long domination (since 1821) of the governor's chair; indeed all of the rival candidates in the 1840s were Middle Tennesseans. Additionally, in the latter part of the decade, intrastate sectional hostilities surfaced when the parties chose their standard-bearers. Concerning party machinery, the use of nominating conventions first occurred in 1841, when the Whigs gathered to choose their candidate. As illustration of the still tentative nature of such party mechanisms, however, the Democrats did not stage a convention in 1841 or in 1843 and the Whigs abandoned theirs in 1843. It was not until 1845 that dependence upon nominating conventions developed. The argument used in 1841 and 1843 to justify the absence of such conventions—that it was already common knowledge who the candidates would be—was not employed in 1847 by the Democrats or in 1849 by the Whigs, though both times it was obvious that the incumbent would seek reelection.

In these contests for governor there was a shift away from state and local concerns to matters of national and regional importance. This trend bespoke the mounting tension over Texas annexation, the Mexican War, territorial acquisition, and, of course, the slavery question. This new mood became apparent in the 1845 debates between Aaron V. Brown and Ephraim Foster but even more visible in the discussions between the contenders in 1847 and 1849. Whig leaders in Tennessee had to walk the proverbial tightrope between the proannexation and pro-Mexican War feelings in the state, on the one hand, and their general lack of enthusiasm for either, on the other hand. That they succeeded in doing so—consider especially their victories in the 1844 presidential and 1847 gubernatorial races—is testimony of their skillful talents and of the stability of party allegiance. In Tennessee, as elsewhere in the nation, by the latter half of the decade the old issues of national bank, tariff, internal improvements were threadbare; newer, more volatile, more emotional problems replaced them.

That both parties were beset by internal squabbling and dissension should not be surprising. The battles over Senate seats frequently gave vent to such feelings; similarly, intraparty disputes erupted in some of the gubernatorial contests, particularly in the latter part of the period. That factional fighting became a fact of life is related to the smouldering Senate seat controversy, to personal ambitions and animosities, and to the unique problems related to presidential patronage. Tennessee Democrats could hardly have avoided internal bickering after one of their own—James K. Polk—went to the White House in 1845; for not surprisingly Polk played favorites with federal appointments in Tennessee. Those not favored—such as A.O.P. Nicholson, Andrew Johnson, and George W. Jones—quickly began expressing their unhappiness.[18] This attitude was hard to shield when Polk's man, Aaron V. Brown, elbowed his way to the top of the ladder of party leadership. So the love feast that seemed to characterize the Tennessee Jacksonian party during the campaigning of 1844 did not last much beyond election day in August 1845.

Disgruntled Whigs were also to be found in the state. The well-recognized antipathy between Bell and Foster that began in the 1830s retained its force and impact throughout the 1840s, though with lessening intensity after Foster's gubernatorial defeat in 1845 and Bell's election to the Senate in 1847. Foster personally contributed some unpleasantness by complaining that the party had let him down in 1845, but there were other sources of discontent—such as sectional antagonisms—which became evident in the latter years of the decade. For example, both East and West Tennessee (strongholds of the Whigs party) became increasingly restive about being shut off from supplying candidates for the governor's races. Additional Whig unhappiness was related to the Henry Clay-Zachary Taylor competition; almost until election day in 1848, for example, a small but vocal group of Whigs objected to Taylor as presidential nominee. And subsequently, much like the Democrats in the days of the Polk administration, various Tennessee Whigs became displeased with the handling of patronage by the Taylor administration.

But despite frequent lack of unanimity among party leadership, voter interest and voter participation remained incredibly high throughout the period. The great boosts of 1839 and 1840 made a long-lasting imprint, for during the 1840s the voter participation level never dropped below 80 percent (see Table 4.3). The highest degree of voter turnout in the governors' races occurred in the 1843 rematch between Polk and Jones (87-90 percent range). The gubernatorial races immediately following presidential contests experienced a drop in actual statewide vote (see Table 4.1). Without question, fierce two-party competition had a very healthy effect upon the turnout of voters at the polls; similarly, engaging personalities and special key issues further encouraged the citizenry to participate in the elections.

For a review of the specific gubernatorial campaigns there is merit to considering the 1841 and 1843 races together, since the same two contenders were involved both times. The Whig party held a nominating convention in March 1841, but the Democratic party did not. The principal reason for a Whig conclave was the necessity of selecting someone to run against the Democratic incumbent, Polk. The Bell-Foster rivalry resulted in a surfeit of hopeful contenders, not the least of whom was Bell's brother-in-law, David Dickinson of Murfreesboro. Newton Cannon, discredited by his loss in 1839, naturally had no support in 1841 from fellow Whigs. At one stage both Bell and Foster tried to push the other into the gubernatorial race which, had it worked, would have been very shrewd strategy. Basically those who were antagonistic to Bell at this time united in an effort to block Dickinson's nomination; to succeed they had to agree upon an alternative nominee. James C. Jones, a Wilson County politician who had just completed one term in the legislature, emerged as their man. His admirable talents as a stump speaker were well established and duly noted in the 1840 contest, when Jones, a presidential elector, toiled for the national Whig ticket. In reality this was his only claim to fame, but it was enough. Democratic leader Samuel H. Laughlin tried to make light of Jones by dismissing him as "a weak vain man—a mere bag of wind." Jones's Democratic opponent, Governor Polk, merely announced in 1840—after having been thwarted in his vice presidential ambitions—that he would seek reelection in 1841. When the 1843 race approached, neither Jones nor Polk seemed particularly anxious to be a candidate. In the Whig camp there was a feeling among some that Jones would be soundly defeated by Polk, but Ephraim Foster took charge of organizational strategy and convinced fellow Whigs that they could win the August elections. In February both Jones and Polk made public announcements of their intentions to carry the Whig and Democratic colors, respectively; therefore no nominating conventions were held by either party.[19]

The Polk-Jones contests displayed a mixture of state and national issues. Polk tried in 1841, for example, to gain ground by talking about the new Harrison-Tyler administration, but all of his noise about "federalism" among the Whigs seemed to have counted for

Table 4.1. Total Votes, 1840–49

Party	1840	1841	1843	1844	1845	1847	1848	1849
Whig	60,194	53,299	58,306	60,169	56,736	61,441	64,623	60,339
Democratic	47,946	50,697	54,474	59,902	58,377	60,704	58,504	61,832
Total	108,140	103,996	112,780	120,071	115,113	122,145	123,127	122,171

little. In fact, there were no issues of great consequence in the initial Polk-Jones battle; instead both candidates depended more on amusing anecdotes and clever repartee. This was not an altogether surprising strategy in a campaign that followed only a few short months after the "Tippecanoe and Tyler too" hoopla. Early in the race, Polk threatened to borrow Jones's joke book after he had exhausted his own supply of stories.[20] In 1843, however, Polk by and large abandoned his attempts to trade humorous jibes with Jones; after all, that practice had not worked very well for him two years earlier. Jones did not have to resort to his usual antics as much in 1843, because he had at least two ready-made issues. The obstructionist course of the "Immortal Thirteen" in the General Assembly furnished Jones with more than ample ammunition; not only had they blocked the election of U.S. senators, but also they had rejected Jones's nominees to the board of the state bank and had refused his request for an investigation of that bank. All of this was grist for the Whigs' mill, and Jones used it very effectively. Since this gubernatorial race occurred on the eve of a national election year, the question of presidential preference was a natural one. Jones was able to take the offensive on this matter, because it was indisputable that Henry Clay would be the party's standard-bearer in 1844; moreover, Jones was apparently willing to gamble that Clay's popularity had improved in Tennessee, especially in relation to Van Buren's. Jones therefore vociferously endorsed Clay in the 1843 debates and pushed a somewhat embarrassed and nervous Polk to declare his presidential favorite. But since there was as yet no certain Democratic nominee, though Van Buren seemed to have the inside track, Polk could afford to say little more than that he would support the candidate chosen by the national convention. Not only did Jones emphatically back Clay for president, but he also championed the traditional Clay program of national bank, protective tariffs, and internal improvements.[21]

What do the 1841 and 1843 election results show? In the first campaign, there was a drop in the level of voter participation as compared to the immediately preceding 1840 presidential and 1839 gubernatorial canvasses (see Tables 4.1 and 4.3).[22] Approximately 104,000 votes were cast in 1841—about 4,000 fewer than in 1840 and about 2,000 fewer than in 1839. But the 1843 Polk-Jones battle saw the statewide voter participation jump to the highest level of all the gubernatorial elections in the decade. In that contest Jones gained more than Polk did from the increased voter turnout, so that the 1843 race became the greatest triumph for the Whig party in the gubernatorial elections of the 1840s (see Table 4.2). In fairness to Polk, it should be pointed out that his accomplishments in 1841 (48.8 percent of the statewide vote) look more impressive when compared to Van Buren's 44.3 percent in the 1840 presidential contest.

The sectional distribution of the statewide vote is worth noting briefly. In both 1841 and 1843 Jones carried East and West Tennessee while Polk held onto Middle Tennessee, but Jones did not secure as high percentage in the eastern and western thirds as the Whig presidential contender had done in 1840 (see Table 4.2). Moreover, Jones's percentage slipped slightly in 1843 in East and West Tennessee, in comparison to his performance in 1841. Perhaps most interesting is the erosion of Polk's strength in Middle Tennessee. To be sure, in 1841 he was hurt (in comparison to 1839) by the thumping Whig victory in 1840, but one must search for additional reasons to explain why his percentage there in 1843 was 1.6 lower than what it had been in 1841. Some credence must be given to the rumors (especially in 1843) that local Democratic politicians in Middle Tennessee made deals with Whig leaders whereby support would be thrown to Jones in exchange for Whig backing of certain Democratic legislative and congressional candidates, although no conclusive proof of that claim is extant.[23]

The 1845 election dramatically reversed the undeniable Whig trend in the state. Without question the biggest advantage enjoyed by the Democrats in that year was the experience of having worked harmoniously and zealously for Polk in the 1844 campaign. If fact a month after the November election, the State Central Committee announced that the first Democratic nominating convention would be held on March 4, 1845 (Polk's inauguration date).[24] In the immediate aftermath of the party's convention, the *Nashville Union* captured the attitude and motivation of Tennessee Democrats in 1845: "The loss of Tennessee . . . seems to impress itself upon every Democratic mind as a circumstance placing the Democracy of the State under the strongest obligations to show their gratitude to their sister Democratic States in a splendid triumph in August. The smallness of the majority by which we were defeated in 1844 gives to every Democrat the most perfect assurance that victory is within our power."[25] The

Table 4.2. Percentage of Democratic Vote by Section, 1840–49

Section	1840	1841	1843	1844	1845	1847	1848	1849
East	40.5	45.1	45.3	46.7	47.2	46.3	42.8	46.2
Middle	49.0	53.1	51.5	53.4	54.2	53.0	51.5	55.0
West	39.2	43.8	45.2	46.3	47.8	47.0	45.0	47.3
STATE	44.3	48.8	48.3	49.9	50.7	49.7	47.5	50.6

Table 4.3. Percentage of Statewide Voter Participation, 1840–49

1840	1841	1843	1844	1845	1847	1848	1849
89.6	84–87	87–90	89.6	85–88	85–88	83–86	81–84

only serious candidate for the gubernatorial nomination mentioned prior to the convention was Aaron V. Brown, three-term congressman from lower Middle Tennessee and Polk's longtime personal and professional friend. When the party assembled in Nashville, Brown had a rival, however, in the person of Frederick P. Stanton, an aspiring West Tennessee politician. But Stanton withdrew from contention, permitting Brown to be chosen unanimously.[26]

Meanwhile Governor Jones had let it be known that he did not wish to seek a third term, thereby opening up the question of a suitable nominee for the Whig party. In February the *Nashville Whig* began making editorial noises in favor of the nomination of Ephraim Foster; in fact, it apparently went so far as to wonder aloud if Foster might be permitted to seek the gubernatorial office without opposition from the Democrats. During the following month there was a sudden interest in the possible nomination of Neill S. Brown, who because of his youth had no political sins for which to answer. But when the Whig convention met in late March, Foster was chosen without difficulty, mainly because of a decade of yeoman service to the party. Probably only John Bell could have raised a voice against Foster, but he chose not to do so.[27]

Given the year and the candidates, it is no surprise that the topic of America's territorial expansion was paramount in the race. Tennessee voters had shown in the immediately preceding presidential election an affinity for the annexation of Texas, but Foster, as U.S. Senator, voted against the Texas annexation treaty in 1844 and subsequently compounded his sin by voting against the joint resolution on Texas in early 1845. With Aaron Brown, Polk's devoted ally, being Foster's opponent, there was no escaping the question of Texas and related expansion issues. Until Foster's vote against the joint resolution on Texas, he had been treated by Democrats as friendly toward annexation, despite his negative ballot on the 1844 treaty. Afterward, however, the Jacksonian press depicted Foster as an inconsistent, untrustworthy man on the Texas question. As one editorial expressed it, "True, Mr. Foster *speaks* for Texas, but he *votes* against it—and actions speak stronger than words!" The *Nashville Union* calculated that both groups within the Whig party—the proannexation and the antiannexation elements—would claim Foster because he was a good deal for Texas and a great deal against Texas. The first Brown-Foster debate took place in Clarksville on April 7, and from that date until election day the candidates argued over the Texas question. Foster attempted to escape harm by contending that he had not backed the joint resolution because there were no guarantees in it to protect slavery in the west. A week or two before election day, word was received that the Texas convention had accepted the terms of Congress' joint resolution—thereby bolstering the position of Brown and the Democrats in the campaign.[28]

Despite a vigorous and strenuous effort by the two contenders, the voters did not turn out in record numbers. Perhaps the *Union* was right when it editorialized that the people had not gotten excited; although not indifferent to the outcome, they were tired of noise and agitation.[29] As Table 4.3 shows, there was a drop in the level of voter participation in 1845 in comparison to 1844 and 1843. Remarkably, Foster lost to Brown by only 1,600 votes, despite recognizable odds against him. Party stability and loyalty almost saved the day for Foster and the Whigs. There is, however, perhaps some merit to the frequently voiced Whig complaint that the party lost because it did not get its people to the polls.[30] When one considers that the Whig vote in 1845 was 3,500 fewer than in 1844 and 1,600 fewer than in 1843, it is understandable why Whigs felt they had only themselves to blame for the defeat of Foster. Still, credit must certainly be given to Brown and the Democrats, for Brown's percentages in East and West Tennessee exceeded those of Polk's in both 1843 and 1844. Most strikingly Brown reestablished Middle Tennessee as a Democratic stronghold, pulling a higher percentage than Polk had in 1841, 1843, and 1844. In many respects (the issues debated and the distribution of votes) the 1845 gubernatorial race was the culmination of the effort that had begun in the summer of 1844 to stem the Whig tide in Tennessee. That mission, which had come within about 300 votes of succeeding in November 1844, finally triumphed nine months later— thanks in large measure to the Texas question which Brown and the Democrats capitalized upon in 1845.[31]

When the 1847 gubernatorial year approached, Whigs tried to get their house in order so that they could stage a comeback. That they were successful, against seemingly difficult handicaps, is both remark- able and praiseworthy. The Mexican War that had begun in 1846 was influential in the gubernatorial campaign, but the election's outcome showed that Tennessee citizens were not unquestioning supporters of the war. Whig leaders worked both sides of the street during the 1847 race: they took credit for the victories of Zachary Taylor at Buena Vista and of Winfield Scott at Vera Cruz, while also criticizing the war itself and Polk's conduct of it.

Since there was no clearly identifiable Whig nominee, several aspir- ants expressed willingness to tackle the assignment of restoring the Whigs to power. The Whig who could easily have secured the nomina- tion and probably just as easily defeated Aaron Brown was former congressman from Middle Tennessee, William B. Campbell. He was on the battlefields of Mexico at this time, a fact that of course con- tributed great luster to his name and candidacy. John Bell feared Campbell's possible candidacy, for he wanted an East Tennessean to get the nod in 1847—at least so he told Thomas A.R. Nelson, one of that section's emerging powers. It has been suggested that Bell took this course because it might make it easier for him to secure the U.S. Senate seat being vacated by Jarnagin of East Tennessee. Not surpris- ingly, Ephraim Foster, Bell's fraternal foe, jumped on the Campbell bandwagon. For various selfish reasons several prominent Whig lead- ers wrote to Campbell declaring that he could have the nomination, but urging him to decline it. Most of the Whig chieftains breathed easier when, in January, Campbell made known his decision not to carry the Whig standard. This left the way clear then for Meredith P. Gentry, Gustavus A. Henry, and Neill S. Brown—all leading Middle Tennessee Whigs—to press their own claims for the nomina- tion. But by the time of the Whig convention, Gentry, a strong oppo- nent of the war, had decided to seek reelection to Congress instead. Neill Brown enjoyed the backing of Foster and his coterie at the conclave, and apparently Bell chose to take a back seat and not get directly involved in pushing one candidate over another. The assem- bled Whigs had little difficulty in agreeing upon Neill Brown; but not all was harmonious within the Whig household, for Henry left town with ruffled feathers.[32]

Although there had been some slight noise among a few Democrats —those unhappy with Polk—that perhaps Governor Aaron Brown was not the best man to make the race in 1847, such talk quickly evaporated when the party gathered for its nominating convention. The *Union*, worried lest the party fail to stage a convention, argued that the convention was necessary to effect party organization, harmony, and unity. Brown, unanimously chosen as the candidate at the April 1 convention, was an arch-defender of the Polk administration and the Mexican War. The party went on record lauding Polk, the independent treasury, the reduction of the tariff, and approving the prosecution of the war against Mexico.[33]

Attention was unavoidably riveted upon national issues and problems, but Neill Brown's moderate stance on the war made him a less vulnerable target than Governor Brown desired. Generally Neill Brown was not an arch-critic of the war in the same mold as two or three of the Whig congressmen from Tennessee. From the very first joint debate, at Nashville on April 3, to the end of the campaign the Mexican War occupied a central place in the speeches of the contenders. The Whig position generally was that the war was unnecessary and had been unconstitutionally brought on by the president. The Democrats tagged Brown and fellow Whig leaders with the label, "Mexican Whigs"—those who opposed the war and sided with Mexico; whereas the Democrats called the rank and file of Whigs, "American Whigs"—those who opposed the treasonous leaders in their party and who volunteered to fight against the Mexicans. Governor Brown and his followers apparently had trouble recognizing that there really was no unanimity in Tennessee in support of the war. But Whig criticism of Polk's appointments of Democratic politicians to high military posts caused a worried Aaron Brown in May to beg the president to elevate Tennessee Whig William B. Campbell to a generalship. Much to the governor's relief, Polk quickly obliged this urgent request.[34]

Whatever attention the war merited in the gubernatorial debates and in newspaper editorials, it had to take second place to the presidential preference question. In the very first joint debate, Neill Brown declared himself in favor of Zachary Taylor for president in 1848, and from then on the Whigs frequently extolled the virtues of Taylor on the battlefield and predicted he would make an excellent president. Democrats fought back, not by attacking Taylor who was extremely popular in the state, but by questioning whether he would in actuality

become the Whig nominee. With telling comments Democratic editorials claimed that the endorsement of Taylor by the Whigs was a
two-fold strategy to cover up their opposition to the war and to take
advantage of the enthusiasm Taylor's successes had fostered. Democratic leaders and their press continued to insist that the national
Whig party would never accept Taylor, for the northern abolition
Whigs did not want him and the northern manufacturers did not want
a low-tariff man. As a June issue of the *Union* declared in exasperation, "He [Taylor] is no more fit for a whig candidate for President
than a pious preacher is to be the keeper of a grog-shop." A month
later this same paper reiterated the theme: "To be *Taylorized* will be
full as heavy a blow to whig principles as to be *Tylerized.*" Despite
continuing criticisms by the Democrats, the idea of Taylor as the
prospective Whig presidential nominee steadily attracted attention
and a following throughout the state. Certainly the Whigs never tired
of trumpeting a military hero as their likely candidate. Democrats,
who had no appealing hero to place in opposition to Taylor, were hard
pressed on this issue. When the noise of the campaign subsided, it
looked as though the 1847 canvass had truly been a proving ground
for the presidential race.[35]

Conversely, the contest was not a forum for an examination of the
strengths and weaknesses of the Wilmot Proviso. Although the proviso had first been introduced into Congress the year before Tennessee's gubernatorial campaign and although it was a continuing and
lively topic in Congress, it enjoyed no serious attention in the governor's race. Perhaps the neglect of the proviso in 1847 may be understood on the basis of the Jacksonian press which minimized the
significance of the measure. The *Nashville Union*, for example, maintained that Congress simply could not legislate on matters of slavery
or nonslavery in territories before the land had actually been acquired.
Even if the present Congress adopted the Wilmot Proviso, such action, argued the *Union*, would not be binding on subsequent sessions
of Congress. Apparently this line of reasoning was fairly typical of the
thinking of Tennessee leaders in 1847, for there was no further mention of the proviso, and the candidates did not deal with it in their
debates and speeches.[36] Two years later, however, the proviso would
seem more important to Tennesseans.

With all the furor over the Polk administration, the Mexican War,
and the potential candidacy of Taylor, the campaign attracted a
healthy increase in voter turnout (see Table 4.1). The Whigs benefited
most from the larger turnout, as Neill Brown received about 4,700

more votes than had Foster in 1845, while Aaron Brown got only 2,300 more votes than he had in 1845. In terms of geographical regions, the Whig candidate's percentages were better in East and West Tennessee in 1847 than Foster's had been in 1845. Middle Tennessee went for Aaron Brown in 1847 but not as strongly as in 1845 (see Table 4.2).[37]

Interpretations of the outcome at the ballot box were varied. The *Nashville Republican Banner* was certain that the voters had voiced their opposition to Polk's conduct of the Mexican War. One very knowledgeable Democrat, Alfred Balch, attributed defeat to the popularity of Zachary Taylor and indicated his dread of the presidential campaign looming on the horizon. President Polk, from the vantage point of Washington, thought that Tennessee Democrats had been over-confident and that they had not dealt boldly enough with "the Taylor feeling" in the state. Polk also conceded that his distribution of federal patronage had offended some state Democratic leaders, which might have made them less than enthusiastic backers of Polk's protégé, Aaron Brown. The *Nashville Union* spent the month of August explaining away the Democratic defeat on the grounds that the party had not been well enough organized and unified, that the Democrats therefore defeated themselves. Perhaps there was some merit in the press's interpretation, for in the extremely competitive situation of 1847 party apathy and inattention to effective statewide organization were critical weaknesses. In the final analysis, it appears that Tennessee Whigs managed to blunt charges of their being strongly antiwar while concurrently promoting Taylor for the presidency. This well-conceived strategy paid off on election day.[38]

As was expected in 1848, Zachary Taylor and the Whigs won handily in Tennessee. Thus when the year 1849 dawned, Democrats confronted some uncomfortable facts: they had suffered notable defections in the 1848 contest; the Whigs held the gubernatorial office and would be seeking to retain it; and of the seven statewide elections in the 1840s the Democrats had been victorious in only one. Meanwhile the Whigs, confident of their ability to secure the reelection of Neill Brown despite his lackluster term as governor, were not fully aware of the emerging importance of the Wilmot Proviso and slavery questions. Instead, they blindly assumed that Brown could hang onto Taylor's coattails in 1849 with little difficulty.

Early noises coming out of the Democratic camp indicated that the party would be faced with several gubernatorial hopefuls. That intrastate sectional considerations were now entering the picture was

shown by slight flurries of activity on behalf of candidates from East
and West Tennessee, such as Landon C. Haynes and Andrew Johnson
and Levin H. Coe. But from early January on attention focused
primarily upon William Trousdale and to a lesser extent upon Gideon
J. Pillow—both from Middle Tennessee. Trousdale and Pillow, renowned for their exploits on the battlefields of Mexico, apparently had
considerable support among certain Democrats. The rumor mills in
late February produced A.O.P. Nicholson as a possible Democratic
nominee, but Nicholson quickly bowed out with a behind-the-times
statement expressing the hope that state issues, such as common
schools and internal improvements, would be central to the campaign.
By the time of the mid-April nominating convention, Pillow had
removed himself from contention, leaving a clear field for Trousdale.
At the convention itself, however, both Trousdale and Haynes were
nominated—much to the surprise of a number of delegates—but the
convention quickly eliminated the Haynes candidacy and strongly
endorsed Trousdale, the military hero.[39]

By the time the Whig nominating convention met, three days after
the Democrats, the selection of Governor Neill Brown seemed assured. Earlier, however, there had been a faint move to push the
candidacy of Thomas A.R. Nelson of East Tennessee—a result of that
region's dissatisfaction. But Nelson, good party man that he was,
withdrew gracefully and urged his friends to back Brown. About two
months before the Whig convention Brown had seemed uncertain
about seeking the nomination, but no rivals emerged to challenge
him.[40] Brown eventually received the nomination almost by de-
fault and apparently without great enthusiasm among his fellow
Whigs.

The two conventions set the tone and topics for the gubernatorial
race. Strongly pressured by the West Tennessee branch of the party,
the Democrats adopted a platform denying the right of the federal
government to interfere with slavery, rejecting outright the Wilmot
Proviso, and urging Tennesseans to take vigorous action against
threats to their sovereignty and their property rights. Although there
was some dispute over these states rights resolutions, they were accepted in full by vote of the convention. Despite the failure of the
Whig conclave to adopt a platform or resolutions, Neill Brown's
acceptance speech adequately typified party attitudes. Brown voiced
opposition to the Wilmot Proviso and aligned himself with the South
on the slavery question; but equally important, Brown opposed any
kind of southern resistance movement, saying that if the proviso
passed, the "south should submit quietly to its operation." Brown and

other Tennessee Whigs were hopeful that the Taylor adminstration would somehow be able to calm growing sectional tensions.[41] In the aftermath of the conventions, the issues of the protection of slavery and the Wilmot Proviso occupied central places in the campaign.

The Democratic press made certain that the Whigs were given no respite from the charge that Brown and his cohorts were submissionists. Brown's "truckling servility to the anti-slavery feeling of the north" was one graphic way the press depicted his position. Trousdale presented the "domino theory" in his speeches—elimination of slavery in the District of Columbia would lead to prevention of slavery's extension into territories, to prohibition of slave traffic, and finally to abolition of slavery in the southern states. Probably the strongest Whig argument charged the Democrats with being disunionists, which they stoutly denied. One new wrinkle in the slavery and Wilmot Proviso debates was introduced by Democrats who argued that southerners should stop commercial intercourse with northern businesses, if laws were enacted injurious to the South.[42] Apart from some squabbles in June over the military credentials of Trousdale and Brown, the public heard little but the claims and counterclaims from the parties about their stance on the slavery question.[43]

When the votes were counted in August, Trousdale came out on top by about 1,500 or a percentage of 50.6. The total statewide vote (see Table 4.1) matched that of 1847 but was lower than that of 1848. Voter participation in 1849 declined from previous record turnouts, making it the lowest in the decade (see Table 4.3). As compared to 1847, Neill Brown managed to hold his own in 1849 in East Tennessee and experienced a very slight decline in the western third of the state (see Table 4.2). The most striking aspect of the election was Trousdale's strength in Middle Tennessee, which he carried by a margin of nearly 5,800 votes or a percentage of 55.0 (the best percentage in the decade). Trousdale's victory is even more impressive in light of the decisive Whig presidential victory the preceding year.

Part of the explanation of the results in 1849 is that Trousdale's military record put him in good stead with the voters—much as Taylor's had in 1848. Moreover, some Whigs were disheartened by the federal patronage squabble taking place in East Tennessee, though this bickering did not adversely affect the Whig percentage there. Compared to 1847 and 1848, apparently a sizable group of Whigs across the state stayed home on election day in 1849, causing Whig leaders to blame apathy for the defeat. The *Nashville Union* admitted that there were a great many Whigs who refused to vote for Brown but emphasized that they did so because of their unhappiness with the position on slavery taken by Brown and the party. But a natural overconfidence among Whigs in 1849 based upon their 6,000-vote victory the preceding year must also be considered. The *Union* had no hesitation in its analysis of the election's outcome, declaring that "the whole South will rejoice with us, for it is a triumph of Southern Rights and of the Union as it is." The election returns seem to indicate that Trousdale's popularity and the Wilmot Proviso and slavery issues helped win back the "Taylor Democrats" of 1848, so that the 1849 vote resembled very closely that of 1847.[44]

Although congressional elections, with the exception of 1841, were held concurrently with the gubernatorial races, they were not necessarily influenced by them. Only in the 1841 Whig victory and in the 1849 Democratic victory does there appear to have been a connection between the gubernatorial and congressional electoral results. In 1841 the Whigs captured eight of the thirteen seats, their greatest success in the decade, and in 1849 the Democrats swept seven of the eleven seats for their best showing. Of the eleven districts from the 1843 election through 1849, only three shifted party allegiance in terms of congressmen elected, while five districts remained consistently Democratic and three were regularly Whig.[45]

While Democrats enjoyed some measure of success in the gubernatorial and congressional campaigns, they failed in the three presidential elections in the 1840s. The incredibly high levels of voter participation (approximately 90 percent in 1840 and 1844 and about 83-86 percent in 1848) demonstrated the enthusiastic response of the people, as did the fact that these presidential elections outpolled the gubernatorial races—a reversal of traditional patterns in Tennessee. The Whigs won handily in 1840 and 1848 (55.7 percent and 52.5 percent, respectively), outstripping their victories in gubernatorial elections. On the other hand, the 1844 presidential battle stands out as the closest election of all the gubernatorial and presidential contests, not only in that decade but in the 1830s and 1850s as well. Furthermore, in 1844 Tennessean James K. Polk was a contender—a return to the tradition begun in 1824, but broken in 1840, of having a Tennessee resident on the presidential ballot. Finally, the 1844 election terminated the Whig party's longest string of consecutive victories in Tennessee, begun in 1840. Never before or afterward were the Whigs able to put together four successive wins.

The three presidential contests lend themselves readily to a topical rather than chronological examination. Given its indispensable and vital nature, party organization was a paramount concern in most of the gubernatorial and presidential elections of the 1840s.

One of the most notable hallmarks of the 1840 contest, for instance, was the development of an organizational network by both parties. What followed in subsequent presidential and gubernatorial campaigns was largely an imitation of the 1840 model. Unlike the situation in a number of states, the Whig party in Tennessee blazed the new trail of party organization, and it seldom surrendered that advantage in later electoral battles. The first state party conventions of the new two-party system were held in 1840—clear evidence of the emphasis that would be given to getting both parties girded for the campaign. The Whig faithful, stunned by Polk's upset victory in August 1839, determined immediately that they must put forth a united, coherent effort in 1840. In fact, before August had ended a County Vigilance Committee was organized by Rutherford County Whigs, and similar committees appeared elsewhere in September and October. The mushrooming efforts to organize the Whigs were boosted by the December 1839 national convention's startling decision to trust "Tippecanoe and Tyler too" with the party's colors. The man saddled with the responsibility of whipping Tennessee Whigs into shape was Ephraim Foster, still smarting from his forced resignation from the United States Senate. Foster took the Whigs into the intensive campaigning of the summer months well prepared and very determined.[46]

On January 4, Whig members of the legislature, plus other party notables, met in Nashville and laid the groundwork for the two state conventions: February 3 in Nashville for Middle and West Tennessee Whigs and February 10-11 in Knoxville for East Tennessee. These conventions agreed upon a slate of presidential electors, thirteen men to represent the congressional districts and two at-large electors— Hugh Lawson White and Ephraim Foster. Upon the shoulders of these fifteen men rested the responsibility of carrying the Harrison flag into every corner of the state.[47] Following the February conventions, great exertions were made in every county to organize the party rank and file. Some counties established central corresponding committees which became the party's sinews and brains at the local level; elsewhere Tippecanoe Clubs sprang up to supplement the more official party structure. As Allen Hall, editor of the *Nashville Republican Banner* put it, "Above all, let the watchword of the Whigs be ORGANIZATION, ORGANIZATION! We must have committees in every county, and Tippecanoe Clubs in every town and neighborhood." Apparently they succeeded in creating an imposing network, for when the election results became known, Polk wrote to Nicholson: "We are *beaten* in the late contest in the state, *beaten* by the superior organization and industry of our opponents."[48]

Given the existence of an established two-party rivalry, Tennessee Democrats responded with alacrity to the stirrings of the Whigs. They were somewhat at a disadvantage because their national convention would not meet until May 1840. Of course, the selection of incumbent Van Buren as the nominee was a foregone conclusion (good reason for not holding a convention, some said); thus Democrats were able to organize locally despite the absence of the party's official imprimatur upon Van Buren. Worried by rumors of secret Whig organizing efforts, Democratic legislators and others assembled in Nashville on January 8 to voice their concern. Emerging from this influential gathering were proposals for the creation of a Democratic State Committee to coordinate the work of prospective county committees and a call for a state convention to be held on February 11 in Nashville. In the following three or four weeks many counties staged meetings to choose delegates to the state convention. That convention designated thirteen district electors, plus two state-at-large electors: Adam Huntsman of West Tennessee and Andrew Johnson of East Tennessee.[49] A Central Corresponding Committee of twelve men, headquartered in Nashville, was established to supervise communications among the various components of the party's structure. Thus, on paper at least, the Democrats hastily erected a framework to conduct the campaign; events would reveal how sturdy and reliable it would be.[50]

As the 1844 presidential year approached, both parties scurried around to solidify and refurbish their organizations. While the results resembled the model created in 1840, there were noticeable variations. This time, for example, it was the Democratic party, rather than the Whig, that got the jump on organizational efforts—doubtless because of its two consecutive defeats in the 1841 and 1843 gubernatorial contests. Two or three weeks after Polk's second gubernatorial loss, Andrew Johnson commended the Maury County Democrats (Polk's home county) for their new organizing work and exhorted all his fellow party members thus: "Then I say, let the Democracy organize and act as one man." Another motivation prompting at least some Democrats to action was the desire to promote Polk's designs on the vice presidential nomination. As early as October 1843, when the new General Assembly met, Polk and other party chieftains conferred repeatedly in Nashville about strategy and organization. A call was issued for a statewide party convention to be held on November 23. When it met, the conclave chose delegates to attend the national convention in Baltimore in May 1844 and authorized the convention president, Leonard P. Cheatham, to appoint three state committees of correspondence which would in turn name the state-at-large presidential electors. These three committees were also expected to do the usual supervision and promotion of communications among the various entities of the party. The November convention further recommended that meetings be held in the eleven congressional districts for purposes of choosing electors.[51] So unlike 1840, the Democratic convention in 1843 left untouched the matter of the presidential electors.

In the aftermath of the November meeting and before the national convention in May, state Democrats busied themselves with organizational concerns. Numerous counties established or revitalized Democratic associations and several of the congressional districts had meetings to select presidential electors. In March the three state committees reached agreement on Hopkins L. Turney (Middle Tennessee) and Levin H. Coe (West Tennessee) as the at-large electors. Of course the selection of Polk in May as the presidential candidate stimulated new excitement and new spurts of organizing activities among Tennessee Democrats: the formation of "Young Hickory" clubs was urged, the slate of electors was finally completed in mid-June, addtional Democratic associations were seen, and new committees to raise necessary funds were evident in the state.[52] Although there had been some sluggishness in the efforts to organize the party, the summer months brought intensified and widespread movement on this front.

Embued with confidence because of their successive victories, Tennessee Whigs waited until the new year to begin shoring up their organizational structure. Whig legislators, meeting on January 8, 1844, chose their two state-at-large electors—John Bell and Gustavus Henry, both of Middle Tennessee. They thus made one of the key decisions, not leaving it to the party conventions as had been done in 1840. Although the legislators called a state conclave to meet on February 22, there were actually three Whig conventions on that date, an obvious decentralization and a bow to sectional realities in the state. These three meetings (Nashville, Knoxville, and Somerville) succeeded in naming the electors from the various congressional districts. By early March the entire slate of electors was complete. As the campaign heated up there was increasing activity among the Whigs to insure a thoroughly organized party, for in addition to the customary paraphernalia of local correspondence and vigilance committees, a State Committee of Correspondence was created, which in September called for county committees and civil district committees within each county. These latter groups were charged with the responsibility of devising a list of all the eligible voters in their respective civil

districts; they were to categorize the voters according to party preference and to work to convert those voters who had indicated no party
identification or allegiance. Clearly the Whigs had no intention of
letting down their guard in that critical election year.[53]

As in 1844, the Whigs of 1848 were somewhat slower than the
Democrats in shaping their campaign. Their tardiness was related in
part to the confidence that they could win without great difficulty
(remembering the 1847 governor's race) and in part to the Clay-
Taylor feud within the Whig ranks in Tennessee. In any event, Whig
leaders gathered in Nashville on January 27 to name their two state-
at-large electors. In recognition of mounting sectional unhappiness,
they chose John Netherland of East Tennessee and Christopher H.
Williams of West Tennessee to head the electoral slate. Pursuant to
the legislators' recommendation, Whig meetings were held in May to
select delegates to the national convention at Philadelphia and to
name presidential electors. After Taylor's nomination there was a
surfeit of county and district Whig meetings to ratify the national
ticket and in some cases to make a decision on electors. When it was
learned that Christopher Williams had declined to serve as state-at-
large elector, the Lawrenceburg meeting recommended a state convention. This call was echoed in early July by the *Republican Banner,*
which urged that such a meeting be held in Nashville on August 7.
In the intervening four weeks various county meetings designated
convention delegates. At the party's long-overdue convention, the
assembled Whigs agreed upon James C. Jones (now of West Tennessee) as a replacement for Williams. The slate of presidential electors
was finally completed and a special five-man Whig Central Committee
was created to give overall direction to the remainder of the campaign.[54]

That the Democratic camp was apprehensive about the 1848 race
may be inferred from the early start given to its organizational efforts.
In mid-November 1847, Democratic legislators set up a State Central
Committee of fifteen men, which in turn appointed two additional
five-man committees, one for East and one for West Tennessee. The
November caucus concluded with a call for a state convention to meet
in January at Nashville. On the appointed day, Tennessee Democrats
assembled to name delegates to the national convention, select the two
state-at-large electors (George W. Rowles of East Tennessee and William T. Brown of West Tennessee), and designate nine of the eleven
district electors. Thus in 1848, unlike 1844, the convention itself
handled most of the matters of party organization. In February, however, Rowles announced his decision not to serve; immediately in

March the State Central Committee, plus the East and West Tennessee committees, named Aaron V. Brown to that post. Brown, who was still grumbling about his hard work in 1845 and 1847 and the party's lack of appreciation of him, had earlier boasted, "I can organize our party in this State better than any other man can & if identified with the coming election I can bring 2000 more votes to the polls than any body else."[55] The election results in November showed the extent of Brown's braggadocio.

There was a flurry of activity, including numerous county rallies, among the state's Democrats immediately after the nomination of the Cass-Butler ticket. The final complete slate of presidential electors was not secured until early June, there having been several changes in the original group as well as the necessity of filling two of the positions left vacant at the January state convention.[56] The Democrats in 1848 were matching the pattern seen in 1844, though they were clearly ahead of what the Whigs were doing in 1848. As the campaign progressed, however, the principal Democratic newspaper, the *Nashville Union,* expressed mounting anxiety about the lack of effective party organization, claiming that in some of the counties nothing had been done.[57] One can speculate that Cass's failure to generate enthusiasm among the state's voters in general and Democrats in particular had a negative impact on the development of party machinery.

The Democrats always staged a single party convention, whereas the Whigs, except in the much-delayed 1848 meeting, had state meetings to accommodate the different sections. Perhaps this reflects the irrepressible hegemony of Middle Tennessee in the Democratic party and, conversely, the Whig strength in both East and West Tennessee. On another front, if one assumes that the selection of presidential electors showed the importance of state conventions, then one is forced to concede the diminishing or at least fluctuating significance of those conclaves. In 1840, for instance, both parties utilized their state conventions to designate all of the presidential electors. But the Democrats abandoned this procedure in 1844, only to return to it four years later. In both 1844 and 1848 the Whig legislative caucuses named the state-at-large electors, whereas the 1844 convention chose the other presidential electors; but in 1848 that task fell upon meetings held in the congressional districts, a stratagem used previously by the Democrats in 1844.

Despite the best efforts of both parties to get a complete list of electors early in the campaign, more often than not they were frustrated by numerous changes in personnel. The Democrats, for example, had to replace three district electors in 1840, two in 1844, one at-large and three district electors in 1848. The Whigs had better luck; in 1840 after the death of Hugh Lawson White in April they had to find a new state-at-large elector and also to replace one of the district electors. In 1848 they substituted Jones for Williams in the at-large post. But in the 1844 campaign the Whigs had their entire slate by early March and did not make any changes thereafter. It is not altogether clear whether the shifting and changing of electoral candidates by Democrats indicated weaknesses in party organization.

While the great concern over political machinery may rightfully be viewed as a positive manifestation of the growing-up process, the factional feuding and disharmony evident from time to time should be considered as a negative sign. One would be hard pressed to claim which party, Whig or Democrat, was more afflicted by schism and disagreement, for both seemed to have had their share. In the 1840 election year there was no recognizable internal division, with the exception of some initial unhappiness among certain Whigs over the selection of Harrison as the presidential nominee. Among Tennessee Democratic leaders there was the expectation that Polk would be rewarded for his 1839 governor's race by being named Van Buren's vice presidential running mate in 1840. Naturally the state's Democrats were keenly disappointed that their efforts came to naught when the national convention decided to have no vice presidential candidate. But like good troopers, Polk and his fellow Democrats shielded their unhappiness and waged battle, however unsuccessfully, for Van Buren.[58]

As the 1844 election year approached, dissatisfaction within the Democratic camp could no longer be hidden. By that time, Polk's unchallenged role as leader of the state's party was questioned by those chagrined over his defeats in 1841 and 1843 and his unquenchable thirst for the vice presidency. Adding strength to the cause of the disenchanted Democrats was Polk's persistent stance in favor of Van Buren for the presidency; after all, many had grown weary of following the New Yorker down the road to defeat in Tennessee. Not surprisingly, much of the latent antagonism toward Polk and his allies boiled over in the crucial months of late 1843 and early 1844.[59]

That some Democrats wanted to abandon Van Buren and switch to Lewis Cass, whereas Polk and his friends needed to stand by Van Buren as the best strategy to secure the vice presidential nomination for Polk, set these two groups on an unavoidable collision course. The widespread notion that Polk lost in 1843 because of shouldering the prospective candidacy of Van Buren played right into the hands of those who were increasingly disgruntled with both Polk and Van Buren. The enfant terrible of the state party, A.O.P. Nicholson, announced his backing of Cass shortly after the results of the August 1843 election were known. In fairness to Cass it should be observed that his cause gained ground in the fall of 1843 because some Tennessee Democrats liked him better than Van Buren; but the principal impetus for the pro-Cass movement came from the anti-Polk faction of the party. When the November 1843 convention met in Nashville, there was ready agreement upon endorsing Polk for the vice presidential nomination. A convention floor fight over the presidential recommendation, however, was avoided through a so-called compromise that had been hammered out in advance: no one should be endorsed for the presidency. The Cass people acceded to this in order to escape a bitter fight which they might possibly lose, not realizing at the time how well they had cooperated with the Polk strategy. Polk and his cohorts had already decided that the tactic of no nomination by the convention would conceivably show Van Buren that he must embrace Polk for his running mate or face the risk of losing in Tennessee. At any rate, the state's delegates to the Baltimore convention went uninstructed on the question of presidential nomination.[60]

The Polk faction's shrewd machinations nearly backfired in the months immediately following the November state convention. As soon as Congress convened in December, questions were raised in Washington about Tennessee's failure to endorse Van Buren. Cave Johnson and others had to devote a good bit of their time to calming the agitated spirits of the Van Buren partisans. In the meantime, Polk, Jackson, and others had written directly to Van Buren, assuring him that he was indeed the choice of the Tennessee Democrats but also informing him that in order to preserve harmony the procedure of having no presidential nomination had been followed. Van Buren was probably unaware that this report was a misrepresentation of both facts and motives. Polk's troubles mounted in January, when the state convention's special committee prepared an address that was so lukewarm toward Van Buren (Nicholson had had a hand in drafting it) that it could not be circulated beyond Tennessee. Furthermore, Polk urged the *Nashville Union* to declare for Van Buren, but it delayed until early February. From that point on Polk's chances as Van Buren's running mate began to diminish. Therefore several of the Tennessee congressmen tried to push or drag Polk into the Cass camp, believing there might be a possibility of a Cass-Polk ticket. The *Nashville Union,* still under the influence of Nicholson, was very friendly toward the suggestion of a Cass-Polk team—which was very embar-

rassing and damaging to Polk, who was still clinging tenaciously to
Van Buren. When Laughlin took over in early March as editor of the
Union, Polk pressured him to condemn those who were linking Polk's
name with Cass's and to declare once again Tennessee's preference for
Van Buren. In the midst of all this confusion Andrew Johnson lamented the no nomination strategy of the November state convention;
had Cass been endorsed then, he argued, it would have given his
candidacy a great boost throughout the nation and caused Van Buren
to withdraw.[61]

The month of May 1844 was an incredibly complicated and difficult
time for both the national party and the state party, especially in the
wake of Van Buren's antiannexation statement. Nicholson and his
allies stood poised to exploit the sudden eruption of Tennessee sentiment antagonistic to Van Buren. Indeed Nicholson effectively reas-
serted his influence over the *Nashville Union* at this critical moment.
Meanwhile, of the six Democratic congressmen from Tennessee only
one—Cave Johnson—stood firm with Van Buren and Polk. The Baltimore convention itself demonstrated the continuing fight among Tennessee Democrats; in fact, eight of the thirteen delegates were clearly
unwilling to play ball with the Van Buren people. They swung the
delegation to Lewis Cass on all the balloting until the end when Polk
emerged suddenly as the new presidential hopeful. Polk's most ardent
supporter and greatest schemer among the Tennessee delegates was
Gideon J. Pillow, who helped engineer the convention's switch to
Polk for president. He complained, however, that he received little or
no help from his fellow Tennesseans in the intrigue to push Polk's
candidacy—an ominous sign about friction within the leadership of
the state's party.[62] Polk took Pillow's grievance to heart and on
occasion later referred to the antagonism displayed toward him at the
Baltimore convention, particularly by Andrew Johnson and George
W. Jones. The story of the factional feuding of 1843-44 ended on a
happy note, however, for as soon as Polk was chosen at Baltimore the
Nicholson-Johnson crowd laid aside its hostilities and eagerly joined
in the task of aiding the Polk campaign in Tennessee.

But between the 1844 and the 1848 elections infighting among the
state's Democrats became quite pronounced. Doubtless Polk's absence from the state gave new boldness to the anti-Polk faction. In any
event, Nicholson, Johnson, et alii were determined to promote vigorously the nomination of Lewis Cass in 1848, but the state party
convention in January did not name a presidential favorite, reflecting
once again the divided mind and motivations of the Tennessee Demo-

crats. Aaron V. Brown, obviously fearing the possible domination of the anti-Polk wing of the party, claimed that he had successfully thwarted a Cass nomination at the January meeting. Some of Polk's allies secretly urged him to consider being a candidate in 1848, while others tried to divert attention to James Buchanan of Pennsylvania or Levi Woodbury of New Hampshire. Distrustful of Polk, Andrew Johnson steadfastly believed that Polk would try at the last minute to get the national nomination. In the meantime, the *Nashville Union* endorsed Cass for the presidency, thereby making it increasingly difficult for the Polk wing to sway Tennessee party leaders to someone other than Cass. At the Baltimore convention the majority of the Tennessee delegates voted for Cass, the victorious nominee. As expected, in the aftermath of the selection of Cass the Nicholson-Johnson stock enjoyed a sudden rise, while such leaders as Brown and Hopkins Turney realized that they had been out-maneuvered.[63] From this presidential election on, the anti-Polk group moved steadily toward a position of domination in the party, though it ran into some difficulties from time to time.

Tennessee Whigs were also beset by internal problems in 1848. As early as the spring of 1847 John Bell declared Zachary Taylor to be his preference for president, and in the governor's race that summer the successful Neill Brown carried the Taylor banner enthusiastically. Moreover, in January 1848 the Tennessee General Assembly voted to recommend Taylor for the presidency. Yet despite such evidence of the pro-Taylor leanings of most Tennessee Whigs, there remained a group committed to Henry Clay. Given Bell's stand, it is not surprising that Ephraim Foster and James C. Jones headed the pro-Clay faction—perhaps for reasons not exclusively related to beliefs about Clay's superior qualifications for the presidency. William G. Brownlow, longtime devotee of both Bell and Clay, found himself in an awkward position but seemingly ignored Bell's enthusiasm for Taylor and stayed with Clay throughout 1848. The most striking example of the rivalry within the state party was the pro-Clay rally staged by Jones in Nashville in April. Democrats, beset by their own problems, doubtless got some enjoyment by standing on the sidelines encouraging the Whig conflict. But immediately after the national convention at Philadelphia chose Taylor, it was none other than Jones who spoke at a special meeting of Clay leaders and others in Philadelphia and declared his support of the Taylor-Fillmore ticket. In Tennessee most of Clay's backers quickly closed ranks with the Bell-Brown faction and jumped on the Taylor bandwagon. So although the frictions may have retarded organizational efforts for a time, by early August the Whigs were united, harmonious, and organized.[64] Doubtlessly, the sweet scent of possible victory had beckoned Whigs of different hues to work together in behalf of the Taylor-Fillmore ticket.

It need hardly be said that in the presidential contests attention was not always focused exclusively upon party organization or party factionalism, for there were issues and concerns raised from time to time that attracted the voting public, but in the initial presidential campaign of the decade there were no serious issues. The "Log Cabin" circus of 1840 left little room for deliberation and debate over issues. This is not to argue, of course, that the press and some leaders failed to address various concerns of the day, but that these attempts counted for little in the campaign. Most of the discussions revolved around the Whig candidate, William Henry Harrison. Obviously worried about the popularity of this quaint folk hero, Democrats in Tennessee made a good bit of noise about Harrison's northern sympathies and abolitionist leanings. In an extremely exaggerated claim the *Nashville Union* declared that Harrison desired the abolition of slavery everywhere and approved the use of public funds to emancipate slaves within the states. The Whig press and Whig leaders were quick to defend Harrison from such charges; the *Nashville Republican Banner,* for example, countered that Harrison had always denied the right of the state or general government to interfere with slavery in the South.[65] Sharing equal billing with the abolitionist discussions were speeches and articles about Harrison's abilities as a military commander and about his long-established Federalist principles.[66] One cannot safely say that any of these three issues were of consequence in the 1840 campaign, for a reading of the correspondence and the newspapers of the time conveys a very strong impression that the mass excitement and hoopla overshadowed serious questions.

But the 1844 presidential battle was different, because both parties had to deal with the Texas annexation issue. Understandably, there was considerable interest in Tennessee over the Texas question—a concern dating back several years to migrations of Tennesseans to Texas and to the 1836 fight for independence which certain Tennesseans helped bring to a successful conclusion. Van Buren and Clay apparently misjudged the importance of the Texas issue when they announced their positions in opposition to annexation. That declaration unleashed a fire storm in the Democratic party which drove Van Buren out of contention and ushered in Polk, a strong annexationist. But the Whigs stood by Clay, for better or worse, because there simply was no one else available in 1844. Eventually, through a series of letters Clay moderated his position so that he inched closer and closer to the Democratic party platform. This strategy helped Clay in places such as Tennessee but hurt him in the northeastern region, an area predisposed to the belief that Texas annexation was directly related to the extension and preservation of slavery.

During the Tennessee campaign, state Whigs worked both sides of the annexation street. John Bell's was probably the most prominent voice raised in support of Clay's position of opposition to immediate annexation. After Democrat Thomas Hart Benton of Missouri made speeches against Texas annexation, Tennessee Whigs circulated Benton's words widely. Various local Whig meetings adopted proannexation resolutions in the early months of the campaign. Whig leaders who attempted to offset the gaining Democratic strength on this question generally argued that the annexation issue was fading in importance as the campaign progressed and that the Democrats were simply using the issue as a political stratagem, not really caring what the consequences of annexation might be. Democrats throughout the state were elated over the Texas question, recognizing the proannexation sentiment that prevailed in the state. Early in the campaign one of the prominent Democratic leaders assured Polk: "The Texas question is a powerful lever in our hands and will give us many Whig votes." The state's Democrats never strayed from a proannexation position and seldom failed to make it the central issue in speeches and newspaper writings.[67] When the voters made know their preferences in November, the Whig candidate Clay emerged as the victor, albeit by a remarkably small margin. The Democrats, however, attracted all the new voters in 1844, statistically speaking, while the Whigs retained the same number of voters they had had in 1840. The Polk-Clay battle was issue oriented, but the tenacious loyalty of voters seems to have carried the day.

Four years later the nation and particularly the South were in a stir over the Wilmot Proviso and the extension of slavery into western territories. But in Tennessee during the 1848 campaign these matters did not assume the importance they perhaps did elsewhere. To be sure, there were speeches and newspaper editorials that treated the proviso and slavery extension, but these concerns received about as much attention as debates over the president's veto power and over the qualifications Taylor possessed for the job of president. In other words, because Tennessee Whigs were trying to be as nonpartisan as possible in 1848 and because their candidate was noncommittal on the matter of the Wilmot Proviso, there was only speculation by both sides as to Taylor's real attitude toward the proviso. Meanwhile Lewis

Cass's famous letter to A.O.P. Nicholson, in which he articulated his belief in popular sovereignty, attracted some attention during the Tennessee canvass. As many observers discovered then and later, such a position could be interpreted as pro-South or as anti-South. Judging by newspaper editorials and campaign speeches, Tennesseans were evidently becoming increasingly concerned about southern rights and related matters of slavery extension.[68] But more important, in 1848 they were caught up in the popular appeal of military hero Zachary Taylor—as they had been during the preceding year's gubernatorial campaign. In this regard then, the presidential race in Tennessee was not truly issue oriented, certainly not as in the 1844 campaign.

That the 1848 contest was something of an aberration may be inferred from the *Nashville Union*, which complained that not since 1832 "has there been so little excitement among the people, at the corresponding period prior to a Presidential election, as at the present time." Whig observer William B. Campbell noted that since both Taylor and Cass lacked personal enemies, not much excitement could be generated. The calmness that pervaded Tennessee in 1848 may also be ascribed to the prevalent feeling that Taylor would win with little or no difficulty; therefore, Democrats were apparently unable to shake off their lethargy while Whigs quietly tried to woo Democrats who were admirers of Taylor's Mexican War activities. Moreover, the state in general and Democrats in particular keenly felt the absence of Polk, the man who had played such indispensable roles in the 1840 and 1844 campaigning. About the only spark of enthusiasm in 1848 came from the joint appearances of two former governors, James C. Jones and Aaron V. Brown, both of whom served as state-at-large electors for their respective parties. When election day arrived, the decline in voter participation (as compared to 1840 and 1844) reflected the relatively tranquil campaign which had just ended.[69]

The 1840 and 1844 campaigns, however, seem to have been about as noisy and exciting as the 1848 race was quiet. In 1840 Tennessee Whigs inaugurated mass rallies as a vital component of their electioneering and in 1844 both parties utilized them. In these elections the Whig state-at-large electors were very instrumental in conducting the campaign. In 1840 Ephraim Foster, for example, did more than yeoman service for the Harrison-Tyler ticket; indeed he was the guiding spirit as well as the most enthusiastic and diligent campaigner. In 1844 the Whig at-large electors, John Bell and Gustavus Henry, led their party's efforts with skill and determination. The Democrats, on the other hand, operated differently, for state-at-large electors Andrew Johnson and Adam Huntsman in 1840 and Hopkins L. Turney and Levin H. Coe in 1844 were not the actual campaign managers. Instead, that leadership role was superbly assumed by none other than James K. Polk; in fact, one gets the impression that the Democrats would not have had a campaign worthy of the name had it not been for Polk. That he was governor during the 1840 contest and presidential candidate four years later doubtless gave him the extra incentive to take to the stump (in 1840 but not in 1844), to arrange speaking tours of other Democratic orators, to plot campaign strategy, to keep the newspapers busy with campaign material, and to carry on an incredible amount of correspondence. The feverish excitement stirred by the campaigners meant that when both parties prepared to stage giant rallies in Nashville in August 1844, a special nonpartisan committee was established to devise certain ground rules in order to avoid possible trouble and disruption. In 1840 one of the Democratic electors, Levin H. Coe, got in a fight at Somerville with a Whig speaker and shot him; luckily the wound was not fatal. When the hoopla of 1840 ended, William G. Brownlow made a typically exaggerated claim about his activities: "I sung louder, jumped higher, and fell flatter and harder than anybody else in the whole state of Tennessee. I wrote upon log cabins, and waved coon-skins and water-gourds high and low."[70] The intensity of feelings fostered by Whig and Democratic electioneering resulted in a remarkable outpouring of voters in both 1840 and 1844.

Information provided in Table 4.1 indicates what these armies of voters did on a statewide basis in the three presidential contests. Some very interesting things happened to the vote captured by each party in these elections. The Whig vote, for instance, jumped from about 36,000 in 1836 to 60,100 in 1840, but stayed at that exact same level in 1844, and then increased by nearly 4,500 in 1848. The Democratic vote on the other hand followed a somewhat different pattern: it leaped from 26,000 in 1836 to almost 48,000 in 1840, jumped by 12,000 in 1844, but then dropped by about 1,400 in 1848. Clearly both parties enjoyed their greatest gains in 1840, both benefiting appreciably from the enlarged voter turnout. An examination of the percentages won by the Whigs shows, however, the reality of declining appeal (see Table 4.2) in 1840 and 1844, when compared to the 58 percent captured in 1836. In 1848, of course, the Whig percentage improved over the 1844 results. From the sectional angle, it was 1844 that firmly established the "tradition" of Democratic victory in Middle Tennessee and Whig triumph in East and West Tennessee in presidential

contests. In the 1836 and 1840 elections the Whigs had swept all three
sections of the state, but they never again enjoyed such good fortune.[71]

Of crucial importance to these presidential elections and other
political battles was the network of partisan newspapers. As in the
1830s the party press in the 1840s carried the burden of promoting
candidates and program, while it also served as a continuing source
of anxiety for party leaders on both sides of the aisle. The maturing
of the two-party system as well as the debilitating factional fighting
in Tennessee were reflected in these newspapers. Both parties relied
heavily and at times exclusively upon the Nashville papers to bolster
their cause. As in the preceding decade, the Whigs in the 1840s
continued to support two newspapers in Nashville, while the Democrats managed to keep only one going. In the spring of 1848, however,
a second Democratic paper, the *Daily Centre-State American,* was
started in Nashville. In its first year and a half of operation, the paper
served initially as a strong voice for the Lewis Cass interests. Both the
Nashville Republican Banner and the *Nashville Union* each had six
different editors in the 1840s. Despite brevity of tenure, running a
newspaper did have its rewards—usually the satisfaction of helping
some candidate win an election. But tangible, direct benefits were
obtained by J. George Harris, Samuel H. Laughlin, and E.G. Eastman, who received federal appointments during the Polk administration, and by Allen A. Hall, who was awarded a diplomatic post in
1841 and an appointment as register of the United States Treasury in
1849.[72]

One cannot discuss the Whig press in Nashville in the 1840s without reference to Hall, for he was the party's most prominent and
important editor. He served the *Republican Banner* until his departure from town in 1841, but upon his return to Nashville in 1845 he
promptly occupied the editor's chair at the old rival, the *Nashville
Whig.* The *Republican Banner* moved into the Ephraim Foster camp
in 1841, giving that faction control of both Whig papers in Nashville.
When John Bell returned to Nashville after resigning from the Tyler
Cabinet, he found the *Whig* and the *Republican Banner* pushing
Foster for the election to the U.S. Senate. Bell, according to one
source, had earlier in the year expended some three thousand dollars
of his own money to keep the *Republican Banner* in operation.[73]

Meanwhile, the *Nashville Union,* though beset with numerous
problems, promoted the Democratic cause as best it could. Its precari-
ous birth and early years were matched by equally hazardous growing-up years. In the first half of the decade, Polk was directly involved

in the affairs of the *Union,* but afterward other Democratic chieftains had the responsibility of sustaining and supporting the paper. The quest for a suitable editor was a continuing search, much as it had been in the 1830s; in addition, the paper changed ownership several times in the ten-year span.[74] An arrangement was worked out in late 1843, for example, through the backing of certain Democratic leaders, whereby John P. Heiss bought out Thomas Hogan. Assured that $1,500 could be raised to pay for a new editor, Polk seized the initiative and offered the job to Samuel Laughlin, renowned for his early days as *Union* editor. Polk and his cohorts felt heavy pressure to move rapidly, because Nicholson and others were breathing down their necks with the pro-Cass threat. But Thomas Hogan, though seriously ill with tuberculosis, stayed on as editor until February 1844. In fact Laughlin did not assume the editor's chair until mid-March, and by that time much harm had already been done to Polk's presidential chances. Heiss, the owner, who did much of the editing in the interim between Hogan and Laughlin, moved into the Cass camp in April and sabotaged some of Laughlin's editorials, much to the dismay of the Van Buren element. In the summer months, various complaints were voiced about Laughlin's work as editor. J. George Harris, who certainly knew what it took to be a good editor, objected to Laughlin's excursions into the countryside and therefore caused Polk, the exasperated presidential candidate, to arrange for Harris to assist Laughlin with the editorial chores.[75]

James G. Shepard bought the paper from Heiss in November 1844 and immediately arranged for Nicholson to become the editor. At this juncture, Nicholson had temporarily "reformed" and was anxious to placate Polk, Aaron Brown, and others. But by the latter months of 1846 Nicholson made known his intention to surrender the editorship. Shepard and certain political leaders turned to E. G. Eastman, former editor of the *Knoxville Argus.* Eastman had won his spurs under the very trying conditions of editing a Democratic newspaper in a heavily Whig town.

Governor Aaron Brown and Democratic members of Tennessee's congressional delegation all took part in the selection of Eastman, along with Shepard of course. One of the congressmen, Lucien B. Chase, defended Eastman from charges about drunken sprees, though he conceded that "while in that infernal Whig hole at Knoxville" Eastman might have gotten inebriated occasionally (shades of Samuel H. Laughlin in the 1830s!). Shepard issued a very pertinent warning to Eastman that as editor he would be expected to "stand aloof from all alliances with cliques" and "stand pledged at all times to support

the action of the party as expressed through properly organized conventions." Eastman assured Shepard that he would conduct the paper
to the satisfaction of Governor Brown and the congressmen, and if
not, he would not expect to receive his salary. Although not wanting
to move until the spring of 1847, he finally relented to the persistent
and urgent pleas that he be in Nashville by January. The following
month Eastman plunged back into the thicket of the political wars in
Tennessee.[76]

Those battles of the 1840s ended with Democratic victory in the
1849 gubernatorial campaign. If a war-weary voter had had the time
and energy to contemplate the fast-paced scenes of political conflict
and intrigue, he doubtless would have recognized how the two-party
system in Tennessee matured throughout the decade. In all likelihood
he would also have sensed the inherent dangers in the internal dissension which disturbed both parties. The delicate balance between the
Whig and Democratic parties in the state was repeatedly demonstrated in the 1840s—with the exception, of course, of at least two of
the presidential contests. Neither party could afford the luxury of
resting on its laurels.

As the decade progressed, more and more attention was focused
upon national events and developments. The 1849 gubernatorial campaign showed the embryonic signs of sectional stress—a harbinger of
the forthcoming decade. While both parties in Tennessee kept their
organization and machinery generally in excellent working condition
and avoided polarization over the slavery issue, no one could be
certain that events and circumstances outside the state might not soon
disturb the political process. Two-party politics definitely came of age
in Tennessee in the 1840s, but this symmetrical and sensible arrangement for conducting politics was placed in jeopardy in the succeeding
years.

V Politics Transformed 1850-59

The decade of the 1850s opened with a brilliant, but fragile, compromise agreed upon by Congress in a valiant effort to deal with the slavery question. For a time the menacing, strident voices of sectionalism were muted, but as the decade progressed the nation found itself caught up in a worsening controversy over slavery. Needless to say, Tennessee did not, indeed could not, escape the swirling crosscurrents of compromise and conflict.

The question of the extension of slavery was the nation's overriding concern. In 1850 Congress dealt with this problem by offering a package containing compromises favorable to both North and South.[1] This action was made necessary because of the territorial acquisition of the Mexican War and also the resulting disputes over the Wilmot Proviso. Tensions over slavery diminished in the wake of the Compromise of 1850, although Nashville hosted two southern protest conventions in that year. The problem of slavery in the territories erupted with intensified fury in 1854 upon the introduction and passage of the Kansas-Nebraska bill. This ill-timed legislation specifically repealed the old Missouri Compromise of 1820 and opened all federal territories to the possibility of being either free or slave. Subsequent events and tragedies in Kansas made a mockery of the notion of popular sovereignty and widened sectional alienation. Both Franklin Pierce and James Buchanan proved incapable of handling the Kansas problem and the consequent divisions within the nation at large. The Supreme Court's Dred Scott decision in 1857, which denied the right of Congress to treat the matter of slavery in the territories, was yet another chapter in the worsening condition of the nation.[2] Economic panic hit the country in 1857 and further contributed to the national malaise by adding a dimension of economic discontent to the already existing anxieties about the permanence of the union. Considering these developments, it is not difficult to perceive a nation being fragmented in ways too serious to repair or heal.

Tennessee was thrust into the somewhat unnatural and uncomfortable position of playing host to a southern convention in June and again in November. During the previous year dissident southern political leaders had urged a conclave to articulate resistance to the federal government's meddling with the slavery issue. When a Mississippi meeting designated Nashville as the site of the proposed convention, it did so despite the lack of extreme southern views in the city or in the state. This prospective meeting naturally evoked partisan attitudes and comments in Tennessee. Newly inaugurated governor William Trousdale, for example, looked with favor upon it, and the Democrat-controlled lower house of the legislature passed a resolution prescribing the appointment of delegates by the governor. But the Whig-dominated state senate blocked the measure, thereby causing the state government's failure to give official sanction to the southern convention. Consequently, the various interested counties had to select their own delegates to the June 1850 meeting. The lack of widespread support in the state may be inferred from the sparse attendance from areas outside Middle Tennessee; in fact, of the approximately one hundred Tennessee delegates nearly half were from two counties —Davidson and Maury.[3]

At the June convention one would have searched almost in vain among the Tennessee delegates to find a Whig. As the 1849 gubernatorial campaign had already shown, some differences between the two parties over states rights and unionism were becoming more visible. Almost to a man Whig leaders in Tennessee condemned the forthcoming southern convention, for they did not want to get their hands sullied with extremism. Besides, they were anxiously waiting for the Whig administration in Washington to resolve the current controversy over slavery. Moreover, the Whig press, with possibly only two exceptions, refused to lend support to the June conclave. Such disdain for consorting with more excessive southern views did not continue to typify all of the Whig chieftains in the state over the next three or four years, but generally speaking it was characteristic of most of the party.[4]

Tennessee Democrats, on the other hand, not only furnished most of the personnel for the state's delegation but also supplied important leadership for the convention itself. To be sure, there was some reluctance among certain Democrats—principally Nicholson and some of his faction—about the proposed meeting, but that was swept aside by the desire to be represented at the June convention. Aaron V. Brown, more and more identified with the burgeoning states rights element in the party, was understandably anxious to have a hand in the proceedings. Nicholson, who at this time abhorred such leanings, attended in order to keep a close watch on his Democratic rivals and also to convey a sense of loyalty to the South. In addition to these leaders, Andrew J. Donelson and Gideon J. Pillow also had active roles at the June meeting. Despite the visibility of Tennessee Democrats it should be noted that they did not share the more radical convictions heard at the conclave. Indeed they seemed to have exerted a moderating impact upon their fellow southerners.[5]

When the Nashville convention reassembled in November, the Compromise of 1850 was about two months old. This time Tennessee contributed only fourteen delegates—all but two of whom had attended the June session and all of whom, with two exceptions, were residents of Davidson County. This more radical November meeting educed very little enthusiasm from the state Democrats in attendance. Both Donelson and Pillow, for example, offered resolutions of their own, and Brown and Nicholson dissented from the convention's final set of resolutions. In fact, the Tennessee delegates were the only ones to vote against the report of the convention's resolutions committee. In the aftermath, both Brown and Nicholson published "addresses" which they had been unable to deliver at the session. Of the two, Brown's was more prosouthern in tone and spirit; although he attacked the Compromise of 1850, he also warned against hasty action by the South. Nicholson placed blame for sectional turmoil equally upon North and South, defended the compromise, and averred that the central question was the preservation of the union.[6] After the June and November meetings doubtless many Tennessee Democrats, fearing that the voters might hold them accountable in some fashion, regretted that their party had been so involved or identified with these sessions.

While Nashville was hosting, however reluctantly, the southern conventions, a very pronounced sentiment in favor of the 1850 compromise was developing in Tennessee. Not surprisingly, the state's Whigs were in the vanguard of those supporting the original Clay proposals as well as the final package agreed upon by Congress in September. Although some Democrats, disposed toward the states rights posture, were suspicious or outright antagonistic toward the compromise, there were plenty who welcomed it on the grounds that it would quiet the mushrooming excitement over the slavery question.[7]

The shake-up in the two Democratic newspapers in Nashville reflected the division of opinion within party leadership over the compromise and the southern conventions. E.G. Eastman editor of the *Nashville Union* since 1847, took a position in 1850 in favor of the forthcoming Nashville convention; and after the June meeting, at which he served as secretary, Eastman commented affirmatively upon its actions and resolutions. But in July the owner of the *Union,*

Harvey M. Watterson, fired Eastman as editor—possibly because of
the influence and insistence of Watterson's close friend, Nicholson.
Eastman was not without journalistic work for long, however, for in
August he became editor of the *Nashville American.* From that point
on, both papers embarked upon an intense rivalry, differing not only
on the compromise and the southern conventions but also on prospective candidates for various political offices. Under Eastman's direction
the *American* attacked the compromise and advocated resistance to
the North; meanwhile the *Union* praised the compromise and unionism. This attitudinal and factional warfare was not halted until May
1853, when the two papers merged to become the *Nashville Union and
American.* [8]

The Kansas-Nebraska bill (1854) stirred sectional tensions over
slavery more than anything previously had done. As one might antici-
pate, the views of Tennesseans about that measure showed marked
differences. Hardly a better example can be found than that of the
state's congressional delegation. Of the two U.S. senators, John Bell
and James C. Jones (both Whigs), the former vigorously opposed the
Kansas-Nebraska bill principally on the grounds that it reopened the
whole slavery question thereby upsetting the accomplishments of the
1850 compromise. Meanwhile Jones, perhaps reflecting West Tennessee attitudes more than Whig party beliefs, threw his support behind
Senator Stephen Douglas's bill, saying that it confirmed and upheld
the Compromise of 1850. In the House of Representatives the four
Tennessee Democrats backed the legislation, as did two of the Whigs,
Felix Zollicoffer and Charles Ready. The other four Whig congressmen, however, lined up behind Bell and refused to countenance the
volatile proposal. The *Nashville Republican Banner* was the most
prominent voice raised against the measure, while its principal rival,
the *Union and American,* gave vent to enthusiastic support of the
legislation and was joined by the *Nashville True Whig.* [9]

In the closing weeks of its 1853-54 session, the Tennessee General
Assembly reacted to the congressional debates over Kansas-
Nebraska. A West Tennessee member of the lower house, E. James
Lamb (Democrat), presented a resolution approving the bill and proposing that Tennessee's senators be instructed and the representatives
be requested to give it "their zealous support." The lower chamber
tabled the Lamb statement, but in the meantime a Middle Tennessee
Democrat, Joel J. Jones, introduced a similar resolution into the state
senate. The Jones proposal breezed through the upper chamber by a
remarkable 20 to 1 vote, obviously enjoying Whig support. It was then
sent to the lower house where it was favored by about a three to one

margin, but there were only forty-seven members of the house present and voting—three short of the required number for a quorum. Therefore House Speaker William H. Wisener (Whig) ruled that the lack of a quorum defeated the measure and voided the proceedings. Those who stayed away from the roll call perhaps did so as the easiest strategy to kill off the Jones resolution and thereby avoid potential embarrassment for John Bell in particular.[10]

The events and circumstances surrounding the controversy in 1854 revealed a more solidified Democratic party in Tennessee and a more divided Whig party. The courageous stand of Bell and four Whig congressmen was to become a subject of much debate in the state. Probably no one perceived the situation better than did the editor of the *Nashville Republican Banner,* who wrote, "The vote *in Congress* on the Nebraska bill will be the great weapon which will be used by our Democratic opponents, from this time forward . . . to cripple and destroy the Whig party in this State."[11]

While momentous developments absorbed the nation's attention, several more local, less dramatic matters competed for notice in Tennessee. For example, the 1835 state constitution underwent its only modification in the antebellum era. In the 1847-48 session of the legislature a bill proposing the popular direct election of state judges and attorneys passed the lower house but was postponed by action of the upper chamber. In the fall of 1849, the new governor, William Trousdale, endorsed a constitutional amendment to effect the election of state judges and attorneys, and both houses of the General Assembly received proposals for such an amendment. Finally, in February 1850 the differences over the proposals were ironed out and the General Assembly endorsed the constitutional amendment.

Because the constitution required that two successive sessions of the legislature had to approve a proposed amendment before it could be presented to the voters, the 1851-52 General Assembly had to deal with the matter. The new Whig governor, William B. Campbell, anxious to be part of a somewhat belated democratization movement, threw his support behind the amendment. Within a few weeks it had been approved by both legislative chambers, which then decided to submit the amendment to the voters at the next gubernatorial-legislative elections, August 1853. According to the report of the secretary of state, Tennessee voters ratified the amendment. It was then incumbent upon the General Assembly to establish a date for the election of state judges and attorneys, and it set the fourth Thursday of May 1854.[12] Thus the 1835 constitution finally caught up with the thrust of Jacksonian democracy.

108 ANTEBELLUM POLITICS

In the economic sphere, an irrepressible railroad mania captured the state. In 1850 there was not a single mile of operational railroad in the state, but ten years later there were approximately 1,200 miles. These startling facts speak volumes about the flurry of activity directed toward the creation of a transportation network. The burgeoning desire for railroads was evident in the late 1840s, to be sure, but it was left to the 1850s to translate those dreams into tangible rails, crossties, and locomotives.

The most significant legislation calculated to aid the railroad boom was enacted in 1852. The Whig-controlled legislature, prodded by Whig Governor Campbell's message, wrestled with the problem of how best to extend government support. The General Assembly finally agreed to provide loans to certain specified railroads in the form of 6 percent bonds at the rate of $8,000 per mile for the purchase of rails and equipment necessary to the actual laying of the rails, a figure that was increased to $10,000 per mile two years later. This then was the pattern of state aid to the railroads in Tennessee; in fact the Nashville and Chattanooga line was the only one built without benefit of state monies.[13]

Given the tradition of intrastate sectionalism, it is not surprising that each section concentrated on the construction of railroad lines that would connect with lines emanating from adjoining states. In fact, the so-called network of railroads did not tie the three sections together.

Concern over banking matters occupied the time and energy of some Tennessee leaders. The antibank hue and cry of the Jacksonians in the 1830s was still alive in the state two decades later. The state bank, established in 1838, was the primary target of attack and defense. Throughout the bank's existence Democratic and Whig leaders alike had learned to live with it and support it, but Democratic tolerance seemed to evaporate in the 1850s, once the party obtained firm possession of the governor's chair. Whereas Whig Governor William B. Campbell had assured the legislature in 1851 that no changes were needed in the operation of the state bank, Democratic governor Andrew Johnson's major legislative messages (December 1853, October 1855, October 1857) repeatedly urged that the state bank be gradually liquidated. Johnson echoed Andrew Jackson when he declared in 1857, "To carry on the business of banking is not one of the objects for which the State was created." The governor, apparently warming to his subject, then revealed that he wanted to see *all* banks in the state shut down—beginning with the state bank! Johnson was assisted in his antibank rhetoric by the president and directors of the state bank who recommended that it should wind up its affairs and be closed. Governor Isham Harris in 1857 and 1859 declared that the state bank must be shut down and urged the General Assembly to fix a date for the commencement of its liquidation. Yet despite the pleas of Johnson and Harris and several bills introduced into the legislature, the bank continued to function throughout the decade.[14]

While banks and railroads earned a niche in the realm of state concerns, and the billowing clouds of antagonism over slavery disturbed the nation at large, the game of politics continued to be played with intensity in Tennessee throughout the 1850s. Almost every election, presidential, gubernatorial, or senatorial, exhibited some degree of factionalism within the parties. After about the middle of the decade, however, internal friction was less apparent, partly because the Whig party had collapsed and been replaced by the American party and partly because the principal dissident element in the Democratic party of the 1840s had emerged as the dominant group in the 1850s.

Apart from the hard feelings generated by ambitious men jockeying for nominations and power, much of the discord was related to patronage problems. The Taylor-Fillmore administration managed to do about as much harm as good with its dispensing of patronage in Tennessee. Senator John Bell, who had the special ear of the national administration, found it quite difficult to keep peace in the Whig family. His handling of federal printing contracts in Knoxville, for example, brought forth the vociferous complaints of William G. Brownlow, who felt entitled to all of the business but found himself having to share the loaf with the rival Whig newspaper, the *Knoxville Register*. The *Register* directed its fire at Bell when he secured an appointment for Oliver P. Temple, Knoxville lawyer and close associate of Brownlow and Thomas A.R. Nelson. Bell attempted, but without success, to woo Nelson by dangling federal appointments in front of him, but Nelson, whose eye was on the U.S. Senate seat available in 1851, resisted such overtures. Those Whig leaders disappointed at not becoming beneficiaries of Bell's patronage naturally coalesced into an anti-Bell clique within the state party. Even long-time personal and political friend William B. Campbell, weary and suspicious of Bell's domination, declared privately, "There does not live a more cold hearted, selfish and artful scoundrel than John Bell."[15] Perhaps it was lucky for Bell that the Whigs did not control the presidency after the 1852 election.

The Democrats likewise had their share of patronage disputes. Beginning in 1853 and continuing throughout the remainder of the decade, the Democratic party held the executive branch of the national government, hence there was abundant opportunity to create unhappiness over appointments and contracts. When the Pierce administration assumed office, there was no Democratic senator from Tennessee to serve as the liaison between it and the state party. President Pierce, mindful of the warring groups in the state, was interested in A.O.P. Nicholson. Had Tennessee gone for Pierce in 1852, perhaps Nicholson would have been offered a prominent Cabinet post; instead Nicholson was asked to accept, but refused, the postmaster generalship. Pierce nonetheless wanted Nicholson in Washington, and by the summer of 1853 the president had arranged for Nicholson to become editor of the *Washington Union.* In his unique position, Nicholson served as the principal consultant on patronage matters for Tennessee. Judging by his complaints to Pierce, however, about too many jobs going to the Aaron V. Brown wing of the state party, Nicholson's role as dispenser of federal patronage must have been short-circuited from time to time. But after some problems along this line, Nicholson apparently entrenched himself securely enough with the Pierce administration that his word on patronage became increasingly indispensable. Shortly after the November 1856 election, Governor Andrew Johnson predicted that Brown was angling for a Cabinet appointment in the Buchanan government, the likelihood of which was thoroughly disgusting to Johnson. Indeed, when James Buchanan became president in 1857, he appointed none other than Brown to be postmaster general. Although Brown moved into the inner circle of the Buchanan administration and exerted influence over patronage for the next two years, Johnson and Nicholson had their day also, for in 1857 both of them were elected to the United States Senate.[16]

To understand how Nicholson and Johnson achieved this distinction it is necessary to examine the Senate contests. The decade began with the two parties sharing the Senate seats—Hopkins L. Turney (Democrat) and John Bell (Whig); then for several years the Whigs held both seats (Bell and Jones); but the period ended with the Democrats holding both positions (Johnson and Nicholson)—an important commentary upon the political transformation in the state. Furthermore, the old traditional sectional alignment of Senate seats did some twists and turns. The 1840s ended with Middle Tennessee being represented in both Senate slots—Turney in the traditional Middle Tennessee seat but Bell in the East Tennessee chair. The 1851 election, however, surprisingly resulted in a West Tennessean, James C. Jones (a transplanted Middle Tennessean, to be sure), capturing the so-called Middle Tennessee seat. This was the first political plum of statewide consequence to fall to the western third of the state, antedating the governorship by some six years. Jones's post was taken over in 1857, however, by Andrew Johnson of East Tennessee. Confusingly, throughout the decade the so-called East Tennessee seat was held by Middle Tennesseans—John Bell and then A.O.P. Nicholson. By comparison with the hectic scramble over the Senate seats in the 1840s the decade of the 1850s appears to have been relatively serene. The only deviation from normal procedures occurred in 1857, when the Democrats riding high from successive victories decided to elect "early"—that is, choose someone in 1857 to replace Bell in 1859. During the two-party system that strategy had been employed only once before—exactly twenty years earlier.

The first of the four Senate elections occurred in 1851, the year Turney's term expired. Given that the Whig party was successful in the gubernatorial and legislative races in August, Democrat Turney stood no chance of securing another term in the Senate. Besides, general unhappiness with Turney among Democrats themselves (a feeling dating back to the circumstances of his election in 1845) insured that Turney would not return to Washington regardless of the outcome of the August elections. When the legislature embarked upon the selection of a senator, recently defeated Governor Trousdale, not Turney, was the Democratic nominee. Prior to the August elections, however, there had been the customary sparring between rival groups within the Democratic party—the result of which was that both Aaron Brown and Nicholson tried to line up support for a possible bid for the Senate seat. Andrew Johnson, anxious to enter the fray in behalf of Nicholson, urged him to make the race against Brown.[17] But all this came to naught when the voters favored the Whigs at the ballot boxes in August.

Quite understandably, then, the principal attention focused on who would emerge as the Whig candidate for the vacated Senate post. Antagonism among the state's three sections was clearly evident in the Whig dispute in 1851. Part of the problem related to the matter that the Turney seat was the traditional Middle Tennessee seat but there already was a Middle Tennessee Whig in the Senate—John Bell. There was even talk among certain Whigs that both Senate seats should be filled in 1851, thus following the dangerous practice of electing "early" and naming someone to take Bell's place in 1853. In that manner East and West Tennessee could each acquire one of the

Senate posts, leaving Middle Tennessee out in the cold. But a more sober analysis of political realities indicated that such a strategy was simply too bold and perhaps too destructive for the party's own good. Hence by the time the General Assembly convened, the Whigs were offering rival candidates for the one seat only. There were three main contenders, one from each section of the state: Thomas A.R. Nelson (East), Gustavus A. Henry (Middle), and James C. Jones (West).[18] Nelson went into the caucus with almost solid backing from his fellow East Tennessee Whigs. That he did not have their unanimous support not only spelled doom for his candidacy but also reflected some degree of factionalism within the eastern branch. Nelson's principal promoter was Brownlow and his *Knoxville Whig,* whereas the rival Whig paper in town eventually decided to support Jones. Nelson was further disappointed by the lukewarmness of Governor Campbell, whose attitude was one of suspicion instead of gratitude because of Nelson's campaigning in the summer of 1851 for an indisposed Campbell. Felix Zollicoffer, editor of the *Nashville Republican Banner,* reflected the governor's position by announcing neutrality in the Senate competition. Senator Bell, with an eye riveted upon the 1853 Senate election, steadfastly refused to take a public stand in favor of Nelson, though it was widely known that he intensely disliked Jones. Gustavus Henry dropped out of the caucus balloting early, recognizing that a Middle Tennessean stood a very slim chance. Henry endorsed Nelson but apparently did not exert enough influence to swing Middle Tennessee votes to Nelson. Jones enjoyed unified support from West Tennessee and considerable backing from the middle section— his native region. After two weeks of caucus voting, Jones won the party's nomination but only by a scant three votes; had four East Tennessee Whigs not defected to the Jones camp on the last ballot, Nelson would have been victorious. The Whigs, having finally agreed upon Jones, hurriedly submitted his name to the General Assembly, which in turn gave him an easy triumph over the Democrat Trousdale.[19] East Tennessee Whigs having nothing to show for their efforts were noticeably unhappy—an attitude that would carry over into the 1852 presidential contest.

Despite a Democratic gubernatorial victory in 1853, the Whigs secured a large enough majority in the legislature's lower house that they could easily override a Democratic majority of only one vote in the state senate. This was of crucial importance on any joint balloting for the United States Senate term. The Democrats were thus consigned to a stalling, delaying role which enabled them to make life miserable for the Whigs.

pleased with the elevation of Nicholson; after many years of being leaders of the dissident element in the state party it was immensely satisfying to be placed in the driver's seat.

An epilogue to the story of Senate elections was added in the 1857-58 session of the legislature when abortive attempts to force Bell to resign, thereby permitting Nicholson to move immediately to the Senate, were made. Resolutions were represented to the General Assembly calling upon Bell to step down because he no longer represented the views of Tennesseans. These strictly partisan measures eventually deleted the clause requiring Bell's resignation but added one which stipulated that Tennessee's senators and congressmen must vote in favor of the admission of Kansas as a state under the Lecompton (proslave) constitution. Senator Bell stubbornly refused to kowtow to such politically inspired developments emanating out of the Tennessee legislature and served out the remainder of his term until March 1859.[27]

Like the contests over the Senate seats, the five gubernatorial races showed important aspects of Tennessee politics during the 1850s. That the Democrats captured four of these indicates a great deal about the transformation occurring in state politics. Instead of the evenly balanced competition seen in the governor's races in the 1840s, Democratic domination (in fact, monopoly) was the theme in the succeeding decade. Part of this was due to the demise of the Whig party nationally and locally by the mid-1850s. Afterward the anti-Jacksonian movement shifted to the American (Know Nothing) party and eventually to a statewide party known simply as the Opposition. These changes eroded the once powerful strength of the Whig movement in Tennessee. While it is indisputable that the vast majority of Whigs gravitated into the Know Nothing and then the Opposition ...ks, some Whigs went into the Democratic party, distasteful as that while others simply abdicated political responsibilities and re... to back any party, regardless of the label. Meanwhile the Demo... party did an amazing job of holding itself together both at th... ...nal and at the state level. Tennessee Democrats were blessed wit... ...ous leadership—principally Andrew Johnson and Isham... ...s. That they represented markedly different elements within t... ...party merely compounded the intrigue of Democratic cont... ...period. Johnson and Harris were able to work together in 18... ...mple, simply on the basis of a mariage de convenance; tha... ...an was in a position to help the other politically at that t... ...en the decade concluded, it was apparent not only that J...

On the Whig side of the chamber discontent over the 1851 Senate election was still apparent in 1853. Thomas A.R. Nelson again became a contender, though he was somewhat uncomfortable about challenging his longtime friend, John Bell. Part of Nelson's hope for victory was based on vague hints and promises by Democrats that they would switch to him at the appropriate time. Meanwhile Gustavus A. Henry, defeated in his 1853 bid for the governor's chair, plunged into the competition on the grounds that the party should reward him for his gubernatorial campaign. But a U.S. Senate seat was a consolation prize too recherché for Henry. Needless to say, John Bell was exceedingly anxious to be reelected, and Allen A. Hall, who had taken over the Nashville Republican Banner, was eager to assist Bell. The incumbent senator shrewdly realized that his greatest threat would probably come from Nelson's East Tennessee, though Brownlow had endorsed him. Bell therefore took steps to solidify his support in West Tennessee; the Whigs there, still content over the election of Jones, did not intend to make trouble this time. But Bell was interested in lining up backing from all of the West Tennessee legislators, Whigs and Democrats alike. His attendance at the commercial convention in Memphis in June 1853 and his strong approval of Memphis as the eastern terminus of a transcontinental railroad were no coincidences.[20]

In 1853 the Whig caucus did not reduce the field to a single candidate; instead, the names of all three Whig aspirants—Bell, Henry, and Nelson—went before the joint convention of the General Assembly. In fact, these three appeared in person in the chamber to patrol the aisles and halls in search of votes. Henry dropped out of contention fairly early, much as he had in 1851. On the forty-ninth ballot Bell finally emerged with a majority of the votes—thanks to West Tennessee Democrats who cast their lot with him in the final hours. This development stirred some controversy in both parties, as one might imagine, but by and large Whigs accepted the Bell election as a positive and fortunate circumstance. The defeated Democrat, Cave Johnson, complained that the Nicholson wing of the party contributed to Bell's success.[21]

There was no reason for Tennessee Democrats to complain in 1857, because they enjoyed a landslide victory in the governor's election coupled with substantial gains in the state legislature. Since Jones's Senate term expired in that year, Democrats were ready to choose someone to occupy that seat. In the latter part of 1856 Andrew Johnson made his decision not to seek a third term as governor; instead he wanted to hold out for higher stakes. As he confided to one of his close friends, "If I continue in public life the true policy is to move upward and onward." Later in this same letter he spelled out his meaning more clearly: "If I make a move for the Senate, now is the time to do it." Johnson encouraged county meetings which selected delegates to the state party convention to propose him for the Senate and several counties did. Without question Johnson worked assiduously in his own behalf over a period of several months—a tactic unique to Tennessee's Senate seat battles.[22] In the legislative races that spring and summer, some Democratic candidates announced their support of Johnson for the Senate, others hedged on the matter, while still others expressed misgivings about sending Johnson to Washington.

With the Democratic triumph at the polls in August 1857, the way seemed to be clear for Johnson to move to the United States Senate. But a possible obstacle existed because the incumbent, Jones, had switched to the Democratic party two years earlier. No one seemed anxious, however, to reward his latter-day conversion; in fact, some Democrats regarded Jones's transfer of loyalty as rank political opportunism. Thus when the legislature assembled in October, it was practically a foregone conclusion that Jones would get no support and that Johnson would be the man. Although Johnson had solicited his Greeneville friend, William Lowry, to come to Nashville to "leg a little" in behalf of his election, such aid was really not needed. The Democratic caucus agreed upon Johnson without dissent, and three days after the legislative session began, Johnson was chosen over Neill S. Brown, the nominal opponent. Johnson showed strength among legislators from all three divisions of the state, but especially West Tennessee. This support in the western third was singular, for that section lost a Senate seat (Jones) with the election of Johnson of East Tennessee. Apparently West Tennessee legislators were willing to tolerate this development, because a West Tennessean, Isham Harris, had just been elected governor.[23] In any event, Johnson got the highest political office ("upward and onward") the state could bestow, thus climaxing an exceedingly difficult climb to power.

No sooner had Johnson been named to take the seat vacated by Jones, than a movement to fill the second Senate chair was launched, a blatant indication of the Democrats' determination to flex their political muscle. Lending great motivation to this unorthodox procedure was John Bell's occupation of the other Senate seat. Ever since his courageous opposition to the Kansas-Nebraska bill in 1854, Bell had been marked by the Democrats as their special target. What

particularly galled the Democrats was Bell's declaration that he would abandon his Senate seat if the state's political sentiment did not support his stance on the Kansas bill. With persuasive merit Democrats vociferously argued that the election results in 1855, 1856, ar 1857 demonstrated beyond doubt that Bell's point of view had be repudiated. The exhilarating notion that they could perhaps force I from the Senate prematurely convinced wavering Democrats th bold strategy of electing "early" was appropriate and desirable. A *Clarksville Jeffersonian* devastatingly put it, "We have our enemy in our hands, and it would be madness, worse than m to let him escape."[24]

Quiet noises about this strategy had been heard since as November 1856. One of the chief promoters was none o A.O.P. Nicholson, who had only recently returned to Tenn his editor's post in Washington. Governor Johnson was one to claim that Nicholson desired one of the Senate seats, time the 1857 legislative races were in full swing Nicho worked for a Democratic sweep of the General Assemb no secret of his eagerness to become a U.S. Senator. In observer surmised that Nicholson's efforts in the sur signed to pave his way to the Senate. There were politicians around, however, anxious to provide Nick petition, the most serious of whom was Gideon quently, Andrew Ewing of Nashville and Wil Columbia crowded into the picture. Once the elec gust were known, public announcement was ma *Union and American* of the intention to have the United States Senators.[25]

Only two days after the election of Johns General Assembly received a resolution callir second seat. The Democratic caucus confront ing a nominee, and after sixteen ballots at la son, though not without noticeable diss Assembly convened the next day, the elect was more or less a formality. There were delay and postpone, but to no avail. I Johnson's influence in behalf of Nichol importance in shaping the decision of th pointed men such as Pillow and Ewin at Johnson's doorstep.[26] Exactly wh remain a matter of speculation. Neve

son and Harris came from opposite ends of the state but also that they stood on opposite sides of the secession question.

Intrastate sectional rivalry contributed to the story of the gubernatorial contests. The stranglehold that Middle Tennessee had exerted on the governor's chair since the very beginning of the two-party system was broken in the 1850s. William B. Campbell, elected in 1851, has the distinction of being not only the last Whig governor but also the last Middle Tennessee governor during the antebellum period. The next four contests resulted in victories for an East Tennessee Democrat, Andrew Johnson, and West Tennessee Democrat, Isham G. Harris. Oddly enough, the anti-Jacksonian party (Whig–Know Nothing) continued to be tied to the Middle Tennessee syndrome, for its defeated candidates were all from that section. But in 1859 the Opposition party offered an East Tennessean, John Netherland. Although Middle Tennessee persisted as the chief source of Democratic votes in the state, the other two sections did not remain consistently in the Whig–Know Nothing–Opposition camp. Andrew Johnson in 1855, for example, came within 200 votes of carrying West Tennessee, and in 1857 and 1859 Harris swept that section by approximately 2,000 votes. Even more surprising was East Tennessee's defection to the Democratic candidate, Harris, in 1857, but two years later the region gave a solid margin to favorite son, John Netherland.

As Tables 5.1, 5.2, and 5.3 show, the electoral results had some characteristics not seen in the 1840s.[28] In terms of the actual vote and percentage differential between the winning and losing candidates, the first three elections (1851, 1853, 1855) followed the pattern of the previous decade fairly well. In 1857, however, Harris captured 54.3 percent of the state's vote—the highest since Newton Cannon's sweep of nearly 61 percent twenty years earlier. Although Harris's percentage slipped in 1859, it still exceeded those seen in the gubernatorial contests of the 1840s. The total vote fluctuated from election to election: the 1853 contest, for example, brought out fewer voters than the 1851 campaign, doubtless suffering from the substantial drop in voter turnout in 1852. But the 1857 race attracted 2,000 fewer votes than the 1855 election, despite an upswing in the statewide vote in 1856. The level of voter participation likewise showed some variation. Whereas it never dropped below 80 percent in the 1840s, it did so in the gubernatorial elections of 1853, 1857, and 1859.[29]

Despite these hints of waning enthusiasm, party machinery apparently remained in good working condition throughout the decade. Not once, for example, did the Democrats fail to stage a convention

Table 5.1. Total Votes, 1851–59

Party	1851	1852	1853	1855	1856	1857	1859
Anti-Democratic	63,333	58,586	61,071	65,860	66,128	59,807	68,216
Democratic	62,293	56,900	63,414	67,139	73,638	71,178	76,237
Total	125,626	115,486	124,485	132,999	139,766	130,985	144,453

for purposes of choosing a standard-bearer, even when the nominee was a foregone conclusion, as in 1855 and 1859, and even though there were some rumblings of discontent among certain Democrats (especially Andrew Johnson) who had begun to question the merit of such meetings. With regard to the opposing party, the 1855 campaign was the only aberration from the norm, for Meredith P. Gentry simply announced that he would run for governor. Various Whig leaders approved his candidacy, and then the American (Know Nothing) party held a secret convention in Nashville to endorse him. The traditional structure of committees so necessary for waging effective campaigns was established, with the new parties—the American and the Opposition—largely borrowing the already existing Whig framework of party structure. But weakened by the transformations taking place in national and state politics, they could not quite match the impressive machinery established by Tennessee Whigs in their heyday.

In the 1850s intraparty factionalism was not as prominent in the gubernatorial battles as it earlier had been. This is partly attributable to the breakup of the Whig party after 1853 and the emergence of two new parties in its place. William G. Brownlow and his East Tennessee allies assumed positions of leadership in the Know Nothing and Opposition parties. Whig Senator James C. Jones, who disliked this turn of events, denounced the Know Nothings in the 1855 contest and cast his lot with the Democrats. Jones was not the only dissatisfied old-line Whig to make this leap into the arms of the former enemy, and the departure of such Whigs enabled the Know Nothing and the Opposition parties to put up a fairly solid front. Meanwhile, the Democratic party was a veritable paradigm of harmony in the various elections. The easy selection of Johnson and Harris as the nominees, for example, was a good indication of the absence of internal friction. Johnson's nomination did not elicit one hundred percent approval from all of the Democratic leaders, but for the most part they kept a civil tongue, recognizing the widespread following that Johnson had cultivated in the state. One might argue, somewhat facetiously, that much of the intraparty discord had been siphoned off into the Senate contests and the presidential campaigns so that there was not much left for the gubernatorial races.

The decade's first statewide electoral contest occurred in 1851, when both parties fielded contenders for the governor's office. In the second week of February, the Democrats' State Central Committee issued a call for a state convention in Nashville on February 25. As the *Nashville Union* indicated, there really was no question that incumbent governor William Trousdale would be chosen by the party to seek reelection. The proceedings of the convention bore out the newspaper's belief, for Trousdale was nominated without opposition. The convention's president, Aaron V. Brown, not only established the central committees for the campaign but also influenced greatly the party's platform. With the meeting coming only about five months after the final adoption by Congress of the Compromise of 1850, it is not surprising that the platform dealt mainly with that topic. The Brown-Nicholson conflict over the southern conventions of 1850 may have spilled over somewhat into the gubernatorial arena, causing Trousdale to run without the energetic backing of all of the Democratic leaders.[30]

Meanwhile in the Whig camp problems arose over securing someone willing to forego his ambition for the U.S. Senate seat, about to become available, in order to seek the gubernatorial office. This led to the somewhat comical situation of potential candidates pushing Campbell's nomination in order to free themselves for the Senate contest. This struggle may have been largely responsible for the Whigs' decision to delay their convention until late March, a full month after the Democrats. Although reluctant to become the party's gubernatorial candidate, Campbell accepted the nomination. Thereafter the party published an extensive address or platform which devoted attention to the Compromise of 1850 and also to internal improvements.[31]

Without question the major issue in the campaign, as revealed in the press and in the debates of the candidates, was the 1850 compromise. In keeping with the Whig address issued by the state convention, Campbell vigorously upheld the compromise in all of its provisions. He and fellow Tennessee Whigs viewed the compromise as the "final settlement" of the slavery question. So steadfastly and enthusiastically did Campbell endorse the compromise that at one juncture Felix Zollicoffer of the *Nashville Republican Banner* admonished Campbell to restrain himself. When attention focused on the fugitive slave clause of the compromise, Campbell stated that he would submit to its repeal or its modification, if Congress so acted. But later Campbell warned that repeal of the compromise in toto would bring about the dissolution of the union. The *Nashville Republican Banner* late in the campaign maintained that Campbell's position on the fugitive slave law was that it must be sustained as it was, without change. The paper apparently feared that Campbell was losing ground in the debates over the compromise.[32]

The Democratic side of the argument on the compromise varied from the Whig, but not drastically. At the February state convention, for example, the party staked out a position of support for the compromise, but only if the North faithfully carried out its provisions. Moreover, said the platform, if further action on the slavery question were sought or if the compromise were altered, the South would be justified in adopting any means of self-preservation. In his campaign speeches, Trousdale backed the compromise as a necessity to preserve the union and steadfastly denied the disunionist label placed on him by Whig speakers and writers, but Trousdale was very explicit about not wanting any alterations of the compromise. He complained that the North got all it wanted in the compromise but nevertheless was still agitating the slavery question. The Democratic press declared that a vote for Trousdale was the only way to show the nation that Tennessee was standing firm on the matter of slavery, the compromise, and in fact on the permanence of the republic.[33]

Closely akin to the recurring debates over the compromise and the union was the discussion over presidential preference. Oddly enough, Trousdale never committed himself to any prospective Democratic presidential candidate, even though Campbell claimed that Trousdale favored Van Buren for the 1852 nomination. The emphasis in the debates and in the press was entirely upon the question of whom Campbell and the Whigs might back in the forthcoming national contest. About a week after the Whig state convention, the *Nashville Union* carried an editorial claiming that certain northern Whigs were trying to bring forth Winfield Scott as the party's nominee, and in the first joint debate of the gubernatorial campaign Trousdale referred to the growing popularity of Scott as a Whig presidential candidate while he also warned of northern schemes to bring about abolition of slavery in the South. Campbell on that same occasion made clear that he preferred Millard Fillmore as the Whig standard-bearer in the presidential contest, and in subsequent debates Campbell defended Fillmore as sound on slavery, whereupon Trousdale read aloud an abolition letter written by Fillmore. A *Nashville Union* editorial in mid-May wondered how Tennesse Whigs could maintain that Fillmore could be relied upon to uphold the constitutional rights of the South. In the latter stages of the statewide campaign the Democratic press claimed that leading Whigs in the state were becoming increasingly alarmed at the prospect of Scott's emerging as their nominee for president. Since Campbell said he favored Fillmore, not Scott, the *Union* eventually took the position that Fillmore was an out and out abolitionist; therefore a vote for Campbell in the governor's race would give aid and comfort to northern abolitionists. Thus the Democrats tied the presidential preference question to the whole issue of slavery and southern rights.[34] How Trousdale managed to escape being pinned down on the presidential question is puzzling; perhaps he kept the Whigs preoccupied with questions about Scott and Fillmore.

The only local issue evident in the campaign was that of internal improvements. With the burgeoning interests in railroad contruction in the state, the issue could hardly be avoided. Democrats had to work to overcome the widely held belief that they were not particularly supportive of improvements. Long before the campaign began, the *Nashville Union* endorsed state aid for important improvements projects. Moreover, the party's platform avowed support for state aid and involvement in internal improvements. An editorial in the *Memphis Appeal* noted that the spirit of improvements was abroad in the land and that it should be encouraged and fostered by state legislation. On the campaign trail, Trousdale favored improvements done mainly by individual enterprise but aided by state government. The Whigs were a bit more secure in their position, for they had increasingly become identified with support of transportation developments and their party platform took a strong stance in favor of state aid to internal improvements projects. On the stump, Campbell repeatedly alluded to the great need for railroads and urged that the state government extend aid or credit to them. When the election year began, differences between the two parties on support of improvements had been more noticeable than they were as the campaign progressed.[35]

When the debates of the canvass were completed, more than 125,-000 voters went to the polls—a 3,400 vote increase over the 1849 gubernatorial race. Clearly the victorious Campbell was the beneficiary of this increase, for he captured 3,000 more votes than had the defeated Whig candidate in the previous governor's contest. A survey of election results by sections shows that Trousdale lost ground (relatively and absolutely) in East and Middle Tennessee in comparison with his showing two years earlier; conversely, he picked up strength in West Tennessee. As in the gubernatorial elections of the 1840s,

Table 5.2. Percentage of Democratic Vote by Section, 1851–59

Section	1851	1852	1853	1855	1856	1857	1859
East	44.8	44.8	49.3	47.1	48.6	50.8	48.2
Middle	53.2	52.6	53.1	53.2	56.0	57.4	56.1
West	48.3	47.6	48.8	49.6	51.5	53.0	52.6
STATE	49.6	49.3	50.9	50.5	52.7	54.3	52.8

when the margin of victory in Middle Tennessee was the chief clue to the statewide results, so it was in 1851. Trousdale carried this section in 1849 and again in 1851, but in the latter year his margin was only 3,800 votes, whereas it had been a remarkable 5,700 in 1849. Campbell's gains in the eastern and middle thirds of the state probably reflected strong procompromise sentiment there, as well as more pronounced interest in railroads. Trousdale's gains, on the other hand, occurred in West Tennessee, an area becoming steadily identified with more extreme southern views. When the defeated Democrats searched for possible explanations, they eschewed the campaign issues and talked instead of the problem of dissension within Democratic ranks in certain counties and gave the usual lament about inadequate party organization across the state. Had they been so inclined, they might have drawn some consolation from the fact that Whigs throughout the South did extremely well in state elections during 1850–51; therefore Tennessee's experience was part of a regional trend.[36]

Two years later questions over the compromise, slavery, and related concerns were not to be heard, for apparently they had been put to rest, at least temporarily. The 1853 contest was influenced by the events of the immediately preceding year, to be sure, but only in the sense that Whig frictions in the 1852 presidential battle in Tennessee left the party barely able to summon strength for the gubernatorial fight. Furthermore, the Whig-dominated legislature redrew congressional district lines so as to make it impossible for Andrew Johnson or any other Democrat to carry the First District, Johnson's political turf since 1843. The Whigs thus unwittingly promoted Johnson for the Democratic gubernatorial nomination in 1853.

The situation might have looked brighter for the state's Whigs if they had been able to convince the popular Governor Campbell to seek reelection, but he wrote a letter to Felix Zollicoffer in early

January stating that for personal reasons he did not intend to make another bid for the gubernatorial prize. This announcement touched off a search for a suitable nominee, or as some thought, a sacrificial lamb. A likely candidate, Gustavus A. Henry, through his hometown newspaper in Clarksville declared that under no circumstances would he be a contender for the nomination, but only two months later William T. Haskell of Jackson, himself considered to be a likely candidate, met with Henry and persuaded him to reverse his earlier position. On April 25 the Nashville convention of the Whig party chose Henry by acclamation to be the standard-bearer. The *Nashville Union* claimed that Henry was agreed upon as a candidate on grounds that he had been an originator of compromise measures. The party went on record in favor of time-honored republican principles, commended the Fillmore administration, and endorsed Henry.[37]

Meanwhile, Andrew Johnson, knowing that his days in Congress were numbered, brooded about the possibility of getting out of politics altogether. But his Democratic allies would not hear of such an unwarranted move; instead, they began to push his name for the gubernatorial nomination. Assisting the Johnson cause at this juncture was some recognition of sectional feelings—namely, the long exclusion of East and West Tennessee from the Democratic ticket. Moreover, in the early months of 1853, there seemed to be a plethora of possible nominees, with no one taking a commanding lead. A.O.P. Nicholson, who had something of a following, eventually stepped aside and refused to compete against Johnson. Near the end of March, the State Central Committee finally issued a call for a nominating convention to be held in Nashville on April 27. Before that date arrived, some thirty-nine counties staged conventions, and of that number, twenty-five announced a preference for gubernatorial nominees. Johnson's name headed the list for twelve of the conventions, Isham G. Harris won the endorsement of six counties, and the remaining seven counties scattered their recommendations among several persons. The Democratic state convention was something of a donnybrook, according to the account given in the *Nashville Whig,* for confusion and disagreement seemed to reign. Several names for nomination were put forward, retracted, and then resubmitted. Out of the chaos finally emerged Johnson's name, along with that of Andrew Ewing of Nashville. Some claimed that Ewing (in a moment of weakness) had promised that he would back Johnson in retaliation for the politically inspired rearrangement of congressional districts. Ewing had difficulty recollecting such a pledge, but he magnanimously withdrew nonetheless, so the convention agreed upon Johnson. The plat-

form gave continued approval to long-held principles, to the election
of Pierce as proof of the party's devotion to preservation of the union,
and to the beliefs set forth in Pierce's inaugural address.[38]

There was no formal campaigning by the candidates during the
month of May, but beginning in June and continuing until election
day in August, Johnson and Henry conducted a vigorous schedule of
speeches and debates. In their discussions and in the press no major
issues emerged, at least nothing comparable to the 1851 contest.
Internal improvements was a ready-made issue, especially in light of
the significant railroad legislation enacted in 1852. Henry applauded
the actions of the legislature and promised continued support of the
railroad boom. Johnson had to overcome the belief, circulated widely
by the Whig press, that he was hostile to all internal improvements,
and the *Nashville Union* defended him from such charges by claiming
that Johnson opposed only ill-timed and defective projects. Johnson,
long a traditional foe of state-supported improvements, hedged during
the campaign by advocating "a judicious system" of such projects.
Thus while there were differences between the two contenders on this
issue, they were blurred and minimized by the Democratic campaign.
Henry also tried to reap advantage out of Johnson's proposal, made
in the 1840s, that congressional districts should be based solely on
white male voters, thereby excluding the Negro population from the
calculations. According to Henry, such a scheme was in violation of
the famous three-fifths clause of the United States Constitution. The
greatest attack directed at Henry by Johnson and the Democrats was
on the matter of Henry's role as the chief promoter of the redrawing
of congressional district lines. They quickly labeled this rearrangement of districts the "Henrymander." The *Union and American* commented that Henry seemed to have consulted only the election returns
when deciding how to redraw the district lines. Certainly many voters
could see the poetic justice of having Henry (the schemer) being
challenged by Johnson (the victim) for the governor's office.[39]

Sometime after Johnson's victory, the Whig party collapsed both
nationally and in Tennessee. This opened the way then for the vitriolic
Knoxville editor, William G. Brownlow, to leap on the Know Nothing bandwagon and assume the position of influential leadership.
Since the antiforeigner and anti-Catholic stances of the Know Nothing movement appealed to Brownlow's prejudices, he welcomed it as
a way of getting back into the thick of politics, after having been
thoroughly exasperated with the election of Jones to the Senate in
1851, the Scott candidacy in the 1852 presidential race, and even
Henry's bid for the governor's chair in 1853. Presumably the alterna-

tive of joining the Democrats never crossed Brownlow's unforgiving mind. In any event, Brownlow and his closest East Tennessee allies quickly launched the Know Nothing crusade, despite the minuscule Catholic and foreign-born population in the state.[40]

It was not long before Brownlow and others began to push the candidacy of Meredith P. Gentry for the forthcoming 1855 gubernatorial contest. Formerly a very prominent Middle Tennessee Whig, Gentry had been a renegade from the party ever since the 1852 presidential race. But in January, he quietly sounded out Whig politicos in and around Nashville to ascertain what kind of support he could muster. Apparently encouraged that it was well worth the gamble, Gentry announced in February his intentions to seek the governor's chair. The *Nashville Union and American* sarcastically interpreted this to mean that former Whigs, anxious to punish Gentry for his past political sins, insisted that he run against Johnson. There were some old-line Whigs who voiced a protest against Gentry's candidacy. Three months later, shortly after the joint Johnson-Gentry debates had begun, a secret meeting of Know Nothings took place in Nashville from which came the endorsement of Gentry as their standard-bearer. With this action, the Know Nothing party replaced the Whigs in Tennessee as the formal rival of the Jacksonians.[41]

Meanwhile, in the Democratic camp all seemed to be quiet and harmonious. There was a flurry of activity early in the year about the advisability of a state nominating convention. The *Union and American* steadfastly advocated one, despite Johnson's hammerlock on the nomination, because a conclave, it argued, promotes harmony within the party. A few newspapers came out in opposition to a state convention, but such agitation came to naught when on February 1 the State Central Committee publicly summoned a convention to be held on March 27 in Nashville. A week prior to that gathering, rumors floated around that the Davidson County delegates would seek to block Johnson's nomination by backing Andrew Ewing. The *Union and American,* however, quickly published a letter from Ewing denying any interest in the nomination. More than a month before the convention, Johnson expressed doubts about his desire to seek the nomination, particularly as he contemplated the physical and mental exertion required for the campaign, "especially in the heat and dust of Summer."[42]

Before the March gathering, more than fifty Democratic county meetings had gone on record in favor of Johnson's selection, so it was no surprise when the delegates at the Nashville convention unanimously chose him. They also adopted a platform which addressed itself mainly to the threat posed by the Know Nothing movement, although there was one plank which noted the party's support of the Compromise of 1850 and of the Kansas-Nebraska bill. The typical organizational structure for the campaign was established by the convention—a State Central Committee, county committees, and civil district subcommittees. Reports on attendance at the convention vary somewhat, but apparently no more than twenty-five to thirty counties were actually represented there, although the low representation was offset to some degree by proxies from about twenty-five additional counties.[43]

The three-month campaign focused upon the tenets of Know Nothingism. The antiforeign and anti-Catholic beliefs of his opponent seemed to bring out the best in Governor Johnson as he traversed the state excoriating these principles. Gentry proved to be surprisingly ineffective in responding to Johnson's attacks, surprising because of Gentry's well-established reputation as an eloquent and impressive speaker. From time to time the press tried to tar the Know Nothings with the abolitionist brush, arguing that Know Nothingism had a strong following among free-soilers and abolitionists of the North. Attempts by Gentry to criticize Johnson's gubernatorial administration or to bring up the old "white basis" argument about congressional districts made little headway. The temperance folk attempted to exert muscle by asking the contenders their position on legislative control of liquor sales. Neither man was a supporter, though Gentry was certainly more sympathetic than Johnson. During the campaign a temperance leader, Philip S. White, entered the state to make speeches that were interpreted by unhappy Democrats as efforts to promote Gentry's cause. Despite this, the temperance question never achieved significance in the race.[44] The remarkable feature about the debates on the stump and in the press is what was omitted: no conflict over the internal improvements question, no direct debates over the Kansas-Nebraska bill, and no mention of presidential preference for the forthcoming 1856 race.

In both of Johnson's campaigns, 1853 and 1855, he seems to have been helped to victory in part by the ineptness of his opponents and certainly by the changing political party situation. In his first race he was able to capitalize upon Henry's role in the infamous redistricting of congressional areas and in the latter election he struck a responsive chord with his attacks upon the secret and bigoted posture of the Know Nothings. In both instances, then, the more traditional issues, either of state or of national concern, faded in importance to give ground to unusual or fleeting matters. None of this is to detract from

Johnson's own abilities as a campaigner and as a stump speaker, but to suggest simply that he was able to take advantage of a political situation that was in flux.

Andrew Johnson was twice victorious, but with a margin of less than 51 percent each time. As Table 5.1 shows, Johnson benefited the most in 1853 from the increased voter turnout, as compared to 1852, whereas in 1855 Johnson and Gentry almost evenly divided the 8,500 increase in total voters. Johnson came within 500 votes of carrying East Tennessee in 1853, and in West Tennessee he steadily whittled away the non-Democratic margins there. Johnson's percentage in 1853 was better in all three sections than the Democratic candidate's in the 1852 presidential election (see Table 5.2). Thanks to his inroads in both East and West Tennessee, Johnson was able to win the 1853 election despite a margin of only 3,600 votes in Middle Tennessee. Heretofore a Democrat had to carry Middle Tennessee by about 4,500 votes to be successful in overcoming his opponent's lead in East and West Tennessee.

In spite of Johnson's statewide victories, there were indications that all had not gone well. Having hoped for a landslide in his 1853 race against Henry, Johnson complained to Nicholson about the lack of unified support among fellow Democrats. In fact, he charged that some Democrats voted against him while some others did not vote at all. Be that as it may, it is clear that the Whigs did fairly well in the 1853 legislative and congressional races which occurred simultaneously with the gubernatorial. Certain Whig leaders claimed that there had been some vote swapping among Whigs and Democrats, so that Whig votes went to Johnson in exchange for Democratic votes for Whig legislative and congressional candidates. The 1855 results in the legislative and congressional races yielded a picture similar to that of 1853. Again there might have been some vote swapping in the August 1855 elections, but there is no conclusive evidence extant.[45] All in all, it is certain that Johnson's successes were not matched by his party's showings in legislative and congressional contests. Things would soon get better, however, for the state's Democrats.

With the dawning of the new year, 1857, Governor Johnson publicly revealed his private decision not to be a candidate for a third term, for he had already fastened his eye on a United States Senate seat and made no secret of his desire to return to Washington. The *Nashville Union and American* announced on the very first day of the new year that Johnson neither expected nor desired the nomination. In December the Democratic presidential electors recommended that the convention be postponed, and subsequently the State Central

Committee set the convention date as April 15. Apparently Johnson had worked behind the scenes for this delay, believing that it would give him more time to build support for his Senate bid and would allow a strong gubernatorial candidate to emerge. As Johnson had predicted, Isham G. Harris quickly gained strength among party leaders as the man best able to lead the ticket. Beginning in January and continuing almost to the time of the state convention, county meetings convened to choose their delegates and also to make known their preferences for the nominee. Harris was the overwhelming choice, although the perennial also-ran Andrew Ewing was endorsed by several counties, the most important being Davidson. But intrastate sectional feelings that had worked to Johnson's advantage earlier seemed to operate again in 1857, this time giving Harris of West Tennessee the advantage over Nashvillian Ewing. Although Johnson was still miffed over Harris's refusal, while a member of Congress, to vote for Johnson's homestead bill, he shielded his antagonism, lest an intraparty feud spoil his senatorial plans and ambitions.[46]

On the appointed day in April, delegates from forty-nine counties assembled in Nashville to choose the Democratic standard-bearer, adopt a platform, and structure the campaign machinery. Harris was the only candidate presented to the convention and was therefore chosen unanimously. The party's resolutions reflected the absence of an overriding issue for the forthcoming battle. More than half of the twelve planks in the platform, for example, were comments about the restrictions placed upon the federal government by the Constitution and praises for the departed Pierce administration and for the newly inaugurated Buchanan presidency. The state Democrats went on record against the antiforeigner and anti-Catholic crusade and the proposal to distribute the proceeds of public land sales to the states. The Dred Scott decision of a month earlier was praised as another example of how the Democratic party's position on sectional issues had been affirmed. In the eyes of state leaders apparently there were no local questions important enough to be treated in the party platform. With these items of business completed, the convention adjourned confident of victory in the emerging contest.[47]

The prime reason for such feelings among the Democrats was the triumphs they had enjoyed in 1855 and 1856 and also the belief that the Know Nothings were so discredited that they might be unable to field a contender. Throughout the early months of 1857 the Democratic press had a good time speculating about possible Know Nothing nominees, preferring of course that Bell be the candidate, but Bell wisely stuck to his senatorial duties and refused to tangle with any Democrat in a statewide election. During the third week of February, the State Central Committee of the Know Nothing party announced a nominating convention for Nashville on May 1, thereby dispelling rumors that the party might not enter the race against Harris. By the time of the convention, the two main contenders for the nomination were William T. Haskell and Robert Hatton. The party chose the latter, for reasons not altogether clear then or now. Some disharmony over the selection of Hatton and rejection of Haskell was made known at the convention and subsequently in the canvass. Before adjourning, the assembly staked out the party's position on several matters. In its platform, the "systematic agitation of the slavery question" was lamented, distribution of public lands monies was approved, modification of naturalization laws was called for, and the federal government's interference in the matter of slavery in the territories was condemned, saying that residents of the territories "have the right to determine the question of slavery." Like their Democratic counterparts, the Know Nothings were unable to identify any local issues of importance.[48]

This latter problem carried over into the campaign itself, both on the stump and in the press. In fact, major issues of any sort, national or local, failed to materialize in the summer's electioneering. Public quarrels over such matters as the distribution to the states of proceeds from sale of public lands and the right of immigrants to vote in the territories failed to generate excitement among the citizenry. In a somewhat convoluted fashion the Democratic press sought to argue that distribution was linked to the abolition of slavery in the states, for such monies would enable the states to provide for compensated emancipation. To use the elaborate words of the *Nashville Union and American,* "Above all, we shall not fail to expose the lurking serpent of Abolitionism which lies concealed among the fragrant flowers, and tempting fruits, and gushing fountains of the garden of 'distribution.' " Whether Tennessee readers took this argument seriously is doubtful, but it does show attempts to cast various questions into relationship to the preservation of slavery. In a slightly different vein Democrats were quick to claim that the Know Nothing party was eventually to be absorbed by the Black Republicans of the North, again trying to warn Tennesseans about the real dangers of the opposition.[49] By July, Johnson and other Democratic leaders had become increasingly dissatisfied with the Harris campaign, fearing that its lack of momentum might jeopardize the legislative and congressional races. They did not, however, doubt Harris's chances for victory. According to some sources, Johnson met with Harris and urged him to heap coals of criticism upon the principles of Know Nothingism. In the closing weeks, Harris did begin to deal more sharply with this issue (reminiscent of Johnson's strategy in 1855) and stirred the voters. The press also began to direct more attention to this topic.[50]

The only noticeable excitement of the campaign occurred at Fayetteville in mid-June. At the joint debate there, Hatton referred to Harris's belief that each state could set voting rights as "infamous." When Harris rose to challenge the use of that label, a vigorous dispute began, resulting finally in Harris knocking Hatton off the platform into the audience followed by fisticuffs between the two men out in the crowd. For the duration of the electioneering, however, the contenders managed to keep their tempers in check, and by the third week of July they had wearied so much of the campaign that they halted it and cancelled the remaining engagements.[51]

The turnout at the polls in August gave evidence of the lackluster campaign, for there was a drop of almost 9,000 votes compared to the 1856 presidential election and a drop of 2,000 votes in relation to the 1855 contest (see Tables 5.1 and 5.2). Despite this apparent hesitancy or apathy of the voters in 1857—the lowest percentage of voter participation in gubernatorial elections in the 1840s and 1850s—those who voted were not reluctant to make known their preference as they gave Harris a stunning victory. The Democratic party had now put together four consecutive victories, matching the record established by the Whigs in the early 1840s.

With that kind of success to its credit the party was not the least bit uncertain that Harris would be its candidate again in 1859. In fact, in December 1858, readers of Democratic newspapers began to learn of the movement in behalf of Harris's renomination. In the middle of that month the party's State Central Committee issued a call for the state convention to be held on March 17. Absent was any debate, as seen in 1855, over whether the party really needed a convention since Harris was the obvious choice. Forty counties sent delegates and sixteen others had proxies available at the conclave, which chose Harris with considerable enthusiasm, set up campaign committees, and adopted a party platform. Unlike the preceding gubernatorial campaign, the Democrats in 1859 found some state questions to address. The platform, reflecting the economic distresses ushered in by the Panic of 1857, favored gold and silver as the only constitutional currency, reform of the state banking system, and the right of the legislature to revoke or modify charters granted by it to businesses. On the national level, the platform endorsed the acquisition of Cuba and reaffirmed the party's support of the Dred Scott decision with regard to slavery in the territories.[52] The convention then adjourned, confident that the party would win a fifth consecutive victory.

The great question was whether a rival party would come into being in time to place a competitor in the field against Harris. But in 1858–59 the tattered remnants of the Know Nothing party and the old Whig party began regrouping, and there was a quiet optimism that such activity could result in a strong new party to carry on the anti-Jacksonian tradition in the state. In fact by the end of 1858 a call had gone out for a state nominating convention to be held in late February. The next question was what man would be chosen to lead this new group. Democratic newspapers were hoping to smoke out John Bell and compel him to confront the Tennessee voters, but the *Union and American* was realistically confident that Bell would avoid such a contest if at all possible, whereupon several names began to appear in the press in January and February as possible candidates, including John Netherland of East Tennessee. The erstwhile leaders of this new political group, known as the Opposition party, decided in late January to postpone the party's convention to some date after the Democratic party conclave. Eventually they agreed upon March 29, twelve days after the Democratic meeting. At that convention Netherland's name was placed into nomination without opposition and he was chosen. Netherland had been one of the doyens of East Tennessee Whiggery and in earlier times had contributed to Whig frictions in his part of the state by opposing the ambitions of Thomas A. R. Nelson. But in 1859 things were different, and Netherland became the first East Tennessean candidate of an anti-Jacksonian party since the two-party system began. The Opposition party established its campaign machinery, with an executive committee in each of the three sections, and also wrote a platform for its supporters to rally around. The adopted document urged the preservation of the union, upheld constitutional rights on slavery, asked for the cessation of further agitation of the slavery question, proposed an extension of time for naturalization of foreigners, endorsed a sound and well-regulated banking system whose notes should be payable, when requested, in hard money, and pledged the party to the overthrow of the Democrats.[53] Without question the platform stood firmly in the Whig-Know Nothing tradition—perhaps old wine in old wine skins.

The two candidates conformed to long-established tradition of twenty-years' standing by conducting a joint canvass throughout the

state. Long before the campaign formally began, there were indications in the press, in county meetings, and in speeches that currency
and banking questions would have a major role in the 1859 election.
In early 1858 the General Assembly took certain steps to alleviate or
minimize some of the economic problems confronting the state. It
sought, for example, to put restrictions upon the note-issuing prac-
tices of the various banks, and it required all banks to resume the
payment of specie on or before November 1.[54] Much of what was
heard in the 1859 campaign was strangely reminiscent of the rhetoric
of the 1830s. State Democrats cast their lot with what they called
"constitutional currency"—gold and silver—and against paper
money. The Opposition party leaders depicted a Democratic party in
disagreement over hard money versus paper currency, and so the
debate raged throughout the spring and summer. Democrats claimed
a strong desire for banking reform or better still an intention to rid
the state of the "present pernicious system of banking." One proposed
reform was to permit the legislature to modify or revoke charters
granted to banks by the General Assembly, an idea that Netherland
and the Opposition party strongly opposed. Harris was lauded by the
Democratic press as the champion of the people's rights, "guarding
them from the oppression of monied monopolies," whereas Netherland was portrayed as anxious to give the banks "dangerous and
despotic control." The so-called pocketbook issue was obviously of
significance to many voters, so the candidates and the press concentrated upon it.[55] In fact, there was some sentiment in Democratic
quarters after the election ended that the party had been hurt somewhat on the banking and currency question.[56]

Vying in importance with questions of economic policy was the
perennial matter of slavery and its related aspects. Democrats strained
themselves from time to time in an effort to depict the Opposition
party as antislavery, but their most successful argument was to link
the Opposition party with the national Republican cause. According
to the Democrats, the only way that Democratic political power could
be overthrown would be for the Opposition in Tennessee and the
South to join up with the Black Republicans. Tennessee voters were
particularly warned that this was the intention of the Opposition
party in the forthcoming presidential election. Speeches by Harris and
other Democratic campaigners, as well as articles in the newspapers,
returned to this theme repeatedly during the race. The *Union and
American* declared the southern Opposition men to be the tails to the
abolition kite. Netherland and his party sought to overcome these
attacks by chiding the Democrats for continually agitating the slavery

question merely for political gain, since there were no abolitionists in Tennessee to hear the Democratic message. Netherland declared in his Nashville speech that a Democrat at that party's state convention had advised that the way to beat the Oppostion party was to throw "nigger" at it. When Opposition leaders claimed that slavery was not an issue in the 1859 state campaign, the Democratic press insisted all the more that it was a lively and significant topic. Netherland further provoked the Democrats in his speech at Charlotte, where he held that nonslaveholders were simply not interested in the slavery question. The *Union and American,* not surprisingly, disagreed with this sentiment and warned Netherland that such an argument would evoke no positive appeal. As the canvass entered its last few weeks, the Democratic press vowed that the Black Republicans and abolitionists of the North were keeping a close eye on Tennessee to see how the Opposition would fare, so they could make appropriate plans and strategy for the 1860 campaign. Interestingly enough, neither Harris nor Netherland ever declared a preference for a candidate in the forthcoming national contest, although there was a report or two in the press about the presidential aspirations of John Bell. Instead, the pending national election was utilized chiefly as a way of treating the slavery question in its various forms.[57]

When the debates ended, the voters gave Harris another resounding triumph. Helping both candidates in 1859 was the tremendous increase in voter turnout, in comparison with the preceding gubernatorial election. Nearly 13,500 new voters showed up at the polls in the Harris-Netherland race, perhaps a tribute to the lively campaign and good organizational efforts. While both candidates benefited, Netherland got the larger share (approximately 8,400 more votes than the Know Nothing candidate in 1857). Although Harris polled more votes in his second victory, he did not win by as large a margin, experiencing percentage decreases in all three sections of the state (see Table 5.2). In 1857 and 1859, Harris swept Middle Tennessee by the largest percentage any Democratic ever carried that section since the two-party system began in 1835. East Tennessee experienced a heavy stay-at-home vote in 1857 which ate disastrously into the Know Nothing vote there and enabled Harris to carry the section, yet in 1859 Netherland swung the eastern section back to its traditional anti-Jacksonian posture. In fact, Netherland made gains in all three sections of the state, compared to Hatton's showing in 1857, but there was no way he could catch Harris.[58]

One should not leave the story of the gubernatorial campaigns without commenting upon the congressional races. The great Democratic triumph of 1857 gave the party seven of the ten congressional seats, but the 1859 contest left only three Democrats among the ten congressmen. In 1859 the Opposition party, holding the three seats previously won by Know Nothing candidates in 1857, added four new ones. Unfortunately, there is no readily available answer to explain these puzzling results. Certainly one can discount the explanation of the *Union and American* to the effect that Democrats were hurt in 1859 by the apportioning done by the Whigs in 1852; this certainly had not been a problem for Democrats in 1857.[59] Whatever one concludes, the fact remains that the anti-Democratic cause still had to be reckoned with in Tennessee despite repeated losses in the gubernatorial elections.

The presidential elections of 1852 and 1856 remain as the final area of description and analysis. They mirrored the disintegration of the highly competitive two-party system. The 1852 contest represented the "last hurrah" of the Whigs in presidential campaigns. Hastening their demise was the selection of Winfield Scott as the candidate in 1852; had the incumbent president, Millard Fillmore, been chosen by the Whigs, the situation might have been different. National Whig leaders learned in 1852, much to their dismay, that they could not always win with a military figure heading the ticket. Without question the Democratic party's tactic of choosing men who were either unknown nationally or else had been out of the public limelight was the best policy to insure success at the polls—at least that is what the Franklin Pierce and James Buchanan candidacies seemed to prove.

In several ways the 1852 and 1856 elections are a study in contrasts, so far as Tennessee was concerned. Already alluded to is the fact that 1852 constituted the last Whig victory in a presidential contest (or any other statewide race, for that matter). But the 1852 success also marked the fifth consecutive triumph for Tennessee Whigs in presidential elections—a record that only three other states in the nation could match. Conversely, 1856 was the first victory for Tennessee Democrats in presidential races since 1832, the presidential contests having remained an elusive goal for the state's Democrats. The 1852 and 1856 contests differed from each other in another respect: the latter was the state's first experience with a new political party in a presidential contest in twenty years, or since the initial "revolt" against Jackson.

In voter turnout and voter participation, the 1852 and 1856 contests were markedly dissimilar. Of all the presidential elections during the two-party system in Tennessee, 1852 was *the* deviation from the pattern established twelve years earlier when presidential races began

Table 5.3. Percentage of Statewide Voter Participation, 1851–59

1851	1852	1853	1855	1856	1857	1859
80–83	73–75	76–79	80–83	82–85	75–78	76–82

to outdraw the gubernatorial. As Table 5.3 shows, the 1851 and 1853 governor's contests attracted higher percentages of voter participation than did 1852. As a matter of fact, the total vote in 1852 was the lowest of all the elections, presidential or gubernatorial, in the decade. The level of voter participation in the 1852 contest was the lowest for the presidential contests since 1836. The results in 1856, however, demonstrated that the 1852 contest had been a fluke of sorts, for the 1856 election showed a return to the normal pattern of voter turnout. Indeed, the percentage of voter participation was the highest level of all the elections in the 1850s.

Like the presidential elections of the preceding decade, the two in the 1850s lend themselves to topical analysis. Factionalism and internal division within the ranks of the rival parties, for example, were obvious concerns. Although the Whigs had experienced some disharmony and discord in 1848, the pro-Clay group eventually surrendered to the realities of that year and joined in support of Zachary Taylor's candidacy, but in 1852 the Tennessee Whigs were unable to patch together their differences, for they were beset by bickering and hostility in the party leadership and in the rank and file as well. One important factor was the legacy of hurt feelings resulting from the selection in 1851 of Jones, rather than Nelson, as United States senator. This became an influential element in the subsequent year as Jones attempted to convince Tennessee Whigs to embrace Winfield Scott for the national nomination. Difficulties were compounded by Jones's own ambition to capture a spot on the national ticket. Most perturbed by these revelations were East Tennessee Whigs, who feared Jones's rising reputation as a statewide party chieftain and resented his successful race against Nelson for the U.S. Senate.

That the Whigs in the state were in for troubled times was made evident by developments preceding the national nominating conclave. The overwhelming opinion in favor of Fillmore was borne out by the decision of the February state convention to endorse him, a display of unanimity that was upset, however, by the additional recommendation that Jones be placed on the ticket with Fillmore. This measure not only revived latent antagonistic feelings toward Jones, but also seemed to ignore the ironic reality that Jones was known to be a supporter of Scott, not Fillmore. In the aftermath of the state convention there were murmurings among Tennessee Whigs who favored Fillmore's nomination but could not tolerate the prospect of Jones on the ticket. Trying to steer a calm course, Gustavus Henry suggested to Nelson that perhaps the best thing to do would be to concentrate on assisting Fillmore's chances and to ignore Jones. Governor William B. Campbell, no friend of Jones, believed Fillmore to be the only Whig capable of carrying Tennessee in 1852 and particularly disliked the efforts of Jones and his friends to curry favor in behalf of Scott. Doubtless because of his position as governor (and titular head of the party), Campbell was the recipient of letters from both sides of the controversy—those condemning Jones's activities and ambitions and those seeking to win Campbell over to the Scott cause. The governor, who by this time resembled Andrew Johnson in terms of dislike and distrust of fellow party leaders, momentarily seemed to declare a plague on both their houses.[60]

In the interim between the state and the national conventions, Tennessee Whigs displayed ambivalence over the likely presidential nominee. As the time for the Baltimore convention approached, Felix Zollicoffer's paper, the *Nashville Republican Banner,* continued to back Fillmore, while at the same time it attempted to prepare Whigs for the possibility of a Scott nomination. A number of state party leaders likewise adopted this foot-in-both-camps strategy. In April a serious breach in party solidarity occurred when Meredith P. Gentry helped lead a withdrawal of some southern Whigs from the Whig congressional caucus after its failure to sanction the Compromise of 1850 as a final settlement of the slavery question. Another Tennessee Whig congressman, Christopher H. Williams, joined Gentry in this dramatic break with the party. At a meeting in mid-May Nashville Whigs debated the actions taken by Gentry and Williams, conferred about support for Fillmore, but also discussed the desirability of backing any candidate who was sound on the 1850 compromise.[61]

A month later the Scott forces prevailed at the Baltimore convention, much to the dismay of the Tennessee delegates. Gentry and Williams declared their intention to withhold support from Scott and were joined by William G. Brownlow, another party stalwart. Though this indeed spelled trouble for the Whig campaign in Tennessee, it could have been worse. Fortunately Senators Bell and Jones and Governor Campbell eventually announced their endorsement, albeit without enthusiasm, of the Scott-Graham ticket. Campbell confessed to Congressman William Cullom his belief that Scott would not carry the state, especially in view of the party's internal dissension. Doubtless capturing the attitude of numerous Whigs, Campbell wrote: "I however am too old to change or equivocate & expect to go to the devil with the Whigs, but I may go along more quietly than I have in days gone by."[62]

In the Democratic ranks there were differences of opinion also, but not nearly so serious as the Whigs'. Among leaders of the state party there was no consensus about a possible presidential nominee. In fact some of the county meetings, staged in December 1851, went to ludicrous extremes by naming five or six men as acceptable for the national ticket. Curiously enough, none recommended Franklin Pierce, the relatively obscure New Hampshire politician who eventually won endorsement as the candidate. While Tennessee Democrats were fishing about for prospective nominees, their main attention was actually focused upon the vice presidential spot. Prior to the January 1852 state party convention, several names were mentioned as worthy of second place: A.O.P. Nicholson, William Trousdale, and Gideon J. Pillow. In fact, both the new editor of the *Nashville Union,* John L. Marling, and Congressman Andrew Johnson tried to stir up interest in a Nicholson nomination. But when the party assembled for its state convention, agreement could not be reached on recommendations for either the presidential or the vice presidential nomination. The competing desires of Trousdale, Pillow, and Nicholson forced the party to withhold advocacy of anyone for the vice presidential slot, and apparently the plethora of potential presidential nominees caused the state convention to avoid this matter altogether.[63] Thus in 1852, as in the 1840s, Tennessee delegates to the national convention were to go uninstructed.

Yet despite these circumstances, Tennessee Democrats readily assented to the Pierce nomination at Baltimore. Andrew Johnson, however, had misgivings about the new Democratic ticket and feared that the Whigs might win with Scott. He lamented the failure of the Tennessee delegates to take a united position in favor of Houston and voiced his suspicions that the ambitions of Brown and Pillow for the vice presidential nomination had precluded support of Houston for the presidency, since that would have resulted in southerners occupying both places on the ticket.[64] In spite of Johnson's characteristic rumblings, state Democrats presented a coherent, unified campaign in behalf of Pierce.

Four years later, however, it was the Democrats' turn to be troubled by internal division. Conversely, leaders of the Know Nothing party in Tennessee (composed mainly of former Whigs) eagerly embraced the 1856 national ticket of Fillmore-Donelson. After all, they had wanted Fillmore in 1852, and now they had him, although under different conditions and a different party label. Among Democrats the Aaron Brown faction, generally deprived of federal patronage by virtue of Nicholson's intervention as the liaison between the Pierce administration and the state party, approached the 1856 election year with a determination to back a candidate who might be more responsive to its own needs and demands. Shortly the Brown clique, perhaps influenced by Cave Johnson's longtime friendship with James Buchanan, agreed to lend its support to Buchanan—a decision in direct conflict with Nicholson's efforts to promote Pierce for nomination and reelection in 1856. Another disruptive factor was Governor Johnson, who nourished a desire either that his own name be brought forward at the state convention as a favorite son nominee or else that no one be recommended. He had already confided his conspiratorial notions that Brown and Pillow were hoping for a presidential or vice presidential nomination themselves.[65]

The competing goals of various Democrats were displayed at the party's January state convention. At least one source reports that at the caucus, held one day prior to the convention, Johnson's lieutenants made an abortive attempt to force an endorsement of him for the presidential nomination. The long and short of the disharmony in the Democratic family at this juncture was that the state convention once again decided upon no preferences. Governor Johnson was noticeably piqued by Nicholson's pro-Pierce advocacy and activity; correspondingly Nicholson was irritated by Johnson's nonsupport of Pierce.[66] This was the first serious disagreement between the two allies, but they subsequently took steps to mollify their hurt feelings.

The outward manifestations of Democratic dissension in the state were terminated once the decision of the Cincinnati convention in favor of Buchanan was reached—with the exception of Governor Johnson. In exasperation he asked why the state's delegates had aided the Buchanan cause. To Johnson, Buchanan was "the Slowest man of the four" candidates and was the last one he would have backed. Certainly Aaron Brown's affinity for Buchanan colored Johnson's remarks at this point. The governor, reserving some of his harshest comments for Brown, was particularly alienated by Brown's determination to acquire a presidential appointment should Buchanan be successful.[67] Not long after Johnson made these blunt observations, however, he was forced to reassess his coolness toward the Buchanan candidacy. After all, given the weakened condition of the anti-Jacksonian contingent, it began to look as though the Democrats might carry the state for the first time in twenty-four years. Moreover, the governor surely realized that he must stir himself in behalf of the ticket if he expected to enhance his chances for a United States Senate seat in 1857. Therefore, as the campaign heated up in the summer months, Johnson joined a host of Democratic leaders actively working for a Buchanan victory.

Obviously, an examination of only the internal disagreements in 1852 and 1856 would yield a warped understanding of these elections, for such problems were offset to some extent by effective party organizations. The rival parties fashioned campaign machinery in the image of the proven and successful examples of the 1840s. In view of their loss at the polls in August 1851 (a "disgraceful thrashing which the Whigs gave us," said Nicholson) it is not surprising that Tennessee Democrats got the jump in organizational matters. In fact the November 1, 1851, issue of the *Nashville Union* carried the announcement that the Democratic caucus in the General Assembly had met and agreed to call a state convention for January 8. Numerous December county meetings chose delegates to the convention which would name delegates to the national convention and take steps toward establishment of the traditional party structure. The state convention approved three executive committees (one for each section) and empowered them with the authority to appoint additional committees, fill certain vacancies in the electoral slate, and in general supervise the campaign. Moreover, the January meeting designated A.O.P. Nicholson and Joseph C. Guild as state-at-large electors, but no attempt was made to select district electors. Despite the difficulties that prevented the convention from agreeing upon preferences for the presidential and vice presidential nominations, *Nashville Union* editor John L. Marling praised the spirit of unity and harmony at the party's conclave.[68]

That the editor was glossing over some unpleasant realities may be inferred from the inactivity of the state party until after the Baltimore national convention and from the "address" issued by the Democratic legislators in late February which, among other things, warned: "Let us beware of divisions in our ranks." Actually by the time of the Baltimore convention, three districts had chosen presidential electors, but not until almost mid-July was the entire electoral slate completed. Problems with electors that plagued the Democrats in the 1840s were also experienced in 1852, when three of the original group of ten had to be replaced. In September the executive committee from Middle Tennessee unveiled its plan for a systematic opinion poll. It proposed to name a central committee in each Middle Tennessee county, which in turn would appoint three-man committees in each civil district. These civil district boards were instructed to talk with every voter, in the process of which they were to determine three things: if there were Democrats unwilling to vote for Pierce and the reasons for this; the number of Whigs in the civil district not supporting Scott; and what Whig charges were most detrimental to the Democratic campaign. The Middle Tennessee executive committee urged its East and West Tennessee counterparts to devise similar plans of information gathering. In addition to these and other trappings of party machinery, young men's associations helped promote the Democratic cause.[69]

The Whig party in Tennessee approached 1852 with a mixture of confidence and apprehension—the former related to successes in August 1851 and the latter a result of contradictory noises over possible nominees for the national ticket. But whatever their feelings, the Whigs knew that their party had to be prepared to compete against the Democrats. Apparently the impetus for a state convention came from the *Nashville Republican Banner,* which in late December 1851 urged that a conclave be held in February and that in the interim county meetings should take steps preparatory for it. Accordingly, the Whig faithful gathered in their respective counties to select delegates to the state meeting and also to declare preferences for president and vice president. Of the county meetings surveyed, only Warren County Whigs went on record favoring Winfield Scott for the presidential nomination. The February state convention appointed delegates to the national convention and instructed them to vote for Fillmore and Jones. Then, with perhaps some irony, the party chose Gustavus A. Henry and Thomas A.R. Nelson to serve as state-at-large electors— the two men who had been unsuccessful contenders against Jones for the U.S. Senate seat in 1851. To complete the initial organizational efforts, the February conclave established three central or executive committees which were authorized to handle the usual matters of party machinery, including the appointment of other committees deemed necessary for the campaign.[70]

The national Whig convention was not scheduled to meet until mid-June; thus, like the Democrats, Tennessee Whigs had trouble generating organizational activity prior to the national assembly. Whig fears surfaced in the spring when Nelson made public his intention not to serve as one of the at-large electors, yet it was not until late July that the party's three central committees selected William T. Haskell to replace Nelson. In the meantime, the Baltimore convention had named Scott to head the Whig ticket, and in response to this a number of ratification meetings were held throughout the state to bolster wavering Whig spirits. Experiencing more difficulty with electors than they had ever had in the 1840s, Tennessee Whigs had to replace one at-large elector, as well as three of the district electors.[71] Perhaps this unprecedented shifting of personnel was indicative of internal troubles. In any event, despite obvious disharmony within the party, it was able to erect a campaign structure closely resembling that of previous presidential canvasses.

The 1856 contest seems to have been characterized by more intensive organizational efforts than seen in 1852—perhaps because there was a new party competing and because the state's Democrats smelled victory in the air. Whatever the chief motivation, both the Know Nothings and the Democrats devoted considerable attention to devising the proper campaign machinery. In fact, the Democratic state convention in March 1855 adopted a resolution specifying January 8, 1856, as the date for the party conclave that would prepare for the presidential campaign. This was the only example in the whole period of a gubernatorial party convention issuing a call for a subsequent meeting. The Democrats issued a reminder in early November 1855 that a state convention was scheduled for January. The pervasive optimism that typified Democratic attitudes at this juncture was expressed by an editorial in the *Nashville Union and American:* "A better feeling than now exists with the democracy of this State has never been known in Tennessee."[72]

The state convention in early January dealt with several organizational matters: it designated delegates to the national convention; it chose William H. Polk and Isham G. Harris as the state-at-large electors; and it authorized the convention president to appoint three central committees to handle the chores of supervising the campaign. The president in turn selected seven men from each of the state's three sections to function as the central committees. No less a luminary from the enemy camp than William G. Brownlow commented favorably upon the Democratic convention and singled out the party's efficient organization.[73]

With the *Nashville Union and American* serving as the journalistic cheerleader ("You must prepare yourselves—organize yourselves thoroughly.") Democrats far and wide responded in the spring months. One of the congressional districts, getting the jump on the convention's decree about April meetings, held its conclave in March and chose its presidential elector. Similar district conventions followed in April and May with the quite remarkable result that by the time of the Democratic national convention, the entire electoral slate, with one exception, had been secured. Equally impressive is the fact

that there were no changes in the Democratic electoral group in 1856
—for the first time since the development and implementation of
party machinery in 1840. All in all, the beginning of summer found
the Democrats more efficiently and more effectively organized than
they had been at the same juncture in most of the previous presidential
contests. Immediately after the Cincinnati convention, Democratic
ratification meetings across the state acquiesced in the Buchanan-
Breckinridge ticket. Not unimportant was the presence of several
locally prominent Whigs on the speakers' platform at some of those
June and July assemblies.[74]

The Know Nothing party in Tennessee, having tested its mettle in
the 1855 gubernatorial campaign, believed that it had a fighting
chance to capture the state in the presidential contest. Accordingly,
in January 1856 Know Nothing legislators issued a call for a convention to be held in Nashville on February 12, just ten short days before
the national convention at Philadelphia, and county meetings hurriedly chose delegates to the state conclave.[75] The convention apparently made no effort to agree upon preferences for the national ticket,
a circumstance partly understandable in terms of the newness of the
party. The Nashville meeting nevertheless did name a group of delegates to attend the immediately forthcoming national convention; it
chose Thomas A.R. Nelson and John S. Brien as state-at-large electors; and it recommended that the various congressional districts hold
conventions in May to agree upon presidential electors. To supervise
and guide the Know Nothing campaign an eight-man State Executive
Committee (composed entirely of Davidson County residents) was
established with authorization to handle the usual responsibilities
incumbent upon such a committee. Furthermore, the state convention
provided that three-man committees should be appointed in every
county of the state to assist the executive committee and to serve as
the party's organizational network.[76] Clearly the Know Nothings
imitated previously existing models of party structure; this was evidently no time for new departures or innovations.

In the wake of the Philadelphia convention, Tennessee Know Nothings set about to complete their campaign machinery and to foster
enthusiasm for the Fillmore-Donelson ticket. Fillmore had long enjoyed support in the state and his nomination in 1856 created new
excitement about the possibility of victory in Tennessee. Not surprisingly, there were some audible reservations about having Donelson,
long so steadfastly and intimately identified with the Democratic
party, as the vice presidential nominee. In fact, at the Philadelphia

convention Brownlow had not hesitated to voice his disapproval of Donelson. But by the time Donelson and the Tennessee delegates returned home, various Know Nothing leaders and newspapers were busily drumming up support for Fillmore and Donelson. The *Republican Banner,* for example, praised the nominations, claiming that they represented "the sound, conservative, patriotic and anti-ultra spirit of both the Northern and Southern sections of the Union." In March and April county rallies expressed approval of the Philadelphia convention's decisions, and thereafter district conventions chose their presidential electors; but the organizational structure was shaken by public announcements in June that Brien and Nelson had declined to serve as state-at-large electors. By mid-June, however, the State Executive Committee replaced Nelson with Horace Maynard and Brien with Neill S. Brown.[77] Apart from this shuffling of assignments, the Know Nothing electoral slate remained intact for the duration of the campaign.

A few summary observations about party organization seem warranted. For example, there was a great deal more organizational symmetry in 1852 and 1856 than had been the case in the 1840s: the times of the state conventions were regularized; the conventions chose the at-large electors but never the district electors; the groups of electors experienced much less changing of personnel. In 1852 the Whigs and in 1856 the Know Nothings staged only one party convention rather than two or three, as had been the Whig custom in the previous decade. Although the terminology changed somewhat in the 1850s, the rival parties continued the practice of setting up central or executive committees to oversee the general operations of the campaigns. In 1856 the Know Nothings departed slightly, however, from this pattern by creating a single committee instead of one from each section of the state.

But even the most elaborate party structure was virtually worthless unless it could produce a vigorous campaign. Voter turnout in the presidential elections gives some clue of the level of interest fostered in part by the type of campaigning. As Table 5.3 indicates, the 1852 contest attracted a much lower level of voter participation than did the 1856 election. A survey of newspapers and private correspondence substantiates the conclusion that the 1856 contest outstripped 1852 in terms of electioneering activity and excitement. There was some intensity of feeling exhibited in 1852, to be sure, but the wrong kind— if one recalls the shoot-out in August between the two prominent Nashville editors, John L. Marling and Felix Zollicoffer. In the 1856 campaign the competing parties resorted to mass rallies and barbecues —a tactic that had just about disappeared from presidential electioneering in Tennessee. In the closing weeks of this contest excitement apparently reached such feverish levels in the Nashville area that the responsible committees of both parties intervened to cool down the partisan ardor. They agreed that Wednesdays and Fridays would be reserved exclusively for Democratic speeches and demonstrations, while Thursdays and Saturdays would belong to the Know Nothings.[78]

Unlike the basic experience in the 1840s, the presidential contests in the succeeding decade saw the state-at-large and district electors occupy the role of principal promoters and servants of their respective parties. These designated electors were assisted, of course, by other leaders of the parties, usually congressmen or former governors. Indicative of the changing times was Senator James C. Jones, who served as an energetic campaigner in behalf of the Whig ticket in 1852, but worked diligently in 1856 in support of the Democratic nominee. Although Andrew J. Donelson took no active part in the 1852 campaign, he supported the Democratic ticket; but in 1856, of course, he was the Know Nothing vice presidential nominee and engaged in limited activities in behalf of this new-found allegiance. Whig efforts in 1852 suffered from the refusal of Brownlow, Gentry, Williams, and others to labor for the party's ticket. Indeed the only campaigning that Brownlow did was to tour several East Tennessee counties to explain why he could not and would not support Winfield Scott. Luckily, most of the other prominent state Whig leaders eventually enlisted in the electioneering work for the ticket. The governors in office at the time of the presidential canvasses—Campbell in 1852 and Johnson in 1856—participated to some extent in the campaigns. In fact, after Johnson got over his initial lukewarmness he was very active in 1856, even swallowing some of his distaste for James C. Jones and consenting to work with him. Despite yeoman service by numerous Know Nothing speakers, all was not well—if one can rely upon reports about the inebriated condition of Donelson and William T. Haskell during some of their public appearances.[79]

Campaign speeches, newspaper editorials, and private correspondence provide a fairly complete record of what questions seemed to occupy the attention of the campaigners and the voters in the state. Actually there were few surprises. In 1852, for example, a Tennessee voter perhaps felt a sense of déjà vu as he listened to and read about the debates over the Compromise of 1850. After all, that same question had played a paramount role in the gubernatorial race between Trousdale and Campbell the previous year. There was didactic merit in the *Nashville Union's* interpretation of the situation in 1852: "The question presented in this canvass, is the *maintenance* of the compromise. . . . The finality of the compromise is the principle democracy contends for." Since Tennessee Whigs had demonstrated their support of the compromise and only one element within the state Democratic party was lukewarm on the matter, no serious breach between the parties was evident. Instead, controversy revolved around the matter of which party could best be entrusted to uphold the compromise and also safeguard the rights of the South. To hear Tennessee Democrats explain it, Franklin Pierce was a southerner in every regard except actual birth; Winfield Scott, on the other hand, was a tool of northern abolitionists. As one Tennessean expressed it: "In my opinion, Scott will never suit the South. . . . He is antipodes to our interest—to our feelings—to every thing that belongs to us." The unhappiness of certain Tennessee Whigs over the Scott nomination merely added weight to the Democratic charges. Gentry, one of those unhappy Whigs, declared that to support Scott would be to offer *"Bounties for Anti-Slavery Agitation and Aggression."* Whigs trying to shore up the party's cause questioned Pierce's background and asserted that he possessed abolitionist leanings. They backed Scott as a devoted advocate of the union and a strong proponent of the compromise, although the latter claim was a bit of an exaggeration, given Scott's taciturn stance on the compromise.[80]

When the 1856 election year arrived, it could not escape the disturbing drama of the events surrounding the Kansas-Nebraska bill, the turmoil in Kansas itself, and, of course, the new anti-Catholic, antiforeign movement exemplified by the American (Know Nothing) party. As the *Union and American* put it, "No man can blind his mind to the fact that the principle contained in the Kansas Nebraska act is the only issue now before the country." Tennessee Democrats devoted much of their verbiage to pressing the point that southern interests were best represented by James Buchanan and the Democratic party. In their examination of Buchanan's long record of public service, they found no hint of a refusal by him to defend the institution of slavery or a failure to uphold the view that Congress could not interfere with slavery in the territories. Moreover, with much cogency they charged that the Know Nothing candidate, Millard Fillmore, stood no chance of being elected president, therefore making a vote for him tantamount to a ballot in behalf of the Republican party's nominee, John C. Fremont. Furthermore, as a carry-over from the 1855 gubernatorial race, state Democrats attacked the bigoted principles of Know Nothingism.[81]

Know Nothing speakers and journalists tried valiantly to respond to the withering barrage directed at them. Not surprisingly, their review of Buchanan's career afforded little comfort to those seeking reassurance about his protective concern for the southern region. Moreover, perhaps as a desperation move, Know Nothing spokesmen revived the hoary charge that Buchanan had participated in the corrupt bargain and intrigue in the 1824 election. To counter Democratic allegations that Fillmore sympathized with abolitionists, the Know Nothings depicted him as a moderate on the slavery question and as a man devoted to the entire union. Finding a mote in the Democrats' eye, the opposition declared that Tennessee Democrats were shielding from the voters the free-soilism evident in the northern wing of the national Democratic party. How safe, asked the Know Nothings, were southern interests in the hands of such a party?[82]

This and other questions were answered by the voters in November of 1852 and 1856. It is generally believed that the precipitous drop in voter turnout in 1852 hurt the Whigs much more than it hurt the Democrats. While it is true that in 1852 Scott secured approximately 5,700 fewer votes than Taylor in 1848, a comparison with the 1851 governor's race does not yield so convincing a picture. An examination of vote totals in Table 5.1 for 1851 and 1852 shows that in fact the Democratic party lost 5,400 voters in the latter election, whereas the Whig party lost only 4,700.[83] Not surprisingly, in 1852 Scott received 4,000 fewer votes in East Tennessee than the Whig candidate in 1851, but on the other hand Pierce got 3,300 fewer votes in 1852 in East Tennessee than did the Democratic incumbent in 1851. These facts raise questions about how seriously Whig dissension in the eastern third of the state hurt the party at the ballot box in November.

There is little room for doubt, however, that in 1856 the swelling numbers of voters redounded to the credit of the Democratic party. The victorious Buchanan, for example, polled 16,700 more votes than Pierce in 1852 and about 6,500 more than Andrew Johnson in the 1855 gubernatorial contest. By comparison, Table 5.1 indicates that Fillmore in 1856 secured 7,500 more votes than Scott in 1852 but only about 300 more votes than the Know Nothing candidate in the 1855 governor's race. It is of significance to note that in 1856 the Democratic ticket made gains in percentages in all three sections of the state (see Table 5.2), though it failed to carry East Tennessee.[84]

It is far easier, of course, to report how the voters reacted in the 1852 and 1856 presidential elections than it is to illumine why they voted as they did. Given the voter apathy which afflicted both parties in Tennessee in 1852 and the internal friction within the Whig ranks, the Whig victory stands as impressive testimony of the tenacity of party identification and loyalty. Although there was a significant decrease in voter turnout in 1852, the Whig party nevertheless emerged victorious with a margin of 50.7 percent, compared to 50.4 percent in 1851 (see Table 5.2). The collapse of the Whig party after 1853 makes comparisons between the 1852 and 1856 campaign difficult, but this much seems certain: Andrew Johnson's successes in 1853 and 1855 had a bearing on the 1856 outcome. West Tennessee's shift from Whig-Know Nothing support to Democratic began with the Johnson races and succeeded in 1856. By the time of that election the Democratic party was identified in the minds of many voters as the one most sympathetic to states rights leanings. West Tennessee was, of course, the region exhibiting the most affinity for extreme views, but Buchanan's astounding showing in Middle Tennessee might indicate similar feelings in that part of the state. In any event, in 1856 there was hardly any way the Democrats could lose. It should not be forgotten, however, that some 66,100 voters embraced the Know Nothing party in that election—evidence of the continuing impact of the anti-Jacksonian element in the state.

In the story of ten years of Tennessee politics from 1850 to 1859, several salient points come into focus. One is that the dual theme of factional discord and organizational unity, so evident and so novel in the 1840s, retained a prominent role in the political drama of the 1850s. Its somewhat diminished impact and luster in the latter decade resulted in part from the expiration of the Whig party and consequent rise of new parties. An analysis of state politics in the 1850s furthermore reveals both the breakup of the smooth functioning, fiercely competitive two-party rivalry of the preceding decade and the emergence of Democratic hegemony. But the anti-Jacksonian tradition in the state showed remarkable persistence. Despite impressive Democratic victories in the latter half of the decade, the party never captured more than 54 percent of the statewide vote. Although the vicissitudes of sectional travail steadily made an impact upon Tennessee voters, their electoral behavior demonstrated the strength and tenacity of traditional political loyalties and allegiances. The slavery question did not greatly disturb state politics in this period, though the menacing issue of the preservation of the union gradually began to divide Tennesseans.

VI   Conclusion

Although Tennesseans at the time did not know it, after the 1859 campaign results had been tallied the so-called antebellum era was essentially over. The next year would bring a national crisis of distressing proportions, with the tragic result that the union began to dissolve. If a mythical Tennessee voter had paused on the eve of the year 1860 to make an assessment of the preceding twenty-five years, he might have raised these two questions: Who were the Democrats, who were the anti-Democrats? What themes and topics characterized this extraordinary period of political conflict in Tennessee?

The first question—Who were the Democrats, who were the anti-Democrats?—brings to mind three fairly recent works that have in various ways dealt with the problem of identifying the rank and file of the parties in Tennessee. In an article published in 1973, Burton W. Folsom II analyzes Davidson County political elites during the antebellum two-party system. Considerably more comprehensive and exhaustive is the dissertation by Lowrey in which he scrutinizes some 6,000 Tennessee voters. Moreover, Ralph A. Wooster provides some important information on Tennessee, especially its legislators, in his study of the seven states of the Upper South.[1] On the basis of these works in particular one is able to say a great deal more about the state's voters and political leaders.

Although his own analysis of Tennessee congressmen showed remarkable similarities of occupational alignments, place of birth, and age between Whig and Democratic officials, Milton Henry nonetheless declared: "The Whig Party in Tennessee in the period 1845-1861 derived the major portion of its strength and personnel from the industrial and planter interests. The Democrats were more dependent for support and personnel upon the small farmers and artisans."[2] Claims such as these have perpetuated persistent and nearly unshakable interpretations, but recent quantitative research enables one to raise serious questions and shed new light.

One obvious point of departure for an analysis of individual voters is occupation. Wooster's study reveals that 67.5 percent of the Democratic legislators were farmer-planters, while only 48.9 percent of the Whigs claimed this occupation. He also found that 20.9 percent of the Whig and 15.0 percent of the Democratic legislators were lawyers. But in his examination of 105 political leaders in Davidson County,

Folsom found no significant differences between the two parties in terms of occupation: 31 percent of the Whigs and 28 percent of the Democrats were lawyers; 35 percent of the Whigs and 23 percent of the Democrats were farmer-planters; 13 percent of the Whigs and 19 percent of the Democrats were businessmen (merchants); and other occupational groups were evenly divided.[3] Somewhat different fingings emerge from Lowrey's investigation of nearly 3,400 individuals during the 1836–54 period. Statewide, 68 percent of the Democrats and 58 percent of the Whigs were farmer-planters; 11 percent of the Whigs and 8 percent of the Democrats were merchants; 12 percent of the Whigs and 7 percent of the Democrats were artisans; 6 percent of the Whigs and 5 percent of the Democrats were lawyers; and so forth. In his analysis of slightly more than 2,300 men for the 1855–60 period, Lowrey again found the farmer-planter category leading all others to a considerable extent: 62 percent of the Democrats and 54 percent of the anti-Democrats fell into this group—not an important variation from the earlier time period. In fact the only change of significance in the 1855–60 bloc was in the artisan group, a point to be dealt with below.[4]

Given the prominence of the farmer-planter group in both parties, it is mildly surprising to learn how noticeably the farmer-planters dominated the Democratic, rather than the Whig, ranks. For the 1836–54 segment this was especially true in Middle and West Tennessee, the most prosperous agricultural regions of the state. In Middle Tennessee, for example, 68 percent of the Democrats and 52 percent of the Whigs were in this occupational group; in West Tennessee, 66 percent of the Democrats and 47 percent of the Whigs were so identified. For these two sections of the state there is at least a hint of occupational influence upon party alignment. Interestingly, in the 1855–60 period the percentage gap narrowed in both Middle and West Tennessee, especially in the latter where 57 percent of the Democrats and 52 percent of the anti-Democrats claimed to be farmer-planters. But the trend in East Tennessee went the other way; that is, an even greater differential (75 percent to 56 percent) was found among Democrats and anti-Democrats who were agriculturalists.[5]

Subjecting these farmer-planters to further scrutiny yields other informative findings. For the 1836–54 period Lowrey found, for example, that Whig farmer-planters were more likely than their Democratic counterparts to be nonlandowners or small landowners (less than $1,000 in real estate). This tendency was particularly true among the younger farmers; hence the tentative conclusion that less wealthy young men were inclined to become Whigs.[6] Combining real estate and personal estate information (available in the 1860 federal census) one gets some clues for the 1855–60 period about the party affiliations of the farmer-planters who owned slaves. Lowrey found that the agriculturalists claiming real estate valued at $10,000 and above and personal property at $10,000 and above were more likely to be found in the Democratic camp, 87 percent of whose farmer-planters were in this category (compared to 79 percent of the anti-Democrats). Meanwhile, farmer-planters of middle-range real and personal estate were very slightly inclined to be in the anti-Democratic column.[7] Despite all the varied analyses of the farmer-planter group in antebellum Tennessee, however, one must be cautioned that there are no firm, definitive conclusions about the political preferences of this group; there are instead only some hints and suggestions. The main message is that there were no substantial differences between Democratic and anti-Democratic farmers.

As noted earlier, throughout the 1836–60 period a higher proportion of anti-Democrats, rather than Democrats, were merchants. This was particularly true from 1836 to 1854 in Middle Tennessee, where 14 percent of the Whigs and 8 percent of the Democrats were merchants; the percentage differential was not as great, however, in East and West Tennessee. In the 1855–60 time bloc the percentage of partisans who were merchants increased in both parties. The proportion of anti-Democrats who were merchants exceeded that of the Democrats everywhere—except in West Tennessee, where 16 percent of the Democrats and 12 percent of the anti-Democrats were merchants. (These figures represent a notable switch in West Tennessee, for in the 1836–54 period 8 percent of the Democrats and 11 percent of the Whigs were merchants.) An important gain occurred in East Tennessee, where 14 percent of the anti-Democrats and 8 percent of the Democrats were classified as merchants; it had been 6 percent to 5 percent in the 1836–54 period. Given the fact that merchants were a town-based group, this development in East Tennessee may reflect the tendency of the urban areas there to respond negatively to the emerging extremism of the state's Democrats. When merchants across the state are analyzed further with regard to wealth, age, and place of birth no distinctions worth noting arise; the only exception is that foreign-born merchants increasingly identified with the Democratic party—an expected trend in view of the nativist principles espoused by the Know Nothings in the mid-1850s.[8]

Contrary to a traditional view that the Jacksonian party had a higher percentage of its members who were working men ("mechanics") than did the anti-Jacksonian party, the facts show that in Tennessee in the 1836-54 period 12 percent of the Whigs and 7 percent of the Democrats were artisans. (Only in West Tennessee did both parties have the same percentages of working men.) In the 1855–60 period, however, the occupational distinction disappears, for statewide 6 percent of the Democrats and 6 percent of the anti-Democrats were categorized as skilled laborers. Lowrey speculates that Andrew Johnson, "a militant champion of the artisan interests," might have been responsible for winning much of that crowd over to the Democratic party in the 1850s. What is not clear is why both parties in the 1855–60 period showed lower percentages in the artisan category than had been the case in the earlier 1836–54 period. Particularly interesting for the 1836-54 period is that a much higher percentage of the Whig artisans (43 percent to 28 percent Democrat) were nonlandowners, whereas a greater proportion of the Democratic laborers (28 percent to 16 percent) reported real estate valued at less than $1,000. As Lowrey suggests, these findings may reflect differences in the requirements for certain kinds of skilled labor, more than anything else. In the 1855–60 period a mixed picture appears: based on real estate, the anti-Democrats had a higher percentage of poorer artisans than did the Democrats; yet based on personal property, the Democrats had a greater percentage of poorer workers than did the anti-Democrats. In the five years before the Civil War, young artisans were decidedly in the Democratic camp (20 percent of the Democrats versus 6 percent of the anti-Democrats) and the same was true of foreign-born workers (13 percent of the Democrats compared to 4 percent of the anti-Democrats).[9]

The professions of physician and lawyer constitute the only other occupational groups of consequence in this examination of individual voters. In the 1836–54 analysis it appears that both parties had almost the same proportion of doctors, although the Democrats enjoyed a slight edge everywhere except in West Tennessee. But according to the 1855–60 study, the situation changed throughout the state. The anti-Democrats emerged with a percentage lead in all three sections, the most noticeable being in East Tennessee (7 percent to 3 percent) and in West Tennessee (10 percent to 6 percent); there is a hint of occupational influence upon political preference. It should be noted that in the 1855–60 period both parties experienced increases in the proportion of their numbers who were physicians. Scrutinizing these doctors with regard to wealth, age, or place of birth shows very few differences between Democrats and anti-Democrats. During the entire period, 1836–60, however, it appears that wealthier physicians exhibited a slight tendency toward the Whigs or anti-Democrats.[10]

Relative to lawyers, the 1836–54 study shows that the Whigs had a higher percentage than did the Democrats, except in East Tennessee, where 6 percent of the Democrats and 3 percent of the Whigs were attorneys. In West Tennessee the Whigs had a substantial advantage, 17 percent to 7 percent—a suggestion of the influence of occupation upon party alignment. In the 1855–60 period a dramatic change took place in East Tennessee, where 16 percent of the anti-Democrats and 5 percent of the Democrats were lawyers. As was claimed earlier about East Tennessee merchants, perhaps also lawyers who were concentrated in the towns reacted strongly against the extremism of Tennessee's Democrats. Conversely, in West Tennessee the gap between the percentages of anti-Democratic and Democratic lawyers was narrowed. About the only distinguishing characteristic between Democratic and anti-Democratic lawyers in the antebellum period is that the latter tended to be somewhat wealthier.[11]

Overall it appears that during at least part of the antebellum period town-based occupations inclined a voter to the anti-Democratic ranks, while farming exerted an opposite pull. Generally the wealthier farmers were found in the Democratic column, while wealthier merchants and lawyers were in the anti-Democratic camp. The poorer artisans, measured by real estate, sought refuge in the anti-Jackson party, not the Jacksonian. In the years immediately before the Civil War, there was a noticeable trend in the urban occupation groups toward the anti-Democratic party in East Tennessee but toward the Democratic party in West Tennessee. The question whether occupation exerted an influence upon party affiliation is not susceptible to firm answers, however; at times there are hints of it, but at other times the evidence merely gives testimony to the impossibility of answers. What is clear is that there were relatively few socioeconomic differences between adherents of both parties in Tennessee. In his examination of the political elite of Davidson County, Folsom found this to be the case, and he indicates that this was probably characteristic of the rank and file as well.[12]

A second major category of individual voter analysis is wealth, both real estate and personal property. Wooster found the median value of real estate held by Whig legislators to be $3,000 compared to $1,500 for Democratic legislators. For the 1836–54 period, Lowrey reports that statewide 37 percent of the Whigs and 28 percent of the Democrats claimed real estate of $1,000 or less in value. West Tennessee was the only part of the state to deviate from this pattern, for there 26 percent of the Democrats and 20 percent of the Whigs reported real estate of $1,000 or less in value. Moving up the scale of wealth, one finds a slightly larger percentage of Democrats. One noticeable feature is that East Tennessee had smaller percentages in both parties who owned $5,000 or more in real estate than did the other two sections. In Middle Tennessee 32 percent of the Democrats and 28 percent of the Whigs had $5,000 or more of real estate value, while in West Tennessee, 34 percent of the Democrats and 40 percent of the Whigs were so classified. Based on occupation, age, and place of birth of nonlandowners and small landowners, one finds few distinctions between parties, but an examination of large landowners ($5,000 or more in real estate) reveals some noteworthy differences. For example, 74 percent of the Democrats and 60 percent of the Whigs in this group were farmer-planters by occupation, but 16 percent of the large landowning Whigs and 8 percent of similar type Democrats were merchants. There is a suggestion here that wealthier merchants preferred the Whig party. Among the wealthy, a much higher percentage of Whigs than Democrats was born in Tennessee, while Democrats dominated on the matter of Upper South and Lower South birthplaces.[13]

Indicative of rising prosperity in Tennessee, the 1855–60 study shows noticeably diminished percentages in both parties with $5,000 or less in real estate (45 percent of the Democrats and 43 percent of the anti-Democrats) than had been the case in the 1836–54 period (71 percent of the Democrats and 76 percent of the Whigs). By the same token the percentages of those with real estate valued in excess of $5,000 in the 1855–60 period were 56 percent of the Democrats and 57 percent of the anti-Democrats. The nearly identical percentages in this latter time bloc mean that distinctions were virtually nonexistent. But in comparison to the statewide picture, the West Tennesseans analyzed showed higher percentages in both parties holding real estate in excess of $5,000 (69 percent of the Democrats and 61 percent of the anti-Democrats); in the 1836–54 period West Tennessee Whigs had had a greater proportion of its members who were large landowners than had West Tennessee Democrats. Examining the different groups of nonlandowners and landowners during 1855–60 with regard to occupation, age, and place of birth adds little or nothing to an analysis of party alignments, except that the earlier inclination of artisans of any level of wealth to be Whigs does not appear to be evident in the five years prior to the Civil War.[14]

Concerning personal property holdings of voters in the 1855–60 period, it may be assumed that those with $1,000 or less of personal estate were nonslaveholders. This being the case, there was no real distinction between Democrats (16 percent) and anti-Democrats (15 percent) statewide. East Tennessee deviated somewhat from the overall picture (16 percent of the Democrats and 21 percent of the anti-Democrats), but such a small number of individuals is in the sample as to cast doubt upon the significance of the findings. As with real estate, the percentages of those holding $5,000 or more of personal property increased across the state from East to West Tennessee: for example, anti-Democrats vis-à-vis Democrats, 45 percent to 42 percent in East; 59 percent to 55 percent in Middle; and 83 percent to 73 percent in West. The West Tennessee figures on personal property over $5,000 are rendered puzzling, if one recalls that the Democratic percentage led in the matter of *real estate* of $5,000 or more value. Generally speaking, an analysis of personal estate holdings indicates little or no connection to party alignment; certainly one cannot claim slaveholding as a characteristic of one party. Wooster found that in 1850 only one third of the Whig legislators owned slaves, while nearly one half (47.9 percent) of the Democrats held slaves. But he also reports that 47.1 percent of the Whig and 39.6 percent of the Democratic legislators came from counties in which slaves accounted for 25 percent or more of the total population. Folsom found no distinctions among the Davidson County elite on the matter of owning slaves, except a tendency for those with largest numbers of slaves to be Democrats.[15]

A third major area of investigation of individual voters is place of birth. The 1836–54 analysis showed that 53 percent of the Whigs and 42 percent of the Democrats had been born in Tennessee. Among the Upper South group, 45 percent of the Democrats and 36 percent of the Whigs were to found, while 7 percent of the Democrats and 3 percent of the Whigs claimed birth in the Lower South. This latter fact was evident, however, chiefly among lawyers, physicians, and to some extent artisans, but not farmer-planters. Consequently, the Lower South natives who were Jacksonians tended to be urban, not rural. In the 1855–60 time bloc, 51 percent of the anti-Democrats and 48 percent of the Democrats were Tennessee natives; one would have expected both parties to have had much higher percentages than in the 1836–54 period. Among the Upper South natives, anti-Democrats counted 38 percent while Democrats counted 36 percent, but the Democrats continued to have a higher percentage who were born in the Lower South (8 percent) than did the anti-Democrats (5 percent). The pattern of Democrats with Lower South origins being urban-based was less apparent in the five years before the Civil War than it had been in the 1836–54 period. The most important shift was among the foreign-born; not unexpectedly they moved into the Democratic camp (4 percent of the Democrats; 2 percent of the anti-Democrats). In fact, all of the foreign-born men identified by Lowrey in West Tennessee were Democrats. In his study of Davidson County elites, Folsom found hardly any variation between leaders of both parties on the matter of place of birth.[16] Overall, that is essentially what Lowrey's more detailed and comprehensive survey uncovered.

Age is a personal characteristic that may have some bearing on one's political leanings. In his examination of the 1836–54 period, Lowrey found that statewide the majority of the Whigs were young (based on ages taken from the 1850 federal census): 51 percent of the Whigs and 45 percent of the Democrats were men under forty years of age in 1850. This was the pattern except in West Tennessee, where 55 percent of the Democrats and 50 percent of the Whigs were in this category. Generally speaking, the younger voters were the ones most likely to have felt the impact of the "revolt" against Jackson and the development of the two-party system. That the Whig party had a higher percentage of younger men than did the Democrats (except in West Tennessee) may be mildly indicative of the appeal an insurgent group sometimes has among younger people. Considering age and occupation together, the Democrats enjoyed advantages among both the younger and older farmer-planters and physicians during the 1836–54 period, when compared to Whig percentages. Conversely, the Whigs dominated the merchant, lawyer, and artisan groups of voters under forty years of age, as well as those over forty. Whatever else might be said about age, it should be noted that when it is combined with considerations of occupation, wealth, or birthplace it seems to exert little or no influence upon party affiliation.[17]

When examining the voters during the 1855–60 period, Lowrey utilized the 1860 census to determine their ages. The voters were older, of course, than those seen in the 1836–54 analysis: only 36 percent of the Democrats and 33 percent of the anti-Democrats were forty years of age and under. Perhaps most interesting of all are the facts about the 21–30 years of age group: East Tennessee, 7 percent of the anti-Democrats and 1 percent of the Democrats; West Tennessee, 4 percent of the anti-Democrats but 11 percent of the Democrats. Although the number of individuals being compared is small, one can argue that the more pronounced states rights position of Tennessee Democrats in the 1850s repelled young men in East Tennessee but attracted them in West Tennessee. In the 1855–60 period, the evidence shows that younger artisans and younger members of the foreign-born contingent were finding their political home among the Democrats. This apparent movement of younger artisans into the Democratic ranks may help explain the fact that, unlike the earlier period, Democrats now had a very slight edge over anti-Democrats (19 percent to 18 percent) among the young men who claimed to hold no real estate.[18]

Other areas of investigation might be pursued to arrive at an even more detailed picture of Tennessee voters, but it is doubtful that much of significance would emerge. In his analysis of Davidson County elites, for example, Folsom considered ethnic and religious factors, but he found little or no correlation between denominational and political preferences. He discovered also that ethnocultural homogeneity was the rule in Davidson County, thus discounting ethnic factors in relation to voting behavior. Lowrey's study (which included Davidson County) involves thousands of individuals and offers much more of an in-depth analysis as well as a much broader geographical coverage. His findings, backed by those of Folsom, indicate that there was a high degree of similarity of voters within both parties and that the various distinctions noted here and there represent only slight variations. Certainly the notion that the Democrats were the party of the "plain folk" while the opposition harbored a disproportionate share of wealthy planters and merchants must be surrendered without hesitation. Lowrey suggests finally that where one lived might "have been more important in determining one's voting behavior than such individual characteristics as occupation, property holdings, age, or place of birth." The point here rests on the claim that in Middle Tennessee the anti-Democratic party enjoyed greater appeal in areas of more advanced economic development, and that across the state the towns leaned toward this party during the antebellum period.[19]

But whatever the various motivations that pushed some men into the Jacksonian and others into the opposition ranks, this much is unquestionably clear: having once made a decision, a voter stayed with his given party for the duration of the two-party period. Lowrey was able to trace nearly 1,600 individual voters through this entire era. Of that number, 738 (or 93 percent) were classified as "continuing" Democrats, while only 58 men (or 7 percent) initially identified as Democrats changed to become anti-Democrats. Similarly, 726 men (or 93 percent) were found to be "continuing" anti-Democrats; whereas 57 men (or 7 percent) switched from anti-Democrat to Democrat sometime before the Civil War. Adding to these remarkable findings is that 81 percent of those who changed from Democrat to anti-Democrat did so after 1854, while 86 percent of those who jumped into the Jacksonian camp from the anti-Democratic group made the leap after 1854. The impressive story hence is one of extreme stability and fidelity among the Tennessee voters; what minuscule change there was occurred in the mid-1850s amidst national party crisis. In case there is any doubt, it should also be pointed out that the changing party labels in the 1850s meant little to those Tennesseans directly affected by these modifications. Lowrey found, for example, that 91 percent of the Know Nothings who could be traced back to an earlier time had been Whigs; 96 percent of the Opposition party previously identified had been Whigs, Know Nothings, or both; and 96 percent of the Constitutional Unionists in 1860 whose earlier affiliation could be determined had been Whigs, Know Nothings, Oppositionists, or some combination thereof.[20] To persevere in the fight against the Jacksonians regardless of the banner under which one waged battle seems to have been the principal concern of these folk.

The intensity of feeling throughout the duration of the two-party system in Tennessee may be measured by the level of voter participation in the gubernatorial and presidential campaigns. As pointed out in the preceding chapters, the percentage of adult white males who voted on election day was very high; in fact, in presidential races few states could match the voter participation levels established in Tennessee (the 1852 contest being the one exception to the rule). Beginning with the 1839 governor's race between Polk and Cannon (an election which brought out about 89 percent of the eligible voters) and continuing through the 1859 gubernatorial contest, the percentage never dropped below 72 percent. In fact, with the exception of some contests in the 1850s voter participation in Tennessee was always 80 percent and above.[21] Hence it is clear that voters not only displayed amazing party loyalty in the two-party era but they also stirred themselves to register their feelings on election day.

In this discussion of voters one must be reminded that the eligible citizenry (adult white males) ranged between 15 and 17 percent of the state's total population. This somewhat startling fact makes even more remarkable the tremendous impact two-party politics exerted upon the Tennessee scene. Obviously, the magnetic pull of the various political battles went far beyond the small number who were actually qualified to vote. The influence of the thousands of nonvoters is one of those imponderables for which one can give little or no accounting. Unquestionably the nonenfranchised played a role, but one can only speculate about its nature and impact. The myriad problems of dealing with those who actually had access to the ballot are enough to discourage one from devoting much attention to the nonvoters.

Turning now to the question about topics and themes, it is appropriate to review briefly the findings, reported in the preceding chapters, about Tennessee's political behavior. The twenty-five-year span has been broken into three chronological blocs, because each decade seems to have demonstrated special features that set it apart. The 1830s, for example, constituted the time of "revolt" against Andrew Jackson and his party. That revolution was *launched* with the electoral contests of 1835 (gubernatorial) and 1836 (presidential); it was *secured* with the gubernatorial election of 1837; and it was successfully, but only momentarily, *challenged* by the governor's race of 1839. Because statewide politics was in a revolutionary phase, it was somewhat chaotic and disorganized. In the latter half of the decade there was no clearly-defined and structured two-party *system;* there were no party nominating conventions or state central committees, for example. These earmarks of partisan competition would evolve shortly thereafter. Further evidence of the confused situation is found in the 1837 campaign, when long-time Democrat Robert Armstrong sought the governor's chair as a "no-party" candidate and garnered support from avowed opponents of the Jacksonian party. Although "revolutionary" things were happening in statewide politics, one tradition remained unchanged in the decade: gubernatorial contests continued to attract higher levels of voter participation than did the presidential. In this regard, it should be noted that in the 1839 battle between gubernatorial aspirants Polk and Cannon the highest degree of voter turnout yet known occurred. During this special period of flux and change, Tennessee voters focused more than ever before upon national alliances. This was quite apparent in the 1835 and 1839 governor's contests, when the issue of presidential preference was uppermost in the minds of the leaders and voters. In the former election this question worked against the Democrats, whereas in the latter it benefited them. Needless to say, the presidential race of 1836 tied Tennesseans to the national scene very directly and securely. The only issue in the latter half of the decade of a local nature was internal improvements; and correctly speaking, it was not a partisan question but rather a sectional one. Both East and West Tennessee evinced great support of state aid for railroad and turnpike companies, and these two sections therefore became linked economically. They also became politically linked, but it is virtually impossible to establish which of these vital connections came first, the economic or the political. In any event, East and West Tennessee "revolted" against Jackson and his party and were joined by a considerable number of like-minded Middle Tennesseans.

By so doing, the voters ushered in the decade of the 1840s as a time of increasingly competitive politics and as a period of the maturing of two-party politics. In one sense the 1840s belonged to the Whig party, for it won six out of the eight statewide contests, a record it would never again match. Yet there is more than meets the eye at first glance, for of the five gubernatorial races, the Whigs captured only three and the highest winning percentage was a scant 51.7. Moreover, the two parties shared United States Senate seats during most of the decade. In terms of statistics, the most impressive Whig victories were the 1840 and 1848 presidential contests. All of this is to say that two-party politics as practiced in the 1840s was fiercely competitive and evenly balanced.

As a part of the maturation of politics the two parties strongly identified themselves with the national structures and left no doubts about their respective alliances. Equally important, both Whigs and Democrats quickly developed impressively organized and effective machines. Both, for example, held party conventions in 1840 to map strategy for the presidential battle of that year, an innovation they again followed in the subsequent presidential canvasses. The first nominating convention to select a gubernatorial candidate was staged by the Whigs in 1841; neither party held one in 1843, but both did in 1845 and thereafter. From the party conventions flowed the typical structure of state central committees, followed by committees for counties or districts. Another example of maturation was the extremely high levels of voter participation in all statewide contests, with the presidential races outpolling the immediately preceding and following gubernatorial races. Accompanying the growth and development of the two-party system in the 1840s was internal friction within each of the partisan camps. Personal ambitions and patronage disputes, rather than ideological disagreements, stirred disharmony from time to time in the leadership of the parties.

As the decade moved along, national issues began to crowd out more local ones. In 1843 and 1847, for instance, the matter of presidential preference was paramount on the eve of forthcoming national elections, and both times the issue worked to the advantage of the Whigs. Following immediately on the heels of the 1844 presidential contest, the 1845 governor's race reiterated the issue of Texas annexation—to the benefit of the Democratic candidate, Aaron V. Brown. In 1847 the Mexican War was second in importance as a campaign topic of dispute, and two years later the decade ended with debates over the Wilmot Proviso and related concerns over slavery. Tennessee Democrats seem to have profited from such debates, as did Democrats in six other states where they were victorious in 1849.

These discussions prefigured the controversies and conflicts of the 1850s. In the first half of the decade, national and regional developments such as the Compromise of 1850, the Nashville conventions, and the Kansas-Nebraska bill found the Tennessee parties exhibiting varying levels of disagreement between each other, as well as within themselves. As the state and the nation were torn by serious difficulties, the symmetrical two-party system as known in Tennessee for years began to fragment. In the process, politics in the Volunteer State was "transformed." But despite the palpable changes taking place, two parties continued to compete in Tennessee until the 1860 presidential contest. Stated very simply, the Whig party collapsed nationally under the burdensome weight of internal friction over slavery's expansion; and because of the tight identity of Tennessee Whigs with the national party, the statewide party could not endure. By the 1855 gubernatorial race, the Whig label was no longer appropriate in the state; but the anti-Jacksonian movement remained strong, albeit in somewhat less imposing fashion. With very few exceptions, leaders and voters of the Whig persuasion in Tennessee hastily found refuge in the American (Know Nothing) party and by the end of the decade in the Opposition party. Changing their hats with disturbing frequency, they were determined nonetheless to fight against the Democratic party as they had been doing for twenty years.

The transforming of statewide politics in the decade resulted in newly labeled parties, accompanied almost expectedly by some voter confusion and apathy. Voter participation levels, for example, dropped in the 1850s, in comparison with the preceding decade, but the most blatant deviation from the norm occurred in 1852, when the Whigs were still waging battle under that banner. Serious disharmony within Whig ranks, dating back to repeated skirmishes over U.S. Senate seats and some disenchantment with the 1851 campaign, erupted in the presidential contest. Yet miraculously—thanks to voter constancy and tenacity—the Whigs carried the state for Winfield Scott in 1852. Further indication of the political transformation in the period was Democratic domination. Early in the decade the Whigs held both U.S. Senate seats, but in the latter half of the period the Democrats captured both. Beginning with Andrew Johnson's gubernatorial victory in 1853 and continuing through the reelection of Isham G. Harris in 1859, the state's Jacksonians swept all the prizes.

Included in this list was the 1856 presidential election, the first such victory for Tennessee Democrats since Jackson's reelection in 1832. Aiding this impressive string of victories was the move by West Tennessee into the Jacksonian camp in 1856, a trend that had begun during the Johnson campaigns for governor. Once both Middle and West Tennessee cast their lot with the Democratic party, the anti-Democratic party, whatever the label, could not expect to win state-wide contests.

Ironically, despite all the furor and excitement of the period, major issues seemed to have a critical role in only the 1851 and 1859 gubernatorial canvasses. To be sure, Johnson blew hot and strong against the principles of Know Nothingism in his campaigns, but in reality those tenets held few charms even for the most active members of the Know Nothing party in Tennessee. At the beginning of the decade debates focused on the Compromise of 1850 as a final resolution of the slavery problem, and at the conclusion of the period, Harris and John Netherland talked about slavery, abolitionism, and disunion. Sandwiched in between were the presidential canvasses of 1852 and 1856; the former was a reiteration of the 1851 campaign, whereas the latter articulated the topic of which party could best be expected to protect southern interests. Increasingly the anti-Jacksonian party became the party of caution and moderation while the Democrats, especially under Harris's tutelage, pushed themselves in the direction of a states rights, pro-South force.

Another ironical twist is that while the Democratic party seized control of state politics in the 1850s, its leadership, particularly in terms of gubernatorial candidates, shifted to East and West Tennessee —which were not the traditional pillars of Jacksonianism. First Andrew Johnson and then Isham Harris undid the long monopoly of the governor's chair by Middle Tennesseans. Sectional tensions within parties had steadily been rising in the preceding decade, so it was not overly surprising to see them blatantly asserted in a period of political transformation.

If Tennessee voters in the 1850s had had the advantage of information provided by a linear regression test (as discussed above in Chapter 2) perhaps they could have readily accepted the Democrats' capture of state political control. Although the takeover appeared suddenly in that decade, it had been developing slowly but steadily across two-and-a-half decades. Knocked back on their heels in the mid-1830s by the whirlwind of revolt against Jackson, the Democrats had to work diligently and feverishly to keep from being swept away. In this regard, Polk performed heroic service to his party with his

victory in 1839, for after all the *lowest* Democratic percentage vote
in all presidential elections was in 1836 and the *lowest* in gubernatorial
elections was in 1837. Exactly twenty years later, however, the *highest*
Democratic percentage in presidential and gubernatorial contests occurred in 1856 and 1857, respectively. Between those lows and highs
were many fascinating, hard-fought electoral battles. For those on the
Tennessee scene who had politics in their blood, it was an exhilarating
quarter of a century. There had never been anything like it before,
because the state had never had a two-party rivalry before. It was a
new day in Tennessee politics and in many respects a glorious one.

Epilogue

Before the outbreak of the Civil War, Tennessee voters had one more opportunity to participate in an election campaign. The climactic presidential contest of 1860 attracted attention and concern in the Volunteer State, as well as across the nation. In April, the national Democratic party split in two at its Charleston convention, with the result that both of the competing wings fielded their own candidates. The Northern Democrats nominated and supported Stephen A. Douglas of Illinois, while the Southern Democrats lined up behind John C. Breckinridge of Kentucky. The stresses that created such serious problems for the Democratic household gave encouragement to the relatively new Republican party, known for its opposition to the extension of slavery. Abraham Lincoln of Illinois won the Republican presidential nomination. A fourth alternative offered to the voters was the newly established Constitutional Union party with John Bell of Tennessee as its standard-bearer. The party hoped to attract the conservative, moderate citizens who abhorred sectional antagonisms over the slavery question and who wanted to preserve the union above all else. With the notable exception of the Republican party, the old and new parties of 1860 found endorsement and commitment in Tennessee.

For the first time in Tennessee's presidential politics there was a three-way race, a new development that doubtless bothered and confused at least some of the voters. Old-line Whigs, however, had minimal difficulties with the somewhat altered political situation, for they simply changed hats (again) and embraced Bell's Constitutional Union party—with obvious satisfaction and enthusiasm. In the divided Democratic camp the preponderant majority of the state's Jacksonians aligned with the Southern Democratic party, while a substantially smaller number endorsed Douglas. Since much has already been written about the 1860 campaign in Tennessee, there is little need to reiterate its details here except to say that the state was a very active center of electioneering by representatives of all three parties.[1] The debates unavoidably centered on the paramount questions of protection of southern property rights (i.e., slavery) and preservation of the union.

What is most striking about the 1860 election in Tennessee is that, despite the volatile circumstances of that contest, the actual voting returns conveyed the theme of politics as usual; this was not true nationwide, of course. John Bell emerged as the winner in the state, but only because the Democratic party was split. He received 68,768 votes, Breckinridge captured 64,406, and Douglas was a very poor third with only 11,410 votes. One slightly surprising feature of the aggregate statewide vote is that it exceeded the 1859 gubernatorial turnout by only 330 votes. Perhaps the extremely small increment mirrored voter confusion that caused some to stay at home on election day. Even a cursory examination of the statistics should enable one to see that 1860 represents continuity rather than change (see Tables 7.1 and 7.2).[2] Not clear from the data in Table 7.1 is that Bell actually carried the Third and Tenth congressional districts, but with only a plurality of the votes. Thus altogether Bell won a total of seven out of the state's ten districts. Bell prevailed in two of the state's sections, East and West Tennessee, in the former by a clear majority of the votes but in the latter by a plurality.

While referring to the state's sections, it should be observed that Douglas's only show of stregth was in West Tennessee. He had a strong following in and around Memphis, which accounted for most of his votes in that region.[3] He won 20 percent of West Tennessee's vote or about 7,500 votes (3,000 of which came from Shelby County). Douglas outpolled Breckinridge in seven West Tennessee counties: Fayette, Hardeman, Haywood, Lauderdale, McNairy, Shelby, and Tipton.[4] Douglas's strength was in counties with heavy percentages of blacks, a fact that seems to run counter to the notion that as the Northern Democratic candidate he could expect little or no backing in such areas (see Table 7.3). Douglas actually carried only one county in the entire state—Tipton. Four of the counties—Fayette, Hardeman, Haywood, and Shelby—were located in the Tenth District, a congressional district which gave Douglas 35.1 percent of its total vote; Breckinridge received only 16.8 percent. Douglas captured nearly 10 percent of the vote in the Ninth District, also located in West Tennessee. Elsewhere in the state, Douglas and the Northern Democrats failed to make a respectable showing. Without design or forethought Douglas succeeded in spoiling the state for the Democrats, thereby giving the electoral votes to Bell and the Constitutional Union party. Throughout the South in 1860, "simply by keeping the Democratic party divided the Douglasites served Constitutional Unionism well."[5]

Comparing again the 1856 and 1860 presidential and 1859 gubernatorial contests, one is impressed with the remarkable stability indicated by the data (see Tables 7.1 and 7.2). The percentages of

Table 7.1. Percentage of Votes for Anti-Democrats, by Congressional
District (1856, 1859, 1860)

District	1856 Fillmore (presidential)	1859 Netherland (gubernatorial)	1860 Bell (presidential)
1	49.9	50.9	50.9
2	51.5	51.7	52.7
3	47.7	47.9	48.1
4	45.4	46.6	44.9
5	52.4	50.9	51.2
6	33.3	33.6	33.7
7	40.7	41.3	42.5
8	54.2	53.1	52.5
9	48.7	48.5	50.1
10	49.7	47.8	48.1

Table 7.2. Percentage of Votes for Anti-Democrats, by Sections (1856,
1859, 1860)

Section	1856 Fillmore (presidential)	1859 Netherland (gubernatorial)	1860 Bell (presidential)
East	51.4	51.8	51.9
Middle	44.0	43.9	44.1
West	48.5	47.4	48.9
STATE	47.3	47.2	47.6

support for the anti-Democratic candidate, regardless of party label,
are so close in these three elections as to be nearly identical. Regardless of how one compares the electoral behavior of the congressional
districts in 1856, 1859, and 1860, there is not a single instance in
which the percentage, from one election to another, varied as much
as 2 percent. Bell's level of proportional support in the districts in
1860 was extremely close to Netherland's in 1859, further testimony

Table 7.3. Data on Counties Showing Douglas Strength in 1860

County	Total population	Black population	Percentage black
Fayette	24,327	15,501	63.7
Hardeman	17,769	7,264	40.9
Haywood	19,232	11,067	57.5
Lauderdale	7,559	2,875	38.0
McNairy	14,732	1,922	13.1
Shelby	48,092	17,229	35.8
Tipton	10,705	5,297	49.5

Source: Population of the United States in 1860 (Washington, 1864), pp. 466–67.

of the continuity. The only district to give a majority to Bell but not to Netherland was the Ninth; even so, Bell's advantage over Netherland was only 1.6 percent.

To argue that Bell's victory in Tennessee (with only 47.6 percent of the statewide vote) represented a break from the Democratic trend evident consistently since the 1853 gubernatorial election is to misread the results. After all, the *combined* Democratic vote in 1860 was 52.4 percent (it had been 52.8 in the 1859 race). Furthermore, to see the state's vote in the presidential election as some sort of referendum on the question of secession is to misread the evidence and to impose an unwarranted interpretation upon the campaign; nor was it a test of secession sentiment elsewhere in the South.[6] To be sure, there were differences in 1860, not the least of which was the fragmentation of the Jacksonian party. Moreover, the questions of slavery and permanence of the union were central to the debates, unlike previous campaigns in Tennessee. But all in all, the voters responded on election day in much the same way they had in the previous presidential race (1856) and in the immediately preceding gubernatorial contest (1859). *Plus ça change, plus c'est la même chose.*

But in 1861 things would be different.

Bibliographical Essay

What follows is a limited, selective discussion of the most pertinent primary and secondary materials upon which I have based my study of Tennessee's antebellum politics. I therefore make no attempt here to replicate the footnotes found in the preceding chapters, though one may search them for a fuller comprehension of the sources utilized.

Two general studies on the pre-Civil War period are especially recommended for providing the larger framework of economic and social developments, as well as political; they are Charles S. Sydnor, *The Development of Southern Sectionalism, 1819-1848* (Baton Rouge, 1948), and Avery O. Craven, *The Growth of Southern Nationalism, 1848-1861* (Baton Rouge, 1953). A much newer work of great importance to the field of southern political history is William J. Cooper, Jr., *The South and the Politics of Slavery, 1828-1856* (Baton Rouge, 1978). Cooper's thesis, which I find debatable, is that antebellum southern politics revolved exclusively around the one central issue of slavery. Cooper's tremendously impressive research in primary materials must be reckoned with, however, as he builds a case for his interpretation. A work of nearly ancient vintage is Arthur C. Cole, *The Whig Party in the South* (Washington, 1913), still the only comprehensive survey of this party. Cole identifies the Whig party's southern branch with the planter, slaveholding aristocracy of the region—a position subsequently challenged by a number of scholars. Regrettably, no one has yet produced a study of the Democratic party in the South, although there are studies of the party in certain states. One other monograph deserving mention here is a study by Ralph A. Wooster, *Politicians, Planters, and Plain Folk: Courthouse and Statehouse in the Upper South, 1850–1860* (Knoxville, 1975). This volume is a companion to his earlier survey of the Lower South. Wooster's is a treasure trove of information on local governments in the region, along with statistical findings about the men who led those governments.

One general work of importance is Richard P. McCormick's *The Second American Party System: Party Formation in the Jacksonian Era* (Chapel Hill, 1966). I have been guided by his depiction of parties as essentially electoral machines. Moreover, his is the best, concise survey of the development of two-party politics in all of the states of the nation. His findings about the newly emerging importance of the presidential elections, vis-á-vis the gubernatorial, are borne out in the Tennessee experience. The McCormick study ends with the 1840 presidential contest which presents an obvious problem for those wishing to follow two-party politics in the important decades of the 1840s and 1850s. In a sense the new book by Michael F. Holt, *The Political Crisis of the 1850s* (New York, 1978), fills part of that void. Holt deals with the nation's political developments from the second half of the 1840s to secession. He argues that the two-party system, as it had been known, broke down or collapsed in the early 1850s because the Whig and Democratic parties had more and more in common, thereby blurring or even eliminating the real differences between them. This trend toward consensus rather than conflict ushered in the demise of the strong, competitive two-party system. Holt's is a fascinating and unique thesis, one that is new grist for the scholars' mills.

Shifting to Tennessee in particular, it must be said that the best starting point is Philip M. Hamer, *Tennessee: A History, 1673–1932* (4 vols., New York, 1933). Hamer's discussion and analysis of nineteenth-century Tennessee has yet to be surpassed. Political and economic circumstances are the subject of Thomas P. Abernethy's *From Frontier to Plantation in Tennessee: A Study in Frontier Democracy* (Chapel Hill, 1932)—a book somewhat marred by the author's bias against Andrew Jackson. The work overall is stronger on developments prior to the "revolt" against Jackson. Eric R. Lacy takes one of the state's three sections and does an able analysis of its political developments in his *Vanquished Volunteers: East Tennessee Sectionalism from Statehood to Secession* (Johnson City, Tenn., 1965). A fairly comprehensive survey of state politics is found in Mary E. R. Campbell, *The Attitude of Tennesseans toward the Union, 1847–1861* (New York, 1961). Actually Campbell's work is much older than the publication date would lead one to believe, for it is a 1937 dissertation. Extremely helpful to an understanding of economic developments and their relationship to politics is the book by Stanley J. Folmsbee, *Sectionalism and Internal Improvements in Tennessee, 1796–1845* (Knoxville, 1939). Unfortunately, Folmsbee's book concludes on the eve of the boom times in Tennessee's railroad construction; what is needed is a companion volume treating the fifteen years immediately prior to the Civil War. The only available study of antebellum banking is Claude A. Campbell, *The Development of Banking in Tennessee* (Nashville, 1932), a work much in need of revision and updating.

One very useful approach to acquiring information about and understanding of Tennessee's antebellum decades is through biography. Indispensable to a grasp of the state's political developments in this period is the biography of James K. Polk by Charles G. Sellers. Two volumes have appeared: *James K. Polk: Jacksonian, 1795–1843* (Princeton, 1957) and *James K. Polk: Continentalist, 1843–1846* (Princeton, 1966). To overlook these volumes would be to miss a rich offering of state political history through the person of James K. Polk, a man in the vortex of political maneuverings and battles. While there are other biographies of Tennessee figures, none gives the breadth and depth of coverage that Sellers's volumes do. Although plentiful, biographical studies of Andrew Jackson do not offer much, so far as Jackson's involvement with state politics in the 1830s and 1840s is concerned. Among his several biographical studies of southern leaders, Joseph Howard Parks had done two that are pertinent for pre-Civil War Tennessee. They are: *Felix Grundy: Champion of Democracy* (University, La., 1940), and *John Bell of Tennessee* (Baton Rouge, 1950). Since Grundy died in 1840, his biography is less valuable on the 1835–60 period than is Parks's study of Bell. Once Bell went to the United States Senate in 1847, however, he was less directly tied to the political battles in the state, excepting his own efforts at reelection. Two other helpful biographies, both of anti-Jacksonians, are Thomas B. Alexander, *Thomas A. R. Nelson of East Tennessee* (Nashville, 1956), and E. Merton Coulter, *William G. Brownlow: Fighting Parson of the Southern Highlands* (Chapel Hill, 1937).

Unpublished biographical studies have proven quite valuable; for example, Patricia P. Clark, "A.O.P. Nicholson of Tennessee: Editor, Statesman, and Jurist" (M.A. thesis, University of Tennessee, 1965); William J. Burke, Jr., "The Career of William Trousdale in Tennessee Politics" (M.A. thesis, Vanderbilt University, 1967); James T. Horton, Jr., "The Evolution of a Whig Editor in Tennessee: Allen A. Hall" (M.A. thesis, Vanderbilt University, 1966); and Charles F. Bryan, Jr., "Robert Hatton of Tennessee" (M.A. thesis, University of Georgia, 1973).

Prominent political figures have been treated in several doctoral dissertations. One of the oldest of these is Lunia Paul Gresham, "The Public Career of Hugh Lawson White" (Ph.D. dissertation, Vanderbilt University, 1943). Clement L. Grant has done a very able study, "The Public Career of Cave Johnson" (Ph.D. dissertation, Vanderbilt University, 1951), and R. Beeler Satterfield has done likewise in his "Andrew Jackson Donelson: A Moderate Nationalist Jacksonian" (Ph.D. dissertation, Johns Hopkins University, 1961). The best work on Andrew Johnson's career as a Tennessee politician is H. Blair Bentley's "Andrew Johnson, Governor of Tennessee, 1853–57" (Ph.D. dissertation, University of Tennessee, 1972).

Apart from these unpublished biographical treatments, there have been a number of other theses and dissertations of much importance to my study. A quite old, but very reliable examination of the state's Whig movement is Powell Moore's "The Establishment of the Whig Party in Tennessee" (Ph.D. dissertation, Indiana University, 1932). A work closely paralleling my own and upon which I have relied frequently is John E. Tricamo, "Tennessee Politics, 1845–1861" (Ph.D. dissertation, Columbia University, 1965). Tricamo's study is particularly strong on the theme of factionalism within the political parties. Of immense importance because of its quantitative approach to state politics is Frank M. Lowrey, III, "Tennessee Voters during the Second Two-Party System, 1836–1860: A Study in Voter Constancy and in Socio-Economic and Demographic Distinctions" (Ph.D. dissertation, University of Alabama, 1973). Although it must be used with some caution (as explained in my Chapter 6 above), it is the best and virtually only work on the problems of economic and social influences upon voting behavior in the state. Replete with scores of tables, it is solidly grounded in immense data gathered and reported by Lowrey. From time to time in my chapters on Tennessee politics, I have referred to my own M.A. and Ph.D. studies—as a sort of shorthand to serve in lieu of a fuller citation of sources. My thesis, "Political Struggles in Tennessee, 1839–1843" (Vanderbilt University, 1962), is an examination of Polk's three gubernatorial campaigns. Restricting myself in the dissertation to the presidential elections, I focused in "The Jacksonian Party on Trial: Presidential Politics in Tennessee, 1836–1856" (Vanderbilt University, 1965) on how those particular campaigns were carried out in the state.

I have depended heavily upon the newspapers of the period, and as the footnotes show, I have confined myself to the papers published in Nashville. This decision was based upon my discovery that the journals in the capital city were clearly the most important ones in the state and second, that they reprinted a great deal of material from other places throughout the state. Thus in reading through the files of Nashville newspapers one is able to get a firm grasp of what is going on around the state. I devoted my research energies to the following: the *Nashville Republican,* the *Nashville Republican Banner,* the *Nashville Whig,* the *National Banner and Nashville Whig,* the *Republican Banner and Nashville Whig,* the *Nashville Union,* and the *Nashville Union and American.* During presidential campaigns, it was sometimes the custom of one of these newspapers to issue a special political paper. One such example was the *Spirit of '76,* which I examined. Since all of the Nashville newspapers were blatantly partisan, political news was top priority for them—making them an impressive source during this period.

Of all the various manuscript collections pertinent to the topic a number were of special merit, among them the following Library of Congress collections: the Andrew Jackson Donelson Papers, the Andrew Jackson Papers, the Andrew Johnson Papers, the James K. Polk Papers, and the Martin Van Buren Papers. As one may readily observe, these collections all involve prominent Democrats; curiously, there are no significant collections involving Tennessee Whigs among the Library of Congress holdings. Other valuable materials on state Democratic politics are found in the Felix Grundy Papers, Southern Historical Collection, University of North Carolina; the William B. Lewis Correspondence, New York Public Library; and the Cave Johnson Correspondence, the Historical Society of Pennsylvania. Luckily for the historian, there are available holdings that focus on the Whig side of the story; for example, the Gustavus A. Henry Papers, Southern Historical Collection, University of North Carolina, and the Thomas A.R. Nelson Papers, Lawson McGhee Library (Knoxville). But the most outstanding collection involving Whig politics in Tennessee is probably the David Campbell Papers, Duke University. For a more complete listing of manuscript materials pertinent to Tennessee's antebellum politics, see the bibliography at the conclusion of my dissertation.

Researchers in nineteenth-century Tennessee have been richly blessed by the appearance over the years, and especially recently, of an outpouring of published primary materials. The oldest of these is Nancy N. Scott, ed., *A Memoir of Hugh Lawson White* (Philadelphia, 1856). It provides information and insight on White's involvement in the revolt against Andrew Jackson and his campaign for the presidency in 1836, as well as subsequent political events. A somewhat surprising source is the *Messages of the Governors of Tennessee* (8 vols.; Nashville, 1952–72), edited by Robert H. White. The surprise is that

White has filled the volumes with all kinds of valuable primary materials (especially excerpts from newspapers), in addition to the actual messages issued by the various governors. An understanding of the Tennessee political scene in the 1850s has been enhanced by the publication of *Pen and Sword: The Life and Journals of Randal W. McGavock* (Nashville, 1959), edited by Herschel Gower and Jack Allen.

Of incalculable and indispensable value to studying Tennessee in the pre-Civil War period are the volumes of edited correspondence, all of which deal with Democrats. Of great worth because of the documents on his postpresidential years are the volumes of the *Correspondence of Andrew Jackson* (7 vols.; Washington, 1926–35), edited by John Spencer Bassett. These are by no means definitive, for Bassett was quite selective; moreover, they do not measure up to the present high standards of historical editing. Nevertheless, the volumes are replete with valuable letters exchanged between Jackson and other political leaders. Currently the University of Tennessee is sponsoring a new publication of Jackson's papers which in time will certainly supersede Bassett's earlier work. Jackson's close political ally, James K. Polk, is another figure on the Tennessee scene whose correspondence is being edited and published. The volumes published thus far are unrivaled in their richness of material on political developments in the state in the 1830s and early 1840s. Therefore one cannot afford to neglect the *Correspondence of James K. Polk* (5 vols. to date; Nashville, 1969–), edited by Herbert Weaver, et al. Closely paralleling the Polk volumes as a cornucopia of information on state politics are the volumes on Polk's rival within the Democratic party, Andrew Johnson. Superbly edited by LeRoy P. Graf and Ralph W. Haskins, *The Papers of Andrew Johnson* (5 vols. to date; Knoxville, 1967–), provide immensely valuable insight on developments in the state. The first three of those volumes are pertinent to the antebellum decades. There is no question that the Jackson, Polk, and Johnson editions of correspondence and papers make the job of the researcher more convenient and more rewarding, although one gets essentially the Democratic point of view. Again, it is regrettable that there is no substantial cache of Whig letters waiting to be edited.

This brief bibliographical essay should provide clues to the kinds of general and specific materials that I have utilized; an examination of the chapters' footnotes will offer further illumination and assistance.

Notes

CHAPTER I

1. For a brief review of Tennessee in the territorial period, see Paul H. Bergeron, *Paths of the Past: Tennessee, 1770-1970* (Knoxville, 1979), pp. 19-26.

2. Richard P. McCormick, *The Second American Party System: Party Formation in the Jacksonian Era* (Chapel Hill, 1966), pp. 223-24. McCormick is incorrect in asserting that John Sevier became an integral part of the William Blount faction.

3. Ibid., p. 226; Charles G. Sellers, *James K. Polk: Jacksonian, 1795-1843* (Princeton, 1957), pp. 68, 69; Thomas P. Abernethy, *From Frontier to Plantation in Tennessee: A Study in Frontier Democracy* (Chapel Hill, 1932), pp. 292-93.

4. Sellers, *Polk: Jacksonian,* pp. 70-71; Abernethy, *Frontier to Plantation,* p. 238.

5. Sellers, *Polk: Jacksonian,* pp. 88-91; McCormick, *Second Party System,* pp. 226-27; Abernethy, *Frontier to Plantation,* pp. 241-42.

6. Sellers, *Polk: Jacksonian,* pp. 137, 197.

7. Ibid., pp. 136, 140, 197.

8. Ibid., pp. 173, 179, 196, 200. For a detailed treatment of individual and group reaction to nullification, see Paul H. Bergeron, "Tennessee's Response to the Nullification Crisis," *Journal of Southern History,* XXXIX (1973), 23-44.

9. Sellers, *Polk: Jacksonian,* pp. 137-38, 198-99. James S. Chase seriously questions the likelihood that Eaton and Overton wanted to block a possible Van Buren nomination; curiously enough, the only information about this alleged plot came from the pen of fellow Tennessean William B. Lewis. See Chase, *Emergence of the Presidential Nominating Convention, 1789-1832* (Urbana, 1973), pp. 270-71. In his discussion of the 1832 Democratic convention, Richard B. Latner makes no mention of the reported efforts by Eaton and Overton to thwart Van Buren's nomination. See Latner, *The Presidency of Andrew Jackson* (Athens, Ga., 1979), pp. 129-37.

10. Voter participation in Tennessee in 1828 was close to 50 percent but dropped in 1832 to 28.8 percent. See McCormick, *Second Party System,* p. 227; Richard P. McCormick, "New Perspectives on Jacksonian Politics," *American Historical Review,* LXV (1960), 292.

11. Sydnor, *The Development of Southern Sectionalism, 1819-1848* (Baton Rouge, 1948), p. 316.

12. The statewide population in 1830 was 681,904; by 1860 it had increased to a total of 1,109,801. It should be pointed out that although East Tennessee had 26.9 percent of the state population in 1860, it had only 25.6 percent in 1850. These census data are gleaned from U.S. Bureau of the Census, *The Fifth Census of the United States, 1830* (Washington, 1832), pp. 109-10; *Seventh Census, 1850* (Washington, 1853), pp. 564-67; *Eighth Census, 1860* (Washington, 1864), pp. 456-59.

13. *Nashville Union,* Oct. 25, 1852.

CHAPTER II

1. To arrive at the percentages shown in Table 2.1, I amassed electoral data from several different sources. For all of the presidential contests I followed the information provided in W. Dean Burnham, *Presidential Ballots, 1836-1892* (Baltimore, 1955), pp. 742-62. For the 1835, 1837, 1841, 1843, 1845, 1853, 1857, and 1859 gubernatorial races I used returns found in the *Tennessee House Journal* or the *Senate Journal.* For the 1847, 1849, 1851, and 1855 elections I utilized the data provided in Mary E.R. Campbell, *The Attitude of Tennesseans toward the Union, 1847-1861* (New York, 1961), pp. 265-74. For the 1839 governor's race I used the figures found in the *Nashville Republican Banner,* Aug. 3-12, 1839, and the *Knoxville Register,* Oct. 22, 1839. There are some minor discrepancies between my statewide percentages and those found in Anne H. Hopkins and William Lyons, *Tennessee Votes: 1799-1976* (Knoxville, 1978), pp. 23-41.

2. I am grateful to Donald L. Winters of Vanderbilt University for his assistance with the linear regression test and with the Democratic mean and standard deviation statistics cited below. The 1839 election saw the most significant increment in Democratic percentage (nearly a full 12 percentage points) during the entire period. Polk's victory in that year seems to stand out as an exception to the slow and gradual growth of Democratic strength.

3. For Tables 2.3, 2.5, and 2.7 the same sources of election statistics cited for the preparation of Table 2.1 were used.

4. For another map of the thirteen districts, see Stanley B. Parsons, William W. Beach, and Dan Hermann, *United States Congressional Districts, 1788-1841* (Westport, Conn., 1978), p. 363.

5. To derive the correlation coefficients, I utilized the Spearman rho rank-order correlation test. This particular test was used, because there are few samples involved and because I am comparing data for one year (voting strength) with data for a period of years (black population, 1835-41). The Spearman correlation coefficients for the other four elections are: $1836 = +.143$; $1839 = -.176$; $1840 = -.148$; and $1841 = -.137$.

6. Brian G. Walton, "The Second Party System in Tennessee," East Tennessee Historical Society's *Publications,* no. 43 (1971), pp. 20-21. I am puzzled at Walton's classification of the Ninth District as a West Tennessee district, for it was composed of five Middle and two West Tennessee counties.

7. Ibid., pp. 22-23, 24-27.

8. This table is based upon data gleaned from *The Seventh Census of the United States, 1850* (Washington, 1853), pp. 573-74. Following the decision of Parsons et al. in *Congressional Districts,* I have included free blacks in with the slave population figures. It is important to note the omission of the six counties that appear on the 1850 census but were not in existence at the time of the congressional redistricting in 1842: Decatur (1846), Grundy (1844), Hancock (1844), Lewis (1843), Macon (1842), and Scott (1849). These six counties had an aggregate population in 1850 of 27,727 and a total slave population (including free blacks) of 2,811. According to state law—which seems to have been observed sometimes and disregarded at other times—counties created after congressional redistricting were to continue to vote with their parent counties in statewide elections until the next reapportionment of the districts.

9. The Spearman coefficients are: $1843 = +.036$; $1844 = -.082$; $1845 = +.009$; $1847 = +.036$; $1848 = +.091$; $1849 = +.091$; $1851 = +.127$.

10. Districts 1, 2, and 3 were East Tennessee districts; districts 4, 5, 6, and 8 were in Middle Tennessee; and districts 9 and 10 were West Tennessee districts. The Seventh District contained both Middle and West Tennessee counties.

11. This table is based upon data from the *Population of the United States in 1860* (Washington, 1864), pp. 466-67. As with the other two tables on population data by congressional districts, this table includes free blacks in with the slave population figures. Five counties were created after the 1852 redistricting and before the 1860 census was taken: Cheatham (1856), Cumberland (1856), Putnam (1854), Sequatchie (1857), and Union (1853). Together they had a total population of 27,513 and a slave population (including free blacks) of 3,205. They are omitted from Table 2.8, since they were supposed to vote with their parent counties until the next redistricting.

12. The Spearman coefficients are: 1852 = +.285; 1853 = −.164; 1855 = −.164; 1856 = −.042; 1857 = −.055; 1859 = +.273.

13. Occasionally in the newspapers one can find voting returns for civil districts or precincts.

14. Lowrey, "Tennessee Voters during the Second Two-Party System, 1836-1860: A Study in Voter Constancy and in Socio-Economic and Demographic Distinctions" (Ph.D. dissertation, University of Alabama, 1973), pp. 28, 33. See his Table 1-1, pp. 29-32, for the listing of counties and their increases or decreases in Democratic percentages.

15. Ibid., pp. 36-37. To arrive at the correlation coefficients, Lowrey used the Pearsonian product moment test.

16. Ibid., pp. 34, 35, 36.

17. Walton, "Second Party System," pp. 23-24.

18. Lowrey, "Tennessee Voters," pp. 38-39. My admittedly less sophisticated analysis of the electoral behavior of the congressional districts (1852-59) gives a somewhat different picture, so far as voter consistency in the 1850s is concerned.

19. Ibid., pp. 195, 196, 198-99, 201-2. Since Burnham, *Presidential Ballots,* reports election returns for 73 counties in 1844, it is not clear why Lowrey deals with only 70.

20. Ibid., pp. 206-9.

21. Ibid., pp. 203-5; Wooster, *Politicians, Planters, and Plain Folk: Courthouse and Statehouse in the Upper South, 1850-1860* (Knoxville, 1975), p. 51. As Lowrey points out, all Tennessee counties experienced increases in land value during the ten years from 1850 to 1860; hence his division into three categories of increase: rapid, moderate, and slight.

CHAPTER III

1. In early 1836 one of Polk's regular correspondents insisted that it had been Bell's intention all along to overthrow the Jacksonian party and become head of the White movement in the state so that Bell might become "the greatest man in Tennessee." See George Gammon to James K. Polk, Jan. 28, 1836, in Herbert Weaver, et al., eds., *Correspondence of James K. Polk* (5 vols. to date; Nashville, 1969-), III, 464.

2. For examples of letters exchanged in 1833 relative to Polk's ambitions to be chosen speaker, see ibid., II, 99ff.

3. Details of the 1834 speakership race are in Charles G. Sellers, *James K. Polk: Jacksonian, 1795-1843* (Princeton, 1957), pp. 234-42; Joseph H. Parks, *John Bell of Tennessee* (Baton Rouge, 1950), pp. 69-72, 74-75. There were personal as well as political scars left by the Polk-Bell rivalry over the speakership. Polk later reported that the two men did not speak to each other again until a specially arranged meeting took place in Polk's presidential office in January 1848. See Milo M. Quaife, ed., *The Diary of James K. Polk* (4 vols.; Chicago, 1910), III, 258-60, 264-65, 284-85.

4. Sellers, *Polk: Jacksonian*, pp. 243-45, 248-49; Parks, *Bell*, pp. 75-77. The flap over Bell's Murfreesboro speech is discussed in letters in Weaver, *Correspondence of Polk*, II, 517ff.

5. Sellers, *Polk: Jacksonian*, pp. 274-75; Parks, *Bell*, pp. 106-8.

6. Laughlin to Polk, Aug. 30, 1835, in Weaver, *Correspondence of Polk*, III, 279; Donelson to Martin Van Buren, Sept. 25, 1835, Martin Van Buren Papers, Library of Congress; Parks, *Bell*, pp. 113-14, 118; Sellers, *Polk: Jacksonian*, pp. 292-95.

7. Sellers, *Polk: Jacksonian*, pp. 296-97; Parks, *Bell*, p. 118; Andrew C. Hays to Polk, Dec. 23, 1835, in Weaver, *Correspondence of Polk*, III, 407; William R. Rucker to Polk, Jan. 17, 1836, in ibid., 443; *Nashville Union*, Dec. 26, 1835.

8. On the 1819 decision against a constitutional convention, see Philip M. Hamer, *Tennessee: A History, 1673-1932* (4 vols.; New York, 1933), I, 318-19. On the 1831 and 1833 votes on the proposed constitutional conventions, see Robert H. White, ed., *Messages of the Governors of Tennessee* (8 vols.; Nashville, 1952-72), II, 427-30, 449-50.

9. Of the sixty delegates elected to the constitutional convention, no more than half a dozen were prominently known in the state. Almost exactly two-thirds of the convention delegates (38) were farmers, while only seventeen were lawyers. A listing of the delegates, accompanied by brief biographical sketches, may be found in White, *Messages*, II, 466-69.

10. In an article by Robert Cassell, "Newton Cannon and the Constitutional Convention of 1834," *Tennessee Historical Quarterly*, XV (1956), 224-42, the importance of the tax controversy is accented. For comments about the new constitution, see Ralph A. Wooster, *Politicians, Planters, and Plain Folk: Courthouse and Statehouse in the Upper South, 1850-1860* (Knoxville, 1975), pp. 17-18, 25, 61, 85, 106, 125. Wooster concludes that Tennessee was among the most democratic of the Southern states.

11. The controversy over depriving free blacks the ballot may be followed in several studies: Chase C. Mooney, *Slavery in Tennessee* (Bloomington, Ind., 1957), pp. 80-82; Mooney, "The Question of Slavery and the Free Negro in the Tennessee Constitutional Convention of 1834," *Journal of Southern History*, XII (1946), 503-6; White, *Messages*, II, 524n, 525n, 601-10.

12. The matter of emancipation of slaves is discussed in: Mooney, *Slavery in Tennessee*, pp. 77-80; Mooney, "Question of Slavery," pp. 489-97, 500-2; White, *Messages*, II, 610-31; and Joshua W. Caldwell, *Studies in the Constitutional History of Tennessee* (Cincinnati, 1895), pp. 134-40. In 1830 Tennessee's slave population was 141,603 and there were 4,555 free blacks. See U.S. Bureau of the Census, *Negro Population, 1790-1915* (Washington, 1918), p. 57.

13. For a county-by-county list of votes on ratification of the constitution, see White, *Messages*, II,658-59.

14. Stanley J. Folmsbee, *Sectionalism and Internal Improvements in Tennessee, 1796-1845* (Knoxville, 1939), pp. 78-80, 84-101; White, *Messages,* II, 288-90.

15. Folmsbee, *Sectionalism and Internal Improvements,* pp. 116-19, 121-26; White, *Messages,* III, 47-48, 58-68, 76-86.

16. Folmsbee, *Sectionalism and Internal Improvements,* pp. 126-28.

17. Ibid., 148-51, 163-69; White, *Messages,* III, 182-85.

18. Folmsbee, *Sectionalism and Internal Improvements,* pp. 170-76.

19. R. Beeler Satterfield, "The Uncertain Trumpet of the Tennessee Jacksonians," *Tennessee Historical Quarterly,* XXVI (1967), 83-84; Frank B. Williams, Jr., "Samuel Hervey Laughlin, Polk's Political Handyman," *Tennessee Historical Quarterly,* XXIV (1965), 359; Sellers, *Polk: Jacksonian,* pp. 247-49; Parks, *Bell,* pp. 77-78; James T. Horton, Jr., "The Evolution of a Whig Editor in Tennessee: Allen A. Hall" (M.A. thesis, Vanderbilt University, 1966), pp. 49-50. A recent study of Alabama politics emphasizes that the party press was an essential element of politics, especially the newspapers in the state capital. See J. Mills Thornton, III, *Politics and Power in a Slave Society: Alabama, 1800-1860* (Baton Rouge, 1978), p. 128.

20. Samuel H. Laughlin to Polk, Oct. 20, 1834, in Weaver, *Correspondence of Polk,* II, 536-57; Samuel G. Smith to Polk, Nov. 20, 1834, Dec. 18, 1834, in ibid., 556-57, 581; Williams, "Laughlin, Political Handyman," pp. 363, 365-67; Satterfield, "Uncertain Trumpet," pp. 84-85; Sellers, *Polk: Jacksonian,* pp. 298-99.

21. Williams, "Laughlin, Political Handyman," pp. 367-68; Satterfield, "Uncertain Trumpet," pp. 86, 87-89; Sellers, *Polk: Jacksonian,* pp. 323-24, 343-44, 360-61.

22. Horton, "Allen Hall," pp. 57-58, 87-88, 94-95; Sellers, *Polk: Jacksonian,* p. 347.

23. Some other southern states staged conventions in the 1830s. Alabama Democrats, for example, held a party convention in 1835 to choose presidential electors for the 1836 contest. Alabama Whigs, however, held a convention in 1839, its only one in the decade. See Thornton, *Politics and Power,* pp. 118, 118n, 119, 119n. Mississippi experienced party conventions with regularity in the 1830s. See Edwin A. Miles, *Jackson Democracy in Mississippi* (Chapel Hill, 1960), pp. 138-40, 163. Richard P. McCormick notes that among the Old South states there had been some use of state conventions before 1839 in Virginia, North Carolina, and Georgia, whereas Kentucky used the convention system in 1828. See McCormick, *The Second American Party System: Party Formation in the Jacksonian Era* (Chapel Hill, 1966), p. 251; for his observations on Alabama, Mississippi, and Louisiana, see ibid., p. 324. Despite the absence of clear-cut party organization and structure in Tennessee in the 1830s, there does not seem to have been an antiparty attitude that characterized political leaders in other states, especially Whigs in Michigan. See Ronald P. Formisano, *The Birth of Mass Political Parties: Michigan, 1827-1861* (Princeton, 1971), pp. 57, 58, 60, 68, 70, 72.

24. The election statistics in Table 3.1 have been drawn from several sources. The 1833 results are from the *Journal of the Senate of the State of Tennessee* (Knoxville, 1833), p. 42. The 1835 and 1837 returns are respectively from the *Senate Journal* (Columbia, 1835), pp. 17-18, and the *Senate Journal* (Nashville, 1837), p. 28. The 1839 totals were compiled from the *Nashville Republican Banner,* Aug. 3-12, 1839 and the *Knoxville Register,* Oct. 22, 1839. The 1836 presidential returns are from W. Dean Burnham, *Presidential Ballots, 1836-1892* (Baltimore, 1955), p. 742. The data in Table

3.2 are drawn from Table 2.1 in Chapter 2 above. The voter participation figures in Table 3.3 are compiled from Richard P. McCormick, "New Perspectives on Jacksonian Politics," *American Historical Review,* LXV (1960), 292; McCormick, *Party System,* pp. 230-31; Brian G. Walton, "The Second Party System in Tennessee," East Tennessee Historical Society's *Publications,* no. 43 (1971), p. 19; and my own calculations. Although McCormick says that the 1835 turnout was approximately 73 percent, my own calculations, based on his figures for the 1836 presidential election, show that the range in 1835 would have to be something like 78-80 percent and in 1837 about 80-82 percent.

25. The expansion of the voting franchise by virtue of the new state constitution seems to have had no impact upon voter turnout in 1835—when compared to the 1833 legislative races which drew nearly 90,800 votes.

26. *Nashville Republican,* July 9, 11, 21, 23, 1835.

27. Ibid., July 18, 1835.

28. Ibid., June 4, 1835.

29. Ibid., March 10, 19, 1835. Newton Cannon's candidacy was not publicly announced in the *Republican* until Apr. 25, 1835.

30. Powell Moore, "The Establishment of the Whig Party in Tennessee" (Ph.D. dissertation, Indiana University, 1932), p. 173; John H. Bills to Polk, May 19, 1835, in Weaver, *Correspondence of Polk,* III, 197; R.H. Barry to John S. Claybrooke, July 18, 1835, Claybrooke Papers, Tennessee Historical Society. See also the *Nashville Republican,* May 26, 1835, concerning Carroll's West Tennessee speech in which he expressed his preference for Van Buren. Cooper is incorrect when he claims that in 1835 Carroll "decided to avoid combining his appeal with one for the unpopular Van Buren." William J. Cooper, Jr., *The South and the Politics of Slavery, 1828-1856* (Baton Rouge, 1978), p. 85.

31. *Nashville Republican,* Aug. 1, 25, 1835; McCormick, *Party System,* p. 229; Polk to Andrew Jackson, Aug. 14, 1835, in Weaver, *Correspondence of Polk,* III, 266.

32. Carroll withdrew from consideration in March, long before the campaign got underway. In his published letter, Carroll decided not to "trouble the public" with his reasons for bowing out of contention. See the *Nashville Republican,* Mar. 16, 21, 1837.

33. *Nashville Republican,* Apr. 18, May 20, 1837; Polk to Andrew Jackson, May 19, 29, June 14, 1837 in Weaver, *Correspondence of Polk,* IV, 121, 130, 143; Polk to Van Buren, May 29, 1837, 132; Polk to William M. Warner, June 19, 1837, 155; Samuel H. Laughlin to Polk, May 24, 1837, 127; Horton, "Allen Hall," pp. 78-79; McCormick, *Party System,* p. 230; Sellers, *Polk: Jacksonian,* pp. 321-23, 325; John Catron to Polk, Apr. 16, 1837, in Weaver, *Correspondence of Polk,* IV, 90–91.

34. *Nashville Republican,* June 3, 29, 1837; Alfred Flournoy to Polk, July 15, 1837, in Weaver, *Correspondence of Polk,* IV, 179-80; Cave Johnson to Polk, July 30, 1837, 195.

35. *Nashville Republican,* May 25, June 1, 3, 6, 8, 10, 24, July 6, Aug. 1, 1837.

36. John Catron to Polk Apr. 16, 1837, in Weaver, *Correspondence of Polk,* IV, 91; Polk to Andrew Jackson Donelson, Aug. 6, 1837, 198; Cave Johnson to Polk, Aug. 7, 1837, 202; Robert B. Reynolds to Polk, Aug. 9, 1837, 206; *Nashville Republican,* Aug. 19, 1837. Mississippi Democrats experienced victory in the 1837 gubernatorial and legislative races, although the statewide contest was a bit confusing; see Miles, *Jacksonian Democracy,* pp. 138-40.

37. Sellers, *Polk: Jacksonian,* pp. 353-55; Paul H. Bergeron, "Political Struggles in Tennessee, 1839-1843" (M.A. thesis, Vanderbilt University, 1962). pp. 13-15.

38. Bell to Clay, May 20, 1839, quoted in Sellers, *Polk: Jacksonian,* pp. 361-62; John W. Childress to Polk, Dec. 12, 1838, in Weaver, *Correspondence of Polk,* IV, 644; Joseph H. Talbot to Polk, Dec. 18, 1838, 656.

39. For detailed summary of the campaigning by Polk and Cannon see Sellers, *Polk: Jacksonian,* pp. 366-73, and Bergeron, "Political Struggles," pp. 25-33. The campaign may be followed by examining the letters found in Weaver, *Correspondence of Polk,* V, 113ff, especially the exchange between Polk and his wife, Sarah.

40. *Nashville Whig,* Apr. 15, 29, 1839. See Bergeron, "Political Struggles," pp. 34-38.

41. Bergeron, "Political Struggles," pp. 40-43, discusses the presidential preference issue as does Sellers, *Polk: Jacksonian,* pp. 363-65, 367-68. The controversy over Van Buren's proposed visit to Tennessee in 1839 may be followed in these letters: Polk to Jackson, Feb. 7, 1839, in Weaver, *Correspondence of Polk,* V, 52-53; Francis P. Blair to Jackson, Feb. 8, 1839, in John Spencer Bassett, ed., *Correspondence of Andrew Jackson* (7 vols.; Washington, 1926-35), VI, 3; Jackson to Martin Van Buren, Mar. 4, 1839, 6. Cooper says that Polk wanted to get Van Buren to postpone or cancel his trip to Tennessee because he had to avoid public endorsement of Van Buren. Cooper, *Politics of Slavery,* p. 143. Yet Polk during the gubernatorial canvass took a strong stand in support of Van Buren.

42. Sellers, *Polk: Jacksonian,* pp. 373-74; Bergeron, "Political Struggles," pp. 51-55; Allen Hall to Henry Clay, Sept. 23, 1839, Papers of Henry Clay, Library of Congress. For comments about Polk's health and stamina see the following: Polk to Sarah Polk, May 5, 8, 12, 18, 22, 24, 28, July 1, 7, 1839 in Weaver, *Correspondence of Polk,* V, 122, 125, 128, 130, 131, 136, 159, 162; and Sarah Polk to Polk, June 25, 1839, 154. Antibank sentiment in Mississippi worked to the advantage of Democrats there who won the governor's race by a 3,000-vote margin. See Miles, *Jacksonian Democracy,* pp. 151, 153, 155. Such an issue did not emerge in Tennessee to contribute to Polk's victory.

43. Sellers, *Polk: Jacksonian,* pp. 284, 373; Hamer, *Tennessee,* I, 294; McCormick, *Party System,* p. 231.

44. Sellers, *Polk: Jacksonian,* pp. 283-84, 325-26, 373; Bergeron, "Political Struggles," p. 46. For an able discussion of Polk's own congressional electioneering in 1835 and 1837, see Joseph M. Pukl, Jr., "The Congressional Campaigns of James K. Polk, 1824-1837" (M.A. thesis, University of Tennessee, 1977), pp. 101-15, 120-24.

45. Balch to Polk, Feb. 21, 1839, in Weaver, *Correspondence of Polk,* V, 76; Sellers, *Polk: Jacksonian,* pp. 358-59, 371; Parks, *Bell,* pp. 157-62; Patricia P. Clark, "A.O.P. Nicholson of Tennessee: Editor, Statesman, and Jurist" (M.A. thesis, University of Tennessee, 1965), p. 35.

46. White, *Messages,* III, 30; Brian G. Walton, "A Matter of Timing: Elections to the United States Senate in Tennessee Before the Civil War," *Tennessee Historical Quarterly,* XXXI (1972), 132-33; Sellers, *Polk: Jacksonian,* pp. 289-90.

47. Walton, "Matter of Timing," pp. 131-34; Parks, *Bell,* pp. 144-45; Sellers, *Polk: Jacksonian,* pp. 342-43.

48. See McCormick, "New Perspectives," p. 292.

49. The pattern of gubernatorial elections outdrawing presidential in the 1830s was widespread throughout the nation. See McCormick, "New Perspectives," pp. 292, 295-96.

50. Jackson later denied having offered the vice presidency to White. See, for example, his letters to Adam Huntsman, Jan. 2, 1837, and to Andrew J. Donelson, Jan. 11, 1837, both in Bassett, *Correspondence of Jackson,* V, 447, 449. But in the spring of 1835 Jackson confided to Polk that if White stayed with the Democratic party, he would in all likelihood be chosen as vice president by the national convention. See Jackson to Polk, May 3, 1835, in Weaver, *Correspondence of Polk,* III, 184.

51. References to early approaches to White are found in Lunia Paul Gresham, "The Public Career of Hugh Lawson White" (Ph.D. dissertation, Vanderbilt University, 1943), pp. 274-75, and in Nancy N. Scott, ed., *A Memoir of Hugh Lawson White* (Philadelphia, 1856), p. 349. The December 1834 meeting of Tennessee congressmen is ably discussed in Sellers, *Polk: Jacksonian,* pp. 259-62, and Parks, *Bell,* pp. 84-88. Polk's version of these stirrings in behalf of Hugh Lawson White is conveyed in two important letters to his brother-in-law; see Polk to James Walker, Dec. 24, 25, 1834, in Weaver, *Correspondence of Polk,* II, 598-601, 603-5. Clement L. Grant argues that Johnson never intended to support White's candidacy; see Grant, "The Public Career of Cave Johnson" (Ph.D. dissertation, Vanderbilt University, 1951), p. 65.

52. Sellers, *Polk: Jacksonian,* p. 279; Eugene I. McCormac, *James K. Polk: A Political Biography* (Berkeley, 1922), p. 81; Polk to Jackson, May 15, 1835, in Bassett, *Correspondence of Jackson,* V, 346, and in Weaver, *Correspondence of Polk,* III, 193; Cave Johnson to Polk, May 1, [1835], 180; Ernest W. Hooper, "The Presidential Election of 1836 in Tennessee" (M.A. thesis, University of North Carolina, 1949), p. 61; *Nashville Republican,* Mar. 10, 1835; Jackson to Polk, May 12, 1835, in Bassett, *Correspondence of Jackson,* V, 345-46, and in Weaver, *Correspondence of Polk,* III, 191.

53. Some students of the period have interpreted Bell's Vauxhall Gardens speech (May 1835) as his "revolt" against Jackson. See, for example, A.V. Goodpasture, "John Bell's Political Revolt, and his Vauxhall Garden Speech," *Tennessee Historical Magazine,* II (1916), 254-63; Hooper, "Election of 1836," pp. 119-20. But Moore, "Establishment of Whig Party," p. 186, downplays the significance of this particular speech.

54. See Jackson to Felix Grundy, Sept. 24, 1835, Felix Grundy Papers, Southern Historical Collection, University of North Carolina Library; Scott, *Memoir,* p. 332; and White, *Messages,* III, 30.

55. Paul H. Bergeron, "The Jacksonian Party on Trial: Presidential Politics in Tennessee, 1836-1856" (Ph.D. dissertation, Vanderbilt University, 1965), pp. 43-44, 51.

56. *National Banner and Nashville Whig,* June 13, 1836. For a cursory review of the Democratic electioneering, see Bergeron, "Presidential Politics," pp. 46-50.

57. Samuel H. Laughlin to Polk, Sept. 8, 1836, in Weaver, *Correspondence of Polk,* III, 719-20. See Bergeron, "Presidential Politics," pp. 52-56.

58. See White's letter to Sherrod Williams, July 2, 1836, as published in the *National Banner and Nashville Whig,* Sept. 16, 1836. For Van Buren's position, see Hooper, "Election of 1836," pp. 112-13.

59. Bergeron, "Presidential Politics," pp. 77-78, 86-87; Satterfield, "Uncertain Trumpet," pp. 82-83.

60. Abernethy, *From Frontier to Plantation in Tennessee: A Study in Frontier Democracy* (Chapel Hill, 1932), p. 299. More recently, William J. Cooper, Jr., has argued that throughout the South the real question was that of slavery—which candidate could be counted on to protect the region's peculiar institution. The Whigs consistently pointed to Hugh Lawson White as the man who best represented southern interests. For Cooper's lengthy, but not altogether convincing, presentation of this viewpoint, see *Politics of Slavery,* pp. 74-97.

61. O.B. Hubbard to William B. Campbell, Aug. 28, 1836, David Campbell Papers, Duke University Library.

62. *Knoxville Register* as quoted in *Nashville Republican,* Sept. 6, 1836; Kenneth L. Anderson to Polk, Mar. 26, 1836, in Weaver, *Correspondence of Polk,* III, 551. See also *Nashville Republican,* Jan. 14, June 16, Aug. 25, 1836; *Knoxville Register,* as reprinted in *National Banner and Nashville Whig,* Aug. 15, 1836; ibid., Aug. 17, 26, 1836.

63. *Jackson Truth Teller* as quoted in *National Banner and Nashville Whig,* Aug. 24, 1836; Campbell to David Campbell, Oct. 6, 1835, Campbell Papers.

64. *Nashville Union,* Jan. 26, Mar. 15, 1836.

65. *Columbia Observer* as reprinted in *Nashville Republican,* Apr. 19, 1836; *Nashville Union,* Feb. 13, 1836; Pillow to Van Buren, Mar. 2, 1836, Van Buren Papers, LC; Hooper, "Election of 1836," pp. 97, 129-30, 137; Faulkner's circular reprinted in *Nashville Republican,* June 4, 1836; *Columbia Observer,* as reprinted in ibid., Apr. 19, 1836. My interpretation of the significance of the slavery question in Tennessee's 1836 campaign is obviously at variance with Cooper's view. Thornton found that in Alabama the southern rights/slavery protection questions were not important in presidential contests until 1848; prior to that time these matters might be introduced into the campaign merely as a strategy or tactic to obscure the real questions. See Thornton, *Politics and Power,* p. 348.

66. See Bergeron, "Presidential Politics," pp. 85-89; James E. Murphy, "Jackson and the Tennessee Opposition," *Tennessee Historical Quarterly,* XXX (1971), 67-68. According to Miles, Van Buren carried Mississippi by a scant 500 votes, this despite some concern in that state about Van Buren being a northerner and White a southerner and how all this related to the problem of slavery. See Miles, *Jacksonian Democracy,* pp. 127-29.

CHAPTER IV

1. Various attitudes of Tennesseans toward the Mexican War have been explored in Billy H. Gilley, "Tennessee Opinion of the Mexican War as Reflected in the State Press," East Tennessee Historical Society's *Publications,* no. 26 (1954), 7-26; and "Tennessee Whigs and the Mexican War," *Tennessee Historical Quarterly,* XL (1981), 46-67.

2. Stanley J. Folmsbee, *Sectionalism and Internal Improvements in Tennessee, 1796-1845* (Knoxville, 1939), pp. 199-209.

3. Philip M. Hamer, *Tennessee: A History, 1673-1932* (4 vols.; New York, 1933), I, 421-23. The decade of the 1840s ended before Tennessee would participate in the railroad boom. Professor Holt observes that "geographical conflict often replaced party conflict." See Michael F. Holt, *The Political Crisis of the 1850s* (New York, 1978), p. 112.

4. Brian G. Walton, "A Matter of Timing: Elections to the United States Senate in Tennessee before the Civil War," *Tennessee Historical Quarterly,* XXXI (1972), 134-35; Charles G. Sellers, *James K. Polk: Jacksonian, 1795-1843* (Princeton, 1957), p. 383. Pertinent Polk letters are found in Herbert Weaver, et al., eds., *Correspondence of James K. Polk* (5 vols. to date; Nashville, 1969–) V, 242ff.

5. Walton, "Matter of Timing," pp. 135-36; Sellers, *Polk: Jacksonian,* pp. 382-84; Joseph H. Parks, *Felix Grundy: Champion of Democracy* (University, La., 1940), pp. 326-28, 332; Alexander O. Anderson to Polk, Nov. 10, 13, 16, 22, Dec. 4, 21, 1839, Feb. 4, 10, 1840, in Weaver, *Correspondence of Polk,* V, 291-92, 297-98, 300-1, 308-9, 326, 354, 378-79, 390; Polk to Martin Van Buren, Nov. 11, 1839, 296-97; John Catron to Polk, Nov. 19 [1839], Jan. 3, 1840, 302-3, 367; Cave Johnson to Polk, Nov. 19 [1839], 305; Robert B. Reynolds to Polk, Nov. 27, 1839, 315-16; Harvey M. Watterson to Polk, Nov. 29, 1839, 319-20; David A. Street to Polk, Dec. 8, 1839, 336; Polk to John W. Childress, Feb. 4, 1840, 384.

6. Walton, "Matter of Timing," pp. 136-37; Patricia P. Clark, "A.O.P. Nicholson of Tennessee: Editor, Statesman, and Jurist" (M.A. thesis, University of Tennessee, 1965), pp. 39-40; Lee Scott Theisen, "James K. Polk, Not So Dark a Horse," *Tennessee Historical Quarterly,* XXX (1971), 384; Sellers, *Polk: Jacksonian,* p. 435. See also Aaron V. Brown to Polk, Dec. 21, 1840, in Weaver, *Correspondence of Polk,* V, 604-5; Hopkins L. Turney to Polk, Dec. 21, 1840, 607; A.O.P. Nicholson to Polk, Dec. 23, 1840, 608; Polk to A.O.P. Nicholson, Dec. 24, 1840, 608; Sarah C. Polk to Polk, Dec. 31, 1840, 609; Harvey M. Watterson to Polk, Jan. 3 [1841], 612.

7. Clark, "Nicholson," p. 40; Walton, "Matter of Timing," pp. 137-38; Sellers, *Polk: Jacksonian,* pp. 435-36; *Nashville Union,* Apr. 1, 1841. See also Aaron V. Brown to Polk, Dec. 21, 1840, in Weaver, *Correspondence of Polk,* V, 605; Hopkins L. Turney to Polk, Dec. 21, 1840, Feb. 19, 1841, 607, 640-41; A.O.P. Nicholson to Polk, Jan. 13, Feb. 12, Mar. 8, 1841, 616, 633, 651; Andrew Jackson to Polk, Feb. 8, 1841, 628; John F. Gillespy to Polk, Feb. 12, 1841, 629; Alexander O. Anderson to Polk, Feb. 17, 1841, 637-39; Robert B. Reynolds to Polk, Mar. 28, 1841, 666; Sarah C. Polk to Polk, Apr. 8, 10, 1841, 674, 675.

8. For a veritable feast of information about the 1841-42 impasse, see Robert H. White, ed., *Messages of the Governors of Tennessee* (8 vols.; Nashville, 1952-72), III, 489-576.

9. Joseph H. Parks, *John Bell of Tennessee* (Baton Rouge, 1950), pp. 195-201; Sellers, *Polk: Jacksonian,* pp. 450-51, 455; J.G.M. Ramsey to Polk, Aug. 25, 1841, in Weaver, *Correspondence of Polk,* V, 736; Julius W. Blackwell to Polk, Sept. 1, 1841, 745; J. George Harris to Polk, Sept. 3, 1841, 752; Bromfield L. Ridley to Polk, Sept. 7, 1841, 755; Samuel H. Laughlin to Polk, Sept. 1, 2, 12, Nov. 13, 1841, 748, 749, 756, 782; Adam Huntsman to Polk, Sept. 15, 1841, 757-58; Polk to Cave Johnson, Sept. 21, 1841, 759-60; Polk to Wm. Moore, Sept. 24, 1841, 761; Robert B. Reynolds, Sept. 27, 1841, 763; Alexander O. Anderson to Polk, Aug. 20, 30, Sept. 28, 29, Oct. 6, 1841, 731,

739, 764-65, 766-67, 769; John F. Gillespy to Polk, [Oct. 1], 1841, 767-68; Harvey M. Watterson to Polk, Oct. 19, 1841, 773.

10. Sellers, *Polk: Jacksonian,* pp. 450-56; Parks, *Bell,* pp. 197, 200-1; Walton, "Matter of Timing," p. 138; Clark, "Nicholson," pp. 44-46; Samuel H. Laughlin to Polk, Nov. 24, 1841, in Weaver, *Correspondence of Polk,* V, 782-83; J. George Harris to Polk, Dec. 13, 15, 1841, 785-86, 788-89; Jonathan P. Hardwicke to Polk, Dec. 15, 31, 1841, 787-88, 793; Hopkins L. Turney to Polk, Dec. 26, 1841, 790-91; Polk to Samuel H. Laughlin, Dec. 29, 1841, 792. Physical violence, including fisticuffs and firing of pistols, accompanied the deliberations of the legislators in 1841.

11. Sellers, *Polk: Jacksonian,* p. 457.

12. Walton, "Matter of Timing," p. 139; Parks, *Bell,* pp. 201-2.

13. Clark, "Nicholson," pp. 52-54; Walton, "Matter of Timing," p. 139; John E. Tricamo, "Tennessee Politics, 1845-1861" (Ph.D. dissertation, Columbia University, 1965), pp. 30, 35; William J. Burke, Jr., "The Career of William Trousdale in Tennessee Politics" (M.A. thesis, Vanderbilt University, 1967), pp. 77-78; Charles G. Sellers, *James K. Polk: Continentalist, 1843-1846* (Princeton, 1966), pp. 311-12; White, *Messages,* IV, 21-29. In an extraordinary interview with Turney, on Dec. 3, 1845, President Polk emphasized how he had avoided all contact with Tennesseans on the Senate election. He confided to his diary his belief that Turney was the man responsible for giving currency to the notion that Nicholson was Polk's candidate in the Senate battle —a strategy calculated to cause Whigs to fight against Nicholson and move toward Turney. See Milo M. Quaife, ed., *The Diary of James K. Polk* (4 vols.; Chicago, 1910), I, 112-15.

14. Tricamo, "Tennessee Politics," pp. 32-35; Walton, "Matter of Timing," p. 139; Clark, "Nicholson," pp. 52-54; Parks, *Bell,* p. 209; White, *Messages,* IV, 30-41.

15. Parks, *Bell,* pp. 211-12; Walton, "Matter of Timing," p. 141; Tricamo, "Tennessee Politics," pp. 51-52; Mary E.R. Campbell, *The Attitude of Tennesseans Toward the Union, 1847-1861* (New York, 1961), pp. 39-40.

16. Parks, *Bell,* pp. 213-15; Walton, "Matter of Timing," p. 141; Campbell, *Attitude of Tennesseans,* p. 40; White, *Messages,* IV, 189-91.

17. Judging from the results in the various legislative races, one must admit that neither party had the upper hand on the General Assembly seats. In 1841 and again in 1849 the Whigs and Democrats each enjoyed a majority in one of the houses of the legislature. The only time in the 1840s that the Democrats controlled both houses was 1845, whereas the Whigs had a majority in both houses in 1843 and again in 1847.

18. Regarding dissatisfaction with the Polk administration among certain Tennessee Democrats, see Tricamo, "Tennessee Politics," pp. 24-26, 34-35; Clark, "Nicholson," p. 59; and Andrew Johnson to Blackston McDannel, July 22, 1846, in LeRoy P. Graf and Ralph W. Haskins, eds., *The Papers of Andrew Johnson* (5 vols. to date; Knoxville, 1967–), I, 331-32.

19. Sellers, *Polk: Jacksonian,* 429-31, 470, 472-73; Parks, *Bell,* pp. 176-77; Paul H. Bergeron, "Political Struggles in Tennessee, 1839-1843" (M.A. thesis, Vanderbilt University, 1962), pp. 60-63, 111-12; Laughlin to Polk, Mar. 12, 1841, James K. Polk Papers, Library of Congress (this letter does not appear in Weaver, *Correspondence of Polk,* V).

20. Bergeron, "Political Struggles," pp. 66-67, 73, 78, 82-85; Sellers, *Polk: Jacksonian*, pp. 433-34, 437-39, 440, 442. Polk's health and stamina were matters of concern during the grueling campaign; see the exchange of letters between Polk and his wife in Weaver, *Correspondence of Polk*, V, 676ff.

21. Paul H. Bergeron, "Tennessee Political Oratory in 1841 and 1843," *Southern Speech Journal*, XXVIII (1962-63), 210-16; Paul H. Bergeron, "The Election of 1843: A Whig Triumph in Tennessee," *Tennessee Historical Quarterly*, XXII (1963), 125-34; Sellers, *Polk: Jacksonian*, pp. 431-34, 437-43, 473-87.

22. The election data in Table 4.1 have been gleaned from several sources. The 1847 and 1849 results, for example, are from Campbell, *Attitude of Tennesseans*, pp. 265-68. The returns for 1841, 1843, and 1845 are from the *Journal of the Senate of the State of Tennessee* (Knoxville, 1841), pp. 46-47 (Knoxville, 1843), pp. 78-79, 89 (Nashville, 1846), pp. 83, 84, 86. The presidential election reports are from W. Dean Burnham, *Presidential Ballots, 1836-1892* (Baltimore, 1955), p. 742. With regard to the 1848 election, however, I have added returns for Decatur County, which are not reported in Burnham. The figures in Table 4.2 are taken from Table 2.1 in Chapter 2 above. The data presented in Table 4.3 are gleaned from Richard P. McCormick, "New Perspectives on Jacksonian Politics," *American Historical Review*, LXV (1960), 292; and Brian G. Walton, "The Second Party System in Tennessee," East Tennessee Historical Society's *Publications*, no. 43 (1971), p. 19.

23. Sellers, *Polk: Jacksonian*, p. 488. See Polk's letter to Robert B. Reynolds, Aug. 19, 1841, in Weaver, *Correspondence of Polk*, V, 728, for his assessment that some Middle Tennessee counties did not get out the Democratic vote to insure his victory. Polk carried that section by a margin of 3,172 votes in 1841 but only by 1,661 votes in 1843, although his total vote increased in the latter year as did the total vote of Middle Tennessee.

24. *Nashville Union*, Dec. 19, 1844.

25. Ibid., Mar. 6, 1845.

26. Ibid., Jan. 10, Mar. 6, 1845. Stanton ran successfully for Congress instead. The Democratic convention adopted no platform.

27. Ibid., Feb. 22, Mar. 8, 20, 1845; Hamer, *Tennessee*, I, 310.

28. *Nashville Union*, Jan. 30, Feb. 20, 27, Mar. 11, 13, 25, 29, Apr. 12, 1845; Hamer, *Tennessee*, I, 311. In the late spring and summer, the press wrote a great deal about the Oregon question, but this issue did not seem to assume importance in the Tennessee campaign.

29. *Nashville Union*, May 31, Aug. 7, 1845.

30. See ibid., Aug. 19, 1845.

31. As it turned out, 1845 was a good year for Democrats, for they were successful in southern elections. See William J. Cooper, Jr., *The South and the Politics of Slavery, 1828-1856* (Baton Rouge, 1978), p. 226.

32. Tricamo, "Tennessee Politics," pp. 43-46; Brian G. Walton, "A Triumph of Political Stability: The Elections of 1847 in Tennessee," East Tennessee Historical Society's *Publications*, no. 40 (1968), pp. 10-11; Campbell, *Attitude of Tennesseans*, p. 37. See also the *Nashville Union*, Dec. 5, 1846, Feb. 6, 27, Mar. 27, 1847. The party adopted no platform.

33. Tricamo, "Tennessee Politics," pp. 43, 46; Campbell, *Attitude of Tennesseans,* p. 37; Walton, "Triumph of Stability," pp. 8-9; *Nashville Union,* Jan. 5, 16, Mar. 4, Apr. 2, 1847.

34. Gilley, "Opinion of the Mexican War," pp. 15-18; Walton, "Triumph of Stability," pp. 12, 16-18; Tricamo, "Tennessee Politics," pp. 42, 47; *Nashville Union,* Apr. 5, 13, June 14, 17, July 21, 29, 1847. Gilley, "Whigs and War," pp. 50-52, 58, 62, 65, sees the Mexican War as the chief issue in 1847.

35. Walton, "Triumph of Stability," pp. 6, 13-14; Tricamo, "Tennessee Politics," p. 49; Gilley, "Opinion of the Mexican War," pp. 18-19; Gilley, "Whigs and War," p. 58; *Nashville Union,* Apr. 6, 7, 17, 21, May 11, 19, June 9, July 6, 14, 1847.

36. See the *Nashville Union,* Mar. 6, 9, 1847.

37. Aaron V. Brown subsequently complained that his fellow Democrats did him an injustice in 1847 by staying away from the polls; furthermore, he charged that he had had to bear the expenses of both the 1845 and 1847 campaigns. See Brown to [?], Feb. 8, 1848, Personal Papers-Miscellaneous, Library of Congress. Table 4.3 shows the same range of voter participation in 1845 as in 1847, although the latter attracted 7,000 more voters. The problem is simply that the 1845 election was probably at the lower end of the 85-88 percent range, whereas the 1847 election was at the upper end.

38. Walton, "Triumph of Stability," pp. 22, 23-24, Balch to Polk, Sept. 3, 1847, quoted in Cooper, *Politics of Slavery,* p. 246; Quaife, *Diary of Polk,* III, 119-20; *Nashville Union,* Aug. 13, 16, 18, 19, 23, 1847. Throughout the South in 1847 Whigs enjoyed successes; Cooper contends that such results can be explained exclusively by conflict over the Wilmot Proviso. See Cooper, *Politics of Slavery,* p. 235. Holt claims that in 1847 and 1848 the parties, both North and South, provided clear alternatives on the controversy over the extension of slavery and thereby retained the loyalty of most of their voters. See Holt, *Political Crisis,* p. 58. My examination of the 1847 canvass in Tennessee, however, does not bear out the contention that slavery, the Wilmot Proviso, or related concerns played a part in the election.

39. White, *Messages,* IV, 270-75; Burke, "Trousdale," pp. 95-98; *Nashville Union,* Jan. 8, Feb. 20, 21, 23, Mar. 12, Apr. 20, 21, 1849. Democrats later claimed that Trousdale had been chosen because of his brilliant military service; see *Nashville Union,* July 7, 1849.

40. Tricamo, "Tennessee Politics," pp. 65-66; Burke, "Trousdale," p. 103; White, *Messages,* IV, 279; Campbell, *Attitude of Tennesseans,* pp. 48-49; *Nashville Union,* Mar. 1, Apr. 23, 1849.

41. Burke, "Trousdale," pp. 99, 103-4, 110-11; Campbell, *Attitude of Tennesseans,* pp. 46-50; White, *Messages,* IV, 275-77, 280; *Nashville Union,* Apr. 20, 21, 25, 1849.

42. *Nashville Union,* Apr. 26, 27, May 1, 3, 9, 10, 11, 12, 14, June 5, 7, July 9, 10, 13, 16, 19, 25, 26, 1849. These are some of the better examples of the discussions over slavery and related concerns, but of course there was hardly a day during the entire canvass that the press did not deal with these matters.

43. The flap over the military qualifications of Trousdale and Brown may be followed in the *Nashville Union,* June 14, 22, 26, 30, July 7, 1849. Naturally the Democrats viewed Whig attacks upon Trousdale's military record as an example of Whig desperation.

44. *Nashville Union,* Aug. 8, 11, 15, 23, 1849; Parks, *Bell,* pp. 234-35; Burke, "Trousdale," pp. 116-17. The Tennessee election should be placed in the larger framework that Democrats won in all seven states where there were elections in 1849. See Holt, *Political Crisis,* p. 71, and Cooper, *Politics of Slavery,* p. 278.

45. For information on Democratic strength in the eleven congressional districts in the 1840s, see Walton, "Triumph of Stability," p. 20.

46. James T. Horton, Jr., "The Evolution of a Whig Editor in Tennessee: Allen A. Hall" (M.A. thesis, Vanderbilt University, 1966), p. 119; Richard P. McCormick, *The Second American Party System: Party Formation in the Jacksonian Era* (Chapel Hill, 1966), p. 232; Sellers, *Polk: Jacksonian,* p. 420; Paul H. Bergeron, "The Jacksonian Party on Trial: Presidential Politics in Tennessee, 1836-1856" (Ph.D. dissertation, Vanderbilt University, 1965), pp. 100, 120. In his book, *The Birth of Mass Political Parties: Michigan, 1827-1861* (Princeton, 1971), Ronald P. Formisano emphasizes that the Whigs in Michigan suffered from a strong strain of antipartyism and therefore did a poor job of organizing themselves into a structured party. The antipartyism attitude was rooted in evangelical and moral reform sentiments. See Formisano, *Birth of Parties,* pp. 57, 58, 60, 72. Tennessee Whigs did not seem to have these attitudes or problems.

47. *Nashville Republican Banner,* Feb. 7, 24, 1840; *Nashville Whig,* Feb. 5, 19, 1840. Of necessity there were some changes in the original group of fifteen electors. See *Nashville Republican Banner,* May 4, 19, 1840; *Nashville Whig,* May 20, 1840.

48. McCormick, *Second Party System,* p. 232; Bergeron, "Presidential Politics," pp. 100-2; *Nashville Republican Banner,* May 13, 1840; Polk to Nicholson, Nov. 7, 1840 in Weaver, *Correspondence of Polk,* V, 578; also Polk to David Burford, Nov. 7, 1840, 576-77; and Polk to Robert B. Reynolds, Nov. 18, 1840, 593-94.

49. Despite the best efforts of the February convention to establish a complete slate of electors, three of them subsequently resigned and had to be replaced. For information about these various changes in personnel, see the *Nashville Union,* Apr. 20, 23, May 11, 14, 28, June 4, 1840.

50. *Nashville Union,* Feb. 14, 1840; McCormick, *Second Party System,* pp. 232-34; Bergeron, "Presidential Politics," pp. 102-4, 150; Sellers, *Polk: Jacksonian,* pp. 420-21.

51. Johnson to Democratic Committee of Maury County, Aug. 29, 1843, in Graf and Haskins, *Johnson,* I, 119; *Nashville Union,* Nov. 25, Dec. 2, 1843; Sellers, *Polk: Continentalist,* pp. 12-14.

52. *Nashville Union,* Mar. 14, 21, May 23, June 13, 15, 18, 1844. At some point in the spring or summer, two of the electors resigned or declined to serve. For a revised list of electors, see *Nashville Union,* Oct. 23, 1844.

53. *Nashville Republican Banner,* Jan. 10, Feb. 23, Mar. 4, July 5, Oct. 2, 1844; *Nashville Whig,* Feb. 24, Mar. 2, 5, June 18, 22, July 25, Sept. 28, Oct. 26, 1844.

54. *Nashville Whig,* Feb. 19, May 13, Aug. 8, 1848; *Nashville Republican Banner,* May 3, 15, June 26, July 3, Aug. 9, 1848.

55. *Nashville Union,* Nov. 17, 29, 1847, Jan. 15, Mar. 7, 1848; Brown to [?], Feb. 8, 1848, Personal Papers-Miscellaneous, LC.

56. In March, Jonas E. Thomas replaced Edwin A. Keeble in the Seventh District; in May, Samuel Turney became the new Fourth District elector in place of Harvey M. Watterson; in that same month, the Fifth District slot went to Robert Farquaharson, who replaced William E. Venable. By mid-June the two vacant districts, the Sixth and

the Eleventh, were filled by Leonard H. Simms and David M. Currin, respectively. See the *Nashville Union,* Jan. 15, Mar. 7, 10, 20, May 20, June 12, Oct. 17, 1848.

57. See the *Nashville Union,* Sept. 4, 1848 for pessimistic comments on party organization.

58. Sellers, *Polk: Jacksonian,* pp. 419-20, 406-7, 410, 411-13, 415-17; Parks, *Grundy,* pp. 333-34, 336. See Andrew Jackson to Martin Van Buren, Feb. 17, Apr. 3, 29, 1840, Martin Van Buren Papers, Library of Congress.

59. A prime example of the anti-Polk feeling is found in Andrew Johnson to A.O.P. Nicholson, Feb. 12, 1844, in Graf and Haskins, *Johnson,* I, 150. The author and the recipient of this letter were the ringleaders of the anti-Polk faction within the Tennessee Democratic party.

60. Clark, "Nicholson," p. 50; Andrew Johnson to Robert B. Reynolds, Sept. 9, 1843, in Graf and Haskins, *Johnson,* I, 121; Sellers, *Polk: Continentalist,* pp. 8-9, 12-14.

61. Jackson to Van Buren, Nov. 29, 1843, in John Spencer Bassett, ed., *Correspondence of Andrew Jackson* (7 vols.; Washington, 1926-35), VI, 245; Polk to Van Buren, Nov. 30, 1843, Van Buren Papers, LC; Sellers, *Polk: Continentalist,* pp. 32, 35-36, 47-48; Johnson to Nicholson, Feb. 12, 1844, in Graf and Haskins, *Johnson,* I, 149-50.

62. Sellers, *Polk: Continentalist,* pp. 74-76, 81, 86, 89-90, 93.

63. *Nashville Union,* Jan. 15, 1848; Aaron V. Brown to [?], Feb. 8, 1848, Personal Papers-Miscellaneous, LC; Tricamo, "Tennessee Politics," pp. 58-59; Johnson to Blackston McDannel, Mar. 24, 1848, in Graf and Haskins, *Johnson,* I, 417; Johnson to Nicholson, May 4, 1848, 424-25; Burke, "Trousdale," p. 95; Clark, "Nicholson," p. 60; David L. Eubanks, "Dr. J. G. M. Ramsey of East Tennessee: A Career of Public Service" (Ph.D. dissertation, University of Tennessee, 1965), p. 203. One should recall Polk's own statements in 1847 that his patronage policies had contributed to friction within the Tennessee Democratic party.

64. *Nashville Whig,* Jan. 8, Mar. 30, Apr. 11, May 25, June 13, 1848; *Nashville Republican Banner,* Jan. 1, June 12, 1848; *Nashville Union,* Apr. 3, 11, 1848; Wm. B. Campbell to [David Campbell] Jan. 23, 1848, David Campbell Papers, Duke University; Tricamo, "Tennessee Politics," pp. 56-57, 61; E. Merton Coulter, *William G. Brownlow: Fighting Parson of the Southern Highlands* (Chapel Hill, 1937), p. 118; Campbell, *Attitude of Tennesseans,* pp. 44-45; Parks, *Bell,* pp. 229-32; Malcolm C. McMillan, ed., "Joseph Glover Baldwin Reports on the Whig National Convention of 1848," *Journal of Southern History,* XXV (1959), 378-79.

65. See the *Nashville Union,* Jan. 15, Feb. 17, June 18, July 2, 1840; *Nashville Republican Banner,* July 14, 31, 1840. In his study of southern politics, Cooper contends that slavery was the essential issue in 1840; see *Politics of Slavery,* pp. 124-48. At one point Cooper writes: "In the antebellum South, that election has a special importance because it confirmed the politics of slavery as a primal force in southern politics" (p. 132). Cooper also cites my dissertation in support of the view that Tennessee Democrats based their campaign on linking Harrison with the abolitionists; see *Politics of Slavery,* p. 139. But I argued in the dissertation that there were no major issues and that Harrison's alleged abolitionist sympathies was merely one of several topics talked about in the Tennessee campaign. I am in basic agreement with Professor J. Mills Thornton III, who in his discussion of Alabama politics in the 1840s maintains

that southern rights questions, though brought up from time to time, did not figure prominently in the elections. Southern rights matters, writes Thornton, were introduced into a presidential campaign simply as a tactic, not as a significant or substantive issue. See Thornton, *Politics and Power in a Slave Society: Alabama, 1800-1860* (Baton Rouge, 1978), p. 348.

66. Bergeron, "Presidential Politics," pp. 132-33, 135-36. Jackson got into the act by castigating Harrison's military leadership. See his letters to Andrew Jackson Donelson, June 18, 1840, Andrew Jackson Donelson Papers, Library of Congress; and to Wm. B. Lewis, May 22, 1840, Wm. B. Lewis Correspondence, New York Public Library. The *Nashville Union* frequently attacked Harrison's alleged Federalism; see, for example, Mar. 26, Apr. 6, 1840. Economic hard times doubtless worked against Van Buren's successes in Tennessee and elsewhere, although the matter never loomed forth as the primary concern of the press or the campaigners. A letter which captured the antagonistic feeling of some Tennesseans toward the Jacksonian party because of the economic distresses is West H. Humphreys to Polk, May 17 [1840], in Weaver, *Correspondence of Polk*, V, 456.

67. *Nashville Whig*, May 16, 30, June 13, 18, 20, July 6, 1844; *Nashville Republican Banner*, May 15, June 14, 17, 19, July 15, Aug. 20, 1844. The quotation is from Adam Huntsman's letter to Polk, June 11, 1844, in Emma Inman Williams, ed., "Letters of Adam Huntsman to James K. Polk," *Tennessee Historical Quarterly*, VI (1944), 360. Another letter conveying the view that the Whigs were moving into the Polk camp is L.C. Haynes to Polk, June 14, 1844, Polk Papers, LC. For an excellent discussion of the Texas issue and its impact upon southern politics in 1844, see Cooper, *Politics of Slavery*, pp. 189-219. Cooper observes that Clay's modification "probably enabled Clay to hang on to Tennessee and perhaps North Carolina" (p. 218). Holt notes that proslavery southern Whigs *opposed* immediate annexation out of fear both of war with Mexico and of Texas competition to cotton and sugar planters in the South; see Holt, *Political Crisis*, p. 43. That argument appears not to have been used by Tennessee Whig leaders who were, with some exceptions, strongly proannexation.

68. *Nashville Union*, Aug. 21, Sept. 9, 25, Oct. 19, 1848; *Nashville Whig*, June 1, July 29, Aug. 8, Sept. 5, 26, 1848. Questions concerning the veto power and Taylor's qualifications for the presidency are treated in Bergeron, "Presidential Politics," pp. 247-53. Cooper views the 1848 campaign as a contest over slavery; see *Politics of Slavery*, pp. 246-67. His contention that southern Democrats hit hardest at Zachary Taylor because of his failure to take a stand on the Wilmot Proviso seems not to have been borne out by the Tennessee campaign. Moreover, since Cooper notes that Taylor ate into Democratic strength in the South (p. 267), one wonders how strong and certainly how effective were the attacks upon Taylor by southern Democrats. Thornton has found that in Alabama questions of slavery and southern rights became central and indispensable in 1848 and thereafter; see Thornton, *Politics and Power*, pp. 348-49. Holt's observation that first-time voters in the South seemed to have gone to Taylor is corroborated by the Tennessee election returns; see Holt, *Political Crisis*, p. 65. For a general discussion of the political and attitudinal reactions, North and South, to the Wilmot Proviso in the second half of the decade, see William R. Brock, *Parties and Political Conscience: American Dilemmas, 1840-1850* (Millwood, N.Y., 1979), pp. 184-275, and David Potter, *The Impending Crisis, 1846-1861* (New York, 1976), pp.

51-89. The best study of the Taylor-Cass contest is Joseph G. Rayback, *Free Soil: The Election of 1848* (Lexington, Ky., 1970).

69. *Nashville Union,* June 23, 1848; Campbell to David Campbell, Aug. 7, 1848, Campbell Papers, DU. Details of the campaigning conducted by both parties may be found in Bergeron, "Presidential Politics," pp. 231-42.

70. The campaigning done by Tennessee Democrats and Whigs in 1840 and 1844 is discussed in Bergeron, "Presidential Politics," pp. 109-27, 171-86, 188-90; Sellers, *Polk: Jacksonian,* pp. 420-26; Sellers, *Polk: Continentalist,* pp. 138-39, 144. The Brownlow quotation is found in Coulter, *Brownlow,* p. 112.

71. For a more detailed analysis, both statewide and sectionally, of the election results in 1840, 1844, and 1848, see Chapter 2 above.

72. Sellers, *Polk: Jacksonian,* p. 429; Coulter, *Brownlow,* p. 39; Jesse Burt, ed., "Tennessee Democrats Employ Editor E.G. Eastman, 1846-1849," East Tennessee Historical Society's *Publications,* no. 38 (1966), p. 84; Sellers, *Polk: Continentalist,* p. 270; Frank B. Williams, Jr., "Samuel Hervey Laughlin, Polk's Political Handyman," *Tennessee Historical Quarterly,* XXIV (1965), p. 388; Horton, "Allen Hall," pp. 136-37. See Thornton's comment about the party press in Alabama in *Politics and Power,* p. 128.

73. James C. Stamper, "Felix K. Zollicoffer: Tennessee Editor and Politician," *Tennessee Historical Quarterly,* XXVIII (1969), 361; Parks, *Bell,* pp. 197-99.

74. R. Beeler Satterfield, "The Uncertain Trumpet of the Tennessee Jacksonians," *Tennessee Historical Quarterly,* XXVI (1967), 90.

75. Williams, "Laughlin," pp. 383-85, 387-88; Satterfield, "Uncertain Trumpet," pp. 90-93; Sellers, *Polk: Continentalist,* pp. 35-36, 74-75; Harris to Polk, July 17, 1844, Polk Papers, LC; Polk to Heiss, July 31, 1844, in St. George L. Sioussat, ed., "Papers of Major John P. Heiss of Nashville," Tennessee Historical Magazine, II (1916), 143; Powell Moore, "James K. Polk: Tennessee Politician," *Journal of Southern History,* XVII (1951), 513.

76. Chase to Eastman, Oct. 9, 1946, in Burt, "Democrats Employ Eastman," pp. 87-88; Shepard to Eastman, Oct. 8, 1846, p. 87; Eastman to Shepard, Oct. 20, 1846, p. 89; Eastman to Aaron V. Brown, Nov. 11, 1846, p. 93; Shepard to Eastman, Oct. 30, 1846, p. 90; Brown to Eastman, Oct. 31, 1846, p. 91; *Nashville Union,* Dec. 17, 1846. Eastman was fired as editor in 1850 by the proprietor of the *Union,* Harvey M. Watterson, who had purchased the paper from Shepard in September 1849.

CHAPTER V

1. For an impressive and convincing discussion of the 1850 Compromise, see David M. Potter, *The Impending Crisis, 1848-1861* (New York, 1976), pp. 90-120. See also Michael F. Holt, *The Political Crisis of the 1850s* (New York, 1978), pp. 76-90; and William R. Brock, *Parties and Political Conscience: American Dilemmas, 1840-1850* (Millwood, N.Y., 1979), pp. 276-316. The standard full treatment of the compromise in Holman Hamilton's *Prologue to Conflict: The Crisis and Compromise of 1850* (Lexington, Ky., 1964).

2. The best general discussion of the problems of the 1850s is found in Potter, *Impending Crisis.* For an unusual interpretation of the political situation in the 1850s, see Holt, *Political Crisis.*

3. Thelma Jennings, *The Nashville Convention: Southern Movement for Unity, 1848-1851* (Memphis, 1980), pp. 78, 93-97, 130-32; William J. Cooper, Jr., *The South and the Politics of Slavery, 1828-1856* (Baton Rouge, 1978), pp. 291-94; Thelma Jennings, "Tennessee and the Nashville Conventions of 1850," *Tennessee Historical Quarterly,* XXX (1971), 73-74. Of the nine states attending the June convention, four of them—Florida, Alabama, Arkansas, and Tennessee—sent unofficial delegates. See Table 7 in Jennings, *Nashville Convention,* pp. 233-50, for a complete listing of Tennessee's delegates, accompanied by data on each individual.

4. Jennings, *Nashville Convention,* pp. 77-78, 93-97; Patricia P. Clark, "A.O.P. Nicholson of Tennessee: Editor, Statesman, and Jurist" (M.A. thesis, University of Tennessee, 1965), p. 65. Of the forty Tennessee delegates whose political affiliation could be established by Jennings, no more than three were Whigs; see Jennings, *Nashville Convention,* pp. 233-50.

5. Jennings, *Nashville Convention,* pp. 132-33; John E. Tricamo, "Tennessee Politics, 1845-1861" (Ph.D. dissertation, Columbia University, 1965), pp. 73-74, 76. For a discussion of the June convention, see Jennings, *Nashville Convention,* pp. 136-54.

6. Jennings, *Nashville Convention,* pp. 194-95, 197; Clark, "Nicholson," pp. 71, 73; William J. Burke, Jr., "The Career of William Trousdale in Tennessee Politics" (M.A. thesis, Vanderbilt University, 1967), pp. 130-32. For a brief discussion of the November meeting, see Jennings, *Nashville Convention,* pp. 191-98. Potter contends that the Nashville convention proved to be an obstacle to secession rather than a vehicle of it; see Potter, *Impending Crisis,* p. 486. Jennings concurs with this assessment but then adds that the convention "paved the way for a Southern Confederacy in 1861"; see Jennings, *Nashville Convention,* p. 210.

7. Jennings, *Nashville Convention,* pp. 185-86; Burke, "Trousdale," pp. 125-27; Tricamo, "Tennessee Politics," pp. 75-76. For a general discussion of southern reaction to the compromise, see Cooper, *Politics of Slavery,* pp. 301-06; and Jennings, *Nashville Convention,* pp. 174-86. Alabama Whigs, like their Tennessee counterparts, lauded the passage of the compromise measures as the cessation of sectional bickering. See J. Mills Thornton III, *Politics and Power in a Slave Society, Alabama, 1800-1860* (Baton Rouge, 1978), p. 187.

8. Jennings, *Nashville Convention,* p. 186; Clark, "Nicholson," p. 74; Burke, "Trousdale," pp. 127-29; Hubert Blair Bentley, "Andrew Johnson, Governor of Tennessee, 1853-57" (Ph.D. dissertation, University of Tennessee, 1972), pp. 44-45.

9. Tricamo, "Tennessee Politics," pp. 132-35; Bentley, "Johnson," p. 242; Cooper, *Politics of Slavery,* pp. 346-56.

10, Joseph H. Parks, *John Bell of Tennessee* (Baton Rouge, 1950), pp. 286-92, 294-95.

11. *Nashville Republican Banner,* June 2, 1854, quoted in Parks, *Bell,* p. 300.

12. Robert H. White, ed., *Messages of the Governors of Tennessee* (8 vols.; Nashville, 1952-72), IV, 301-2, 338-44, 428, 450-55, 589-602. The report of the secretary of state, W.B.A. Ramsey, Oct. 10, 1853, may be found in the Tennessee *Senate Journal,* 1853-

54, pp. 48-51. His report reveals that 55 counties ratified the amendment, while 24 did not. The 1857-58 session of the General Assembly approved a bill calling for a vote for or against a constitutional convention, but the referendum, held on Sept. 2, 1858, opposed the constitutional convention call. See *Tennessee Acts, 1857-58,* pp. 84-86; *Nashville Union and American,* Sept. 26, 1858; White, *Messages,* V, 67-68.

13. White, *Messages,* IV, 423-25, 436-38; Philip M. Hamer, *Tennessee: A History, 1673-1932* (4 vols.; New York, 1933), I, 423-26.

14. White, *Messages,* IV, 427-28, 549, 636-37, 678-81, 684-85; V, 48-49, 110-12; Claude A. Campbell, *The Development of Banking in Tennessee* (Nashville, 1932), pp. 129-33, 141-42, 148.

15. Parks, *Bell,* pp. 264-65; Tricamo, "Tennessee Politics," pp. 78-81. The Campbell quotation is from his letter to David Campbell, Feb. 9, 1851, in Parks, *Bell,* p. 264. Holt notes that disappointment over patronage was widespread among Whigs during the Taylor administration; see Holt, *Political Crisis,* p. 76.

16. Clark, "Nicholson," pp. 82-85, 90-91; Tricamo, "Tennessee Politics," pp. 106-7, 165; Johnson to Samuel Milligan, Nov. 23, 1856, in LeRoy P. Graf and Ralph W. Haskins, eds., *The Papers of Andrew Johnson* (5 vols. to date; Knoxville, 1967–), II, 452.

17. Johnson to Nicholson, May 11, 1851, in Graf and Haskins, *Johnson,* I, 616.

18. Brian G. Walton, "A Matter of Timing: Elections to the United States Senate in Tennessee before the Civil War," *Tennessee Historical Quarterly,* XXXI (1972), 142-43; White, *Messages,* IV, 459-60.

19. Tricamo, "Tennessee Politics," pp. 88-92; Walton, "Matter of Timing," p. 143; Parks, *Bell,* p. 267; Thomas B. Alexander, *Thomas A.R. Nelson of East Tennessee* (Nashville, 1956), pp. 42-45.

20. Parks, *Bell,* pp. 277-79; Tricamo, "Tennessee Politics," pp. 122-25. See also Jere W. Roberson, "The Memphis Commercial Convention of 1853: Southern Dreams and 'Young America,' " *Tennessee Historical Quarterly,* XXXIII (1974), 286.

21. Parks, *Bell,* pp. 280-81; Tricamo, "Tennessee Politics," pp. 126-27; Walton, "Matter of Timing," pp. 144-45; Alexander, *Nelson,* p. 46. There was no Whig caucus in 1853, because East Tennessee Whigs refused to attend and participate.

22. Johnson to Samuel Milligan, Dec. 10, 1856, in Graf and Haskins, *Johnson,* II, 458; Bentley, "Johnson," pp. 574-78, 600-4; Robert G. Russell, "Prelude to the Presidency: The Election of Andrew Johnson to the Senate," *Tennessee Historical Quarterly,* XXVI (1967), p. 154. See also Johnson to Wm. M. Lowry, Dec. 14, 1856, in Graf and Haskins, *Johnson,* II, 461.

23. Johnson to Lowry, Aug. 28, 1857, in Graf and Haskins, *Johnson,* II, 480; Russell, "Prelude," pp. 150, 172, 175-76; Bentley, "Johnson," pp. 624-25; Herschel Gower and Jack Allen, eds., *Pen and Sword: The Life and Journals of Randal W. McGavock* (Nashville, 1959), p. 435; Walton, "Matter of Timing," p. 145. Johnson was elected again to the U.S. Senate some eighteen years later, in January 1875.

24. Russell, "Prelude," p. 169; *Clarksville Jeffersonian,* quoted in ibid., p. 171; Walton, "Matter of Timing," p. 146.

25. Bentley, "Johnson," pp. 578-79, 628-30, 607; Johnson to Samuel Milligan, Nov. 23, 1856, in Graf and Haskins, *Johnson,* II, 453; Clark, "Nicholson," p. 102; Gower and Allen, *Pen and Sword,* pp. 420, 427; Russell, "Prelude," p. 170.

26. Gower and Allen, *Pen and Sword*, pp. 438-39; Bentley, "Johnson," pp. 634-36; Clark, "Nicholson," p. 103; White, *Messages*, V, 24-25; Walton, "Matter of Timing," p. 146. Nicholson had served in the Senate in 1841-42, by virtue of appointment from Governor James K. Polk.

27. Bentley, "Johnson," pp. 637-38; Parks, *Bell*, pp. 320-29; White, *Messages*, V, pp. 36-42; Tricamo, "Tennessee Politics," pp. 178-79.

28. The data for the 1852 and 1856 presidential elections are taken from W. Dean Burnham, *Presidential Ballots, 1836-1892* (Baltimore, 1955), p. 742. Statistics for the 1851 and 1855 elections are from Mary E.R. Campbell, *The Attitude of Tennesseans Toward the Union, 1847-1861* (New York, 1961), pp. 271, 274. Returns for 1853, 1857, and 1859 are from the *Journal of the Senate of the State of Tennessee* (Nashville, 1854), pp. 45-47; *Senate Journal* (Nashville, 1857), pp. 58-59; and the *Senate Journal* (Nashville, 1859), pp. 38-39. The percentages in Table 5.2 are taken from Table 2.1 in Chapter 2. Voter participation figures are derived from my own calculations and from Brian G. Walton, "The Second Party System in Tennessee," *East Tennessee Historical Society's Publications*, no. 43 (1971), p. 19.

29. Holt makes the persuasive point that the increasing similarities or decreasing differences between the Whig and Democratic parties in the early 1850s resulted in widespread voter apathy and virtual collapse of party loyalty; see, for example, Holt, *Political Crisis*, pp. 102-3. Voter participation levels in Tennessee's gubernatorial and presidential contests seem to lend credence to Holt's argument.

30. *Nashville Union*, Feb. 11, 12, 26, 1851; Burke, "Trousdale," pp. 134, 145; Campbell, *Attitude of Tennesseans*, pp. 64-65; see also Andrew Johnson to A.O.P. Nicholson, Apr. 16, 1851, in Graf and Haskins, *Johnson*, I, 614.

31. Tricamo, "Tennessee Politics," pp. 82-84; *Nashville Whig*, Mar. 21, 1851, as reprinted in White, *Messages*, IV, 405-10. See also *Nashville Union*, Apr. 29, 1851.

32. Campbell, *Attitude of Tennesseans*, pp. 65-68; Burke, "Trousdale," pp. 137-39; Tricamo, "Tennessee Politics," pp. 84, 86; *Nashville Whig*, Mar. 21, 1851, as reprinted in White, *Messages*, IV, 407-8; Eric R. Lacy, *Vanquished Volunteers: East Tennessee Sectionalism from Statehood to Secession* (Johnson City, Tenn., 1965), pp. 150-51; *Nashville Union*, May 1, 3, 8, 23, June 26, July 9, 1851.

33. *Nashville Union*, Feb. 26, Mar. 27, May 3, 8, 19, 21, June 26, July 7, 30, 1851.

34. Ibid., Apr. 9, May 1, 3, 8, 16, 23, 29, June 3, July 14, 22, 1851.

35. Ibid., Feb. 10, 26, Apr. 23, May 1, 3, 1851; Lacy, *Vanquished Volunteers*, pp. 150-51; *Nashville Whig*, Mar. 21, 1851, as reprinted in White, *Messages*, IV, 410. Holt claims that the railroad boom helped obliterate "the coherent party lines on economic issues." See Holt, *Political Crisis*, pp. 112-13. But the Tennessee situation was somewhat different; there had never been strong party identification on the internal improvements questions in the 1830s and 1840s. Moreover, the 1851 campaign gave indication that rather recent differences had not been entirely eliminated. On the matter of the state bank, party differences persisted in Tennessee throughout the decade of the 1850s; in fact, they became more pronounced.

36. For more detailed analysis of this and other elections in the 1850s, see Chapter 2 above. Examples of Democratic postmortem discussions may be found in the *Nashville Union*, Aug. 14, 25, Sept. 6, 1851. Whig success in the South is reported in Cooper, *Politics of Slavery*, p. 310.

37. *Nashville Whig,* Jan. 12, 1853, as reprinted in White, *Messages,* IV, 510-11; *Nashville Union,* Jan. 13, 29, Mar. 18, Apr. 26, 27, 1853. Alabama Whigs had been hurt so severely by the 1852 presidential election that their 1853 gubernatorial campaign was badly handled, with their regular nominee withdrawing in the middle of the canvass; see Thornton, *Politics and Power,* p. 352.

38. Bentley, "Johnson," pp. 45, 51, 53; Tricamo, "Tennessee Politics," pp. 114-15; Clark, "Nicholson," p. 84; Russell, "Prelude," pp. 160-61; Burke, "Trousdale," pp. 148-49; *Nashville Whig,* Apr. 29, 1853, as reprinted in White, *Messages,* IV, 512-14; Johnson to David T. Patterson, Dec. 3, 1852, in Graf and Haskins, *Johnson,* II, 94-95; Johnson to Albert G. Graham, Dec. 10, 1852, 97; Johnson to Samuel Milligan, Dec. 28, 1852, 101; *Nashville Union,* Jan. 6, 8, 10, 17, 25, Feb. 19, Mar. 16, 26, Apr. 11, 25, 28, 1853.

39. *Nashville Union,* May 16, 1853; Bentley, "Johnson," pp. 67, 70-75; *Nashville Union and American,* June 21, 1853, as reprinted in White, *Messages,* IV, 516-18; *Nashville Union and American,* May 25, June 5, 24, July 3, 10, 1853. For several of Johnson's speeches, see Graf and Haskins, *Johnson,* II, 139ff.

40. Ralph W. Haskins, "Internecine Strife in Tennessee: Andrew Johnson versus Parson Brownlow," *Tennessee Historical Quarterly,* XXIV (1965), 334; Tricamo, "Tennessee Politics," p. 138. There are no completely reliable figures on the number of foreigners (or foreign-born) in Tennessee at the time of the 1855 campaign. The *Nashville Union and American,* May 3, 1855, cites the 1850 census as showing 5,638 foreigners in the state. Tricamo (p. 143) gives the 1860 census figure of 21,226 foreign-born in Tennessee. Even though the foreign population may have quadrupled in the decade of the 1850s, still it was a very small segment of the total white population, which was approximately 826,000 in 1860. Reliable statistics on the number of Catholics living in the state in the 1850s seem to be elusive. According to the 1850 census, there were three Catholic churches in the state and they could accommodate 1,300 persons. The census taken ten years later reported ten Catholic churches in Tennessee with accommodations for 4,305 worshipers. See *The Seventh Census of the United States, 1850* (Washington, 1853), pp. 595-96; and *Statistics of the United States . . . in 1860* (Washington, 1866), pp. 467, 470.

41. Bentley, "Johnson," pp. 248-53; Tricamo, "Tennessee Politics," pp. 138-40; Gower and Allen, *Pen and Sword,* p. 328; White, *Messages,* IV, 616; *Nashville Union and American,* Feb. 7, 15, 16, 1855. Holt's claim that thousands embraced Know Nothingism "as a vehicle of reform because of its clearly expressed purpose to destroy both old parties, drive hack politicians from office, and return political power directly to the people" overstates the matter, so far as Tennessee is concerned. Tennessee Whigs espoused the Know Nothing party simply because they had nowhere else to go. Holt himself states as much when he says that in the South, "Know Nothingism was largely a vehicle for former Whigs to continue opposition to the Democrats once the Whig party had collapsed"; see Holt, *Political Crisis,* pp. 165-67. Cooper maintains that Know Nothing ideology never mattered much to southerners; instead southern Whigs flocked to the Know Nothing banner because it was a replacement for Whiggery and thus a political base outside of the Democratic party; see Cooper, *Politics of Slavery,* pp. 363-65.

42. *Nashville Union and American,* Dec. 31, 1854, Jan. 14, 16, 20, 21, Feb. 1, Mar. 20, 1855; Johnson to David T. Patterson, Feb. 17, 1855, in Graf and Haskins, *Johnson,* II, 259; Johnson to Wm. M. Lowry, Feb. 24, 1855, 261; Bentley, "Johnson," pp. 255, 257-59, 260-61; Gower and Allen, *Pen and Sword,* pp. 311, 328.

43. *Nashville Union and American,* Mar. 23, 28, 29, 1855; Gower and Allen, *Pen and Sword,* p. 321; White, *Messages,* IV, 616-17; Johnson to Committee of Democratic State Convention, Mar. 31, 1855, in Graf and Haskins, *Johnson,* II, 264-65.

44. Bentley, "Johnson," pp. 277-78, 303-5, 262-65; Gower and Allen, *Pen and Sword,* pp. 326, 327, 336; White, *Messages,* IV, 617-19; *Nashville Union and American,* Apr. 28, May 3, 8, 9, 12, 29, June 5, 21, 29, July 7, 1855. Graf and Haskins reprint several of Johnson's speeches; see *Johnson,* II, 271ff. As Cooper points out, in 1855 throughout the South, Democrats tried to link Know Nothingism with northern abolitionism; see Cooper, *Politics of Slavery,* pp. 366-67.

45. Johnson to Nicholson, Sept. 8, 1853, in Graf and Haskins, *Johnson,* II, 168-69; Bentley, "Johnson," pp. 101-2, 103, 113-15, 333-38; Tricamo, "Tennessee Politics," pp. 121, 145-46. In 1855, Democrats defeated Know Nothings in the South in all seven gubernatorial elections. Democrats won legislative majorities in each of the seven states, except Tennessee; see Cooper, *Politics of Slavery,* pp. 368-69. Holt reports that Know Nothings won in Texas, Kentucky, and Maryland in 1855; see Holt, *Political Crisis,* p. 158. Alabama Know Nothings' gubernatorial candidate received only 42 percent of the statewide vote, compared to Tennessee's 49.5 percent going to the Know Nothing contender; see Thornton, *Politics and Power,* p. 352.

46. Bentley, "Johnson," pp. 571-72, 580-81; Russell, "Prelude," pp. 156, 162-63; White, *Messages,* V, 9-11, 15; Johnson to Sam Milligan, Dec. 10, 1856, in Graf and Haskins, *Johnson,* II, 457-58; Johnson to Wm. M. Lowry, Dec. 14, 1856, 460-61; *Nashville Union and American,* Dec. 6, 13, 1856, Jan. 1, 16, 30, Feb. 8, 10, 11, Mar. 6, 8, 11, 20, Apr. 10, 11, 12, 14, 23, 1857. Much like Johnson, Harris had been discouraged from seeking reelection to Congress in 1853 because of the redrawing of district lines by the General Assembly in 1852.

47. *Nashville Union and American,* Apr. 16, 1857; Gower and Allen, *Pen and Sword,* p. 408. In March 1857 the U.S. Supreme Court declared that Congress had no constitutional right to interfere with slavery in the federal territories. The most recent and most authoritative work on the Dred Scott case is Don E. Fehrenbacher, *The Dred Scott Case: Its Significance in American Law and Politics* (New York, 1978).

48. Bentley, "Johnson," pp. 584-86; Gower and Allen, *Pen and Sword,* pp. 411-12; *Nashville Union and American,* Jan. 13, 17, 27, Feb. 19, 20, 24, Mar. 25, 31, Apr. 19, May 2, 3, 1857; White, *Messages,* V, 11-18; Charles F. Bryan, Jr., "Robert Hatton of Tennessee" (M.A. thesis, University of Georgia, 1973), pp. 48-49. The *Nashville Republican Banner,* May 2, 1857, showed itself adept at whistling in the dark when it referred to the convention's great enthusiasm over a committee report recommending Hatton for the nomination; cited in Bryan, "Hatton," p. 48. Possibly John Bell's alleged influence in behalf of Hatton best explains the convention's selection of Hatton in 1857; see Campbell, *Attitude of Tennesseans,* p. 90.

49. Bryan, "Hatton," pp. 52-60; *Nashville Union and American,* May 12, 16, 29, 30, June 4, 11, July 29, 1857. The newspaper quotation is from the May 30 issue. To some

extent the Know Nothings attempted to make Andrew Johnson an issue. See for example, Bentley, "Johnson," pp. 592-93; Campbell, *Attitude of Tennesseans*, p. 90.

50. Russell, "Prelude," p. 165; Bentley, "Johnson," p. 590; Johnson to Robert Johnson, July 17, 1857, in Graf and Haskins, *Johnson*, II, 473; Johnson to Wm. M. Lowry, July 17, 1857, 475; *Nashville Union and American*, July 14, 15, 1857.

51. *Nashville Union and American*, June 16, 17, 19, 20, 21, 1857; White, *Messages*, V, 20-21.

52. *Nashville Union and American*, Dec. 12, 18, 25, 1858, Jan. 7, 9, 12, 19, 21, Mar. 4, 18, 20, 1859. The Democratic platform is conveniently reprinted in White, *Messages*, V, 89-90.

53. *Nashville Union and American*, Dec. 30, 1858, Jan. 9, 16, 26, Feb. 20, 22, Mar. 30, 31, 1859; the Opposition platform is reprinted in White, *Messages*, V, 91-92; Tricamo, "Tennessee Politics," p. 190. In its platform the Opposition party, like the Democrats, endorsed the acquisition of Cuba. For an extensive analysis of the platform from a Democratic point of view, see *Nashville Union and American*, Apr. 2, 3, 7, 8, 1859.

54. Information about state government and economic problems is found in Campbell, *Banking in Tennessee*, pp. 142-47. Early attention on the banking-currency question is shown in *Nashville Union and American*, Dec. 15, 1858ff. Apparently trying to keep peace in the Democratic family or perhaps somewhat apprehensive about the canvass, Harris urged both Nicholson and Johnson to campaign for him, and it appears that both men did participate to some extent. See Harris to Johnson, July 17, 1859, in Graf and Haskins, *Johnson*, III, 285-86.

55. *Nashville Union and American*, May 3, 4, 8, 11, 29, June 10, 11, 21, 1859.

56. See George W. Jones to Johnson, Aug. 9, 1859, in Graf and Haskins, *Johnson*, III, 288; *Nashville Union and American*, Sept. 10, 11, 1859.

57. *Nashville Union and American*, Feb. 23, Apr. 5, 10, 14, 16, 22, May 3, 4, 13, 17, 21, 27, June 14, 18, July 6, 16, 20, 1859. In Virginia, Kentucky, and Georgia, the Opposition party in 1859 took a strong prosouthern and proslavery stance and fought against any suggestion that it might be linked with the Republican party. See William S. Hitchcock, "The Limits of Southern Unionism: Virginia Conservatives and the Gubernatorial Election of 1859," *Journal of Southern History*, XLVII (1981), 60, 61, 63, 64, 65, 68; John V. Mering, "The Slave-State Constitutional Unionists and the Politics of Consensus," in ibid., XLIII (1977), 396-98.

58. With regard to the 1859 contest, Campbell seems confused. She reports Harris with a total of 72,262 and Netherland with 68,159—thereby robbing Harris of at least 4,000 votes. Her statement that the 1859 election elicited only a few hundred more voters than the 1857 canvass is patently false, as is her assertion that Netherland cut Harris's majority almost in half in 1859; he reduced it from 11,300 to 8,000. See Campbell, *Attitude of Tennesseans*, pp. 94-95. The Opposition party in Virginia, Kentucky, and Georgia lost gubernatorial races in 1859 but reduced the Democratic majorities—like Tennessee. See Hitchcock "Limits of Southern Unionism," p. 71; Mering, "Slave-State Constitutional Unionists," p. 398.

59. *Nashville Union and American*, Aug. 10, 12, 24, 25, Sept. 10, 1859. In the last weeks of the canvass, the *Union and American* began to warn about the tactic of vote swapping between congressional and gubernatorial supporters, whereby Democratic

congressional candidates would be hurt while Harris would be helped. See the following issues of this paper, June 26, July 13, 24, 1859.

60. Tricamo, "Tennessee Politics," pp. 93-96; Paul H. Bergeron, "The Jacksonian Party on Trial: Presidential Politics in Tennessee, 1836-1856" (Ph.D. dissertation, Vanderbilt University, 1965), pp. 274-75; Wm. B. Campbell to David Campbell, Feb. 15, 1852, David Campbell Papers, Duke University Library; Henry to Nelson, Feb. 10, 1852, Thomas A.R. Nelson Papers, McClung Collection, Lawson McGhee Library. See also Christopher H. Williams to [Wm. B. Campbell], Jan. 26, 1852, Campbell Papers.

61. Arthur C. Cole, *The Whig Party in the South* (Washington, 1913), pp. 233-34, 236–38; *Nashville Republican Banner,* Mar. 9, May 12, 18, 29, 1852; *Nashville Union,* Mar. 12, May 17, 1852.

62. *Nashville Republican Banner,* June 23, 28, July 1, 1852; E. Merton Coulter, *William G. Brownlow: Fighting Parson of the Southern Highlands* (Chapel Hill, 1937), p. 119; Campbell to Cullom, June 26, 1852, Campbell Papers.

63. *Nashville Union,* Dec. 6, 1851-Jan. 7, 1852, 9, 10, 12, 14, 1852; Clark, "Nicholson," pp. 77-78; Johnson to Nicholson, Dec. 13, 1851, in Graf and Haskins, *Johnson,* I, 630.

64. Johnson to Samuel Milligan, July 20, 1852, in Graf and Haskins, *Johnson,* II, 67–69; Bentley, "Johnson," p. 43; *Nashville Union,* June 7, 12, 1852.

65. Johnson to Wm. M. Lowry, Dec. 22, 1855, in Graf and Haskins, *Johnson,* II, 350.

66. Clark, "Nicholson," pp. 97-98, 100-1; Bentley, "Johnson," pp. 521-23, 525; Johnson to Nicholson, June 27, 1856, in Graf and Haskins, *Johnson,* II, 389; Gower and Allen, *Pen and Sword,* pp. 345-46; *Nashville Union and American,* Jan. 10, 12, 13, 1856.

67. *Nashville Union and American,* June 7, 1856; Bentley, "Johnson," pp. 527, 529–30; Gower and Allen, *Pen and Sword,* p. 369; Johnson to Wm. M. Lowry, June 26, 1856, in Graf and Haskins, *Johnson,* II, 385-86; Johnson to Nicholson, June 27, 1856, 388.

68. Nicholson to Heiss, Nov. 30, 1851, in St. George L. Sioussat, ed., "Papers of Major John P. Heiss of Nashville," *Tennessee Historical Magazine,* II (1916), 227; *Nashville Union,* Jan. 9, 10, 12, 14, 1852.

69. "An Address of the Members of the Legislature to the Democratic Party of Tennessee," in the *Nashville Union,* Mar. 1, 1852; E.G. Eastman to Adam Fergusson, Sept. 1852, Fergusson Collection, Tennessee State Library and Archives; *Nashville Union,* June 29, July 12, 1852.

70. *Nashville Republican Banner,* Dec. 30, 1851, Feb. 11, 1852.

71. Ibid., Apr. 5, 17, May 20, July 7, 24, Aug. 3, 26, 1852. Alexander, *Nelson,* p. 45, argues that Nelson wanted to serve but could not because of family concerns and business affairs.

72. *Nashville Union and American,* Mar. 28, Nov. 1, Dec. 12, 1855.

73. Ibid., Jan. 10, 12, 13, 1856; Brownlow to [Bell], Jan. 15, 1856, Papers of John Bell, Library of Congress. Brownlow was visiting in Nashville during the time of the Democratic state convention.

74. *Nashville Union and American,* Apr. 6, June 14-July 23, 1856; Gower and Allen, *Pen and Sword,* pp. 358-59.

75. The party's state council had met on October 8, 1855, in Nashville and had agreed to ask the national party to postpone the Philadelphia convention to early June 1856. See *Nashville Republican Banner,* Oct. 7, 11, 1855. W. Darrell Overdyke, *The Know-Nothing Party in the South* (Baton Rouge, 1950), p. 76, erroneously refers to the October 1855 meeting as a state party convention.

76. *Nashville Republican Banner,* Feb. 13, 14, 1856. Prior to the state convention Brownlow had speculated that Fillmore was the preference of Tennessee Know Nothings for the presidential nomination; he told John Bell that Bell was the second choice for the nomination. Brownlow averred that either Fillmore or Bell could carry Tennessee in 1856. See Brownlow to [Bell], Jan. 15, 1856, Bell Papers, LC.

77. R. Beeler Satterfield, "Andrew Jackson Donelson: A Moderate Nationalist Jacksonian" (Ph.D. dissertation, Johns Hopkins University, 1961), p. 503; Wm. B. Campbell to [David Campbell], Apr. 6, 1856, Campbell Papers; *Nashville Republican Banner,* Feb. 28, Mar. 11, Apr. 11, June 12, 25, 1856; Nelson to Oliver P. Temple, May 3, 1856, Oliver P. Temple Papers, University of Tennessee Library. Both Maynard and Brown had earlier served as Whig presidential electors, as had three of the Know Nothing district electors. Both Brien and Nelson pleaded reasons of personal business as the principal consideration in their decisions not to be state-at-large electors in 1856. See, for example, the *Nashville Republican Banner,* May 13, June 12, 19, 1856; Alexander, *Nelson,* p. 57.

78. *Nashville Union,* Aug. 21, 1852; *Nashville Republican Banner,* Oct, 29, 1856; *Nashville Union and American,* Oct. 29, 1856.

79. Bergeron, "Presidential Politics," pp. 283, 287-90, 331-34; Brownlow to Nelson, Oct. 30, 1852, Nelson Papers; James C. Stamper, "Felix K. Zollicoffer: Tennessee Editor and Politician," *Tennessee Historical Quarterly,* XXVIII (1969), pp. 363, 373; Russell, "Prelude," p. 149; Bentley, "Johnson," pp. 538-40; Johnson to Wm. M. Lowry, June 26, 1856, in Graf and Haskins, *Johnson,* II, 385; Johnson to A.O.P. Nicholson, June 27, 1856, 388; Johnson to Robert Johnson, Sept. 28, 1856, 440–42; Cave Johnson to James Buchanan, Aug. 24, Oct. 5, 1856, Cave Johnson Correspondence, Historical Society of Pennsylvania; Wm. B. Campbell to David Campbell, Oct. 5, 1856, Campbell Papers. There were anti-Scott meetings staged by disgruntled Whigs in Knoxville and Chattanooga in early summer; also there was a Daniel Webster electoral slate in Tennessee composed of dissident Whigs, for the October newspapers carried reports of it. See the *Nashville Union,* July 9, 19, Oct. 21. 1852; Coulter, *Brownlow,* p. 119.

80. The *Nashville Union* quotation is from the July 15, 1852 issue; M. B. Winchester to John S. Claybrooke, July 22, 1852, Claybrooke Papers, Tennessee Historical Society; Gentry to Wm. B. Campbell, July 1852, Campbell Papers. In his account of the 1852 election in the South, Cooper builds a case for the continuing controversy between the parties over the protection of slavery and southern rights; see Cooper, *Politics of Slavery,* pp. 322-41. Thornton finds a similar situation in Alabama in 1852; see Thornton, *Politics and Power,* p. 348. Holt, on the other hand, argues that there were no divisive issues in that campaign; see Holt, *Political Crisis,* pp. 104, 119, 125, 127, 134. While it is true that by 1852 practically all Tennessee political leaders accepted the 1850 compromise, still there was much heated discussion in the presidential campaign about the reliability of the candidates on the matter of southern interests.

81. Bergeron, "Presidential Politics," pp. 337-38, 341-42; *Nashville Union and*

American, Sept. 13, 1856. For an excellent example of the Democratic stance in 1856, see Governor Johnson's speech to the Democratic Club, July 15, 1856, reprinted in full in Graf and Haskins, *Johnson,* II, 395-433.

82. Bergeron, "Presidential Politics," pp. 343-45. In 1856, Alabama politics focused on southern rights issues; see Thornton, *Politics and Power,* p. 348. See Holt's discussion of the issues and questions in the 1856 campaign, North and South; Holt, *Political Crisis,* pp. 186-92, 196-98.

83. Cooper emphasizes that in Tennessee the decrease in the Whig vote in 1852 (compared to 1848) was four times greater than the decrease experienced by the Democrats and that the Whig percentage in 1852 declined in every southern state, including Tennessee; see Cooper, *Politics of Slavery,* p. 340. But a comparison with the 1851 gubernatorial election instead of the 1848 presidential contest gives a slightly different interpretation. There is no question that Tennessee in 1852 suffered a substantial stay-at-home vote, but both parties were hurt by it. Moreover, Scott's percentage in 1852 was slightly higher than that of the successful Whig candidate in the 1851 race. See also Holt's analysis of the 1852 vote; Holt, *Political Crisis,* pp. 127-30. He notes that both parties experienced vote erosion in 1852 and that Tennessee's pattern was matched by that seen in several other states.

84. Fillmore and the Know Nothings carried only the state of Maryland in 1856, but ran strong in Kentucky, Louisiana, Florida, and, of course, Tennessee; see Holt, *Political Crisis,* p. 198. In Alabama there were wholesale conversions of Know Nothings to the Democratic cause in 1856, so that Fillmore received only 38 percent of the statewide vote; see Thornton, *Politics and Power,* p. 359. No such experience was seen in Tennessee, although the Democrats were victorious, but Fillmore received 47.3 percent of the Tennessee vote.

CHAPTER VI

1. Folsom, "The Politics of Elites: Prominence and Party in Davidson County, Tennessee, 1835-1861," *Journal of Southern History,* XXXIX (1973), 359-78; Frank M. Lowrey III, "Tennessee Voters during the Second Two-Party System, 1836-1860: A Study in Voter Constancy and in Socio-Economic and Demographic Distinctions" (Ph.D. dissertation, University of Alabama, 1973); and Wooster, *Politicians, Planters, and Plain Folk: Courthouse and Statehouse in the Upper South, 1850–1860* (Knoxville, 1975). For a discussion of how Lowrey amassed his data on some 6,000 individual voters, see his comments, pp. 18-22. It should be made clear at the outset that Lowrey studied individuals from only twenty-four counties, thirteen of which were in Middle Tennessee. His sampling of Middle Tennessee seems much more representative of that region than his sampling of East and West Tennessee. Lowrey analyzes voters from only eight East Tennessee counties, for example; and most of these counties were located in the upper part of that section. He has no East Tennessee counties south and west of Knox County. In West Tennessee, Lowrey deals with only three counties: Haywood, Fayette, and Shelby. These three had numerous similarities, especially in terms of economics and population; but by no stretch of the evidence could it be argued that these three were typical of the rest of West Tennessee.

2. Henry, "Summary of Tennessee Representation in Congress from 1845 to 1861," *Tennessee Historical Quarterly,* X (1951), 141, 147. For a classic statement about southern Whigs being the large planter and slaveowning men of the region, see Arthur C. Cole, *The Whig Party in the South* (Washington, 1913), pp. 58, 69, 71-72, 104.

3. Wooster, *Politicians, Planters, and Plain Folk,* p. 49; Folsom, "Politics of Elites," pp. 368-69. Actually Folsom's figures on the farmer-planter group represent a notable difference between the Whig and Democratic leaders, but Folsom does not make a point of it.

4. Lowrey, "Tennessee Voters," pp. 55, 134.

5. Ibid., pp. 59-60, 61, 133, 135; compare the tables on p. 55 and p. 134. Curiously, Lowrey does not comment on the narrowing percentage spread in Middle and West Tennessee in the 1855-60 period or the widening gap in East Tennessee. The gap in East Tennessee reflects a substantial percentage drop in the anti-Democratic farmer-planter group, rather than an important increase in the Democratic percentage. The West Tennessee situation reflects a gain in anti-Democratic percentage and a decrease in the Democratic percentage.

6. Ibid., pp. 63-64, 67, 70, 76-77.

7. Ibid., pp. 143, 145, 146-47.

8. Ibid., pp. 55, 61, 78, 80, 134, 135, 147, 151, 192. Lowrey suggests (p. 136) that in West Tennessee townsmen "appear to have been experiencing a pressure toward the Democratic party."

9. Ibid., pp. 55, 84-87, 134, 135, 156, 159, 160-61.

10. Ibid., pp. 55, 84-85, 134, 156-57. Lowrey does not deal specifically with the shift in proportional alignments in the 1855-60 period nor does he make any claims about the influence of occupation among the East and West Tennessee doctors.

11. Ibid., pp. 55, 81-82, 83, 134, 135, 151, 154. Lowrey does not make the suggestion of influence of occupation upon West Tennessee lawyers' political preferences in the 1836-54 period.

12. Ibid., pp. 118-19, 136, 192, 214, 216; Folsom, "Politics of Elites," pp. 376, 377. In his study of midwestern states, William G. Shade characterizes Whigs as being "commercial minded," whereas Democrats tended to be "agrarian minded." On the basis of occupations, he found support for the conclusion that Whigs tended to be identified with the towns and Democrats with the agricultural scene; see Shade, *Bank or No Banks: The Money Issue in Western Politics, 1832-1865* (Detroit, 1972), pp. 141, 144, 173. In an analysis of New York during the 1840s, Benson found the lack of an urban-rural cleavage and that neither party was mainly dependent upon the cities; see Lee Benson, *The Concept of Jacksonian Democracy: New York as a Test Case* (New York, 1967), pp. 139, 290, 291. There is a hint, but not much more than this, that Tennessee for a good part of the pre-Civil War period displayed something of a rural-urban cleavage (in terms of occupations).

13. Wooster, *Politicians, Planters, and Plain Folk,* p. 47; Lowrey, "Tennessee Voters," pp. 88-90, 92-93, 94-97, 99, 119. According to Wooster, of the Tennessee legislators in 1850 who claimed no real estate, the Democrats had a significant lead: 43.9 percent to 23.1 percent. In the category of property valued up to $5,000, the Whigs had the upper hand with 53.8 percent versus 43.9 percent of the Democrats. For those

claiming between $5,000 and $25,000 of real estate, the division was: 20.5 percent of the Whigs and 9.8 percent of the Democrats; see Wooster, pp. 175, 46.

14. Lowrey, "Tennessee Voters," pp. 89, 159, 162-63, 164, 166, 168. Lowrey speculates that the large landowners in West Tennessee moved into the Democratic ranks because of the attraction of states rights principles.

15. Ibid., pp. 170-71; Wooster, *Politicians, Planters, and Plain Folk,* pp. 46-51; Folsom, "Politics of Elites," pp. 371-72. (Wooster's figures on Tennessee slaveholding, Table 10, p. 46, are confused with Kentucky's.) According to Wooster, 66.7 percent of the Whig and 52.1 percent of the Democratic legislators in 1850 owned no slaves. Those owning 1-9 slaves were closely matched so far as affiliations were concerned: 23.5 percent of the Whigs; 27.1 percent of the Democrats. Democratic legislators with 10-19 slaves far outdistanced the Whigs: 14.6 percent to 2.0 percent. But in the category of slaveholders with 20-49 slaves, Whig legislators had the lead: 7.8 percent to 4.1 percent. But these latter two categories involve so few legislators as to greatly diminish the importance of the findings. The main point is that the overwhelming majority of the legislators of both parties either owned no slaves or had less than 10 slaves (90.2 percent of the Whigs; 79.2 percent of the Democrats); see Wooster, Table 9e, p. 172.

16. Lowrey, "Tennessee Voters," pp. 109-11, 114-16, 184-85, 190; Folsom, "Politics of Elites," p. 370. In East Tennessee in 1855-60 all of Lowrey's foreign-born were anti-Democrats, but there are something less than two people in the sample.

17. Lowrey, "Tennessee Voters," pp. 100-8. Wooster found Tennessee legislators to be young, with a median age of 39 for the Democrats and 37 for the Whigs; Wooster, *Politicians, Planters, and Plain Folk,* p. 48n.

18. Lowrey, "Tennessee Voters," pp. 178-83, 192, 216.

19. Folsom, "Politics of Elites," pp. 369-71; Lowrey, "Tennessee Voters," pp. 214, 217–18. Folsom found that 12 percent of his Whig leaders were of German background while none of the Democrats claimed such lineage, but he deals here with so few individuals that no significance can be attached to this finding.

20. Lowrey, "Tennessee Voters," pp. 24-27. To qualify as a "continuing" Democrat or anti-Democrat, an individual had to be identified with the same party at least twice over a period of time involving at least two presidential elections. To be labeled a "changer" by Lowrey, a voter simply had to switch party loyalties in a subsequent election, even if it immediately followed an election in which he had supported his traditional party preference.

21. For a convenient listing of voter participation levels, see Table I in Brian G. Walton, "The Second Party System in Tennessee," East Tennessee Historical Society's *Publications,* no. 43 (1971), p. 19. See also Richard P. McCormick, *The Second American Party System: Party Formation in the Jacksonian Era* (Chapel Hill, 1966), pp. 230-31, 234, 235; and Richard P. McCormick, "New Perspectives on Jacksonian Politics," *American Historical Review,* LXV (1960), 292.

EPILOGUE

1. See especially: Marguerite Bartlett Hamer, "The Presidential Campaign of 1860 in Tennessee," East Tennessee Historical Society's *Publications,* no. 3 (1931), pp. 3-22;

Joseph H. Parks, *John Bell of Tennessee* (Baton Rouge, 1950), pp. 346-60, 362, 375-76, 381-88; John E. Tricamo, "Tennessee Politics, 1845-1861" (Ph.D. dissertation, Columbia University, 1965), pp. 205-23; Mary E.R. Campbell, *The Attitude of Tennesseans toward the Union, 1847-1861* (New York, 1961), pp. 105-30. A convenient and enlightening primary source is LeRoy P. Graf and Ralph W. Haskins, eds., *Papers of Andrew Johnson* (5 vols. to date; Knoxville, 1967–), III, 369ff. A thorough, but concise, treatment of the 1860 election nationwide is to be found in David Potter, *The Impending Crisis, 1848-1861* (New York, 1976), pp. 405-47.

2. The 1856 and 1859 percentages in Table 7.1 have been extracted from Table 2.7 in Chapter 2 above; while the 1856 and 1859 percentages in Table 7.2 have been extracted from Table 2.1 in Chapter 2. The percentages for 1860 shown in Table 7.1 have been computed by using the county election returns found in W. Dean Burnham, *Presidential Ballots, 1836-1892* (Baltimore, 1955), pp. 742-62. The percentage figures for 1860 shown in Table 7.2 have been computed from the returns by sections (and counties) found in Campbell, *Attitude of Tennesseans,* pp. 248-87.

3. Without doubt Douglas's candidacy was promoted in Memphis and its immediate environs by the strong support of the *Memphis Appeal.* In fact, Campbell, *Attitude of Tennesseans,* pp. 133-34, credits the newpaper's crusade in behalf of Douglas with influencing votes for him; and Parks, *Bell,* p. 388, echoes this interpretation. They fail to take into account, however, the position of the other three Memphis newspapers: two backed Bell and one endorsed Breckinridge. See David L. Porter, "Attitude of the Tennessee Press Toward the Presidential Election of 1860," *Tennessee Historical Quarterly,* XXIX (1970), 391, 395. Porter unconvincingly concludes: "In all probability, the Tennessee press influenced the electoral outcome considerably"; Porter, "Attitude of Press," p. 395. In his comprehensive study of the *Memphis Appeal,* Thomas Harrison Baker makes little claim about its impact in the 1860 election. Indeed when referring to the *Appeal's* readership and subscribers, Baker says that they were to be found among "that comparatively small group of persons who were financially well off and loyally Democratic." He also declares that "as a political mentor, the *Appeal* does not appear to have acted directly upon the masses of the people"; see Baker, *The Memphis Commercial Appeal: The History of a Southern Newspaper* (Baton Rouge, 1971), pp. 80-82, 41-42.

4. It remains unclear why Douglas was generally popular in West Tennessee. It has been suggested that the Irish immigrant vote in Memphis was pro-Douglas and that the city had strong economic ties with the upper Mississippi Valley which predisposed it toward Douglas of Illinois; see, for example, Tricamo, "Tennessee Politics," p. 227. But even if these explanations are essentially correct, Douglas's following in the other six West Tennessee counties remains something of a puzzle.

5. John V. Mering, "Slave-State Constitutional Unionists and the Politics of Consensus," *Journal of Southern History,* XLIII (1977), 403. In Tennessee, Douglas secured nearly 8 percent of the statewide vote. Yet in Alabama, Georgia, and Louisiana he won 10 to 15 percent of the vote, and almost all of his votes came from nonslaveholders; see Michael F. Holt, *The Political Crisis of the 1850s* (New York, 1978), p. 237. Douglas won 17 percent of the vote in Kentucky and 35.5 percent of the Missouri vote, but in ten of the slave states he did not receive as much as 10 percent of the statewide votes; see Potter, *Impending Crisis,* p. 439.

6. Mering, "Slave-State Constitutional Unionists," pp. 396, 406. Tricamo, "Tennessee Politics," p. 224, says that the combined Bell-Douglas vote was overwhelmingly antisecessionist, but also confesses that many of the Breckinridge supporters likewise opposed secession. That seems to be another way of saying that in 1860 the question of secession was not a real or viable one in the state. Moreover, one must bear in mind that the locale of Douglas's strongest support in Tennessee became probably the state's most rabid secessionist area in 1861. Tricamo rests on firmer ground when he claims (p. 225) that the 1860 contest in Tennessee reflected party regularity and conservative sentiment on sectional issues. E. Merton Coulter misses the point of political continuity when he interprets the 1860 election outcome in Tennessee as essentially a prounion vote—while also saying that the Breckinridge vote cannot be construed necessarily as a disunion vote; see Coulter, *William G. Brownlow: Fighting Parson of the Southern Highlands* (Chapel Hill, 1937), p. 134. Holt maintains that Douglas Democrats in the South generally opposed secession; see Holt, *Political Crisis,* p. 227. But Tennessee's experience does not support his claim.

Index